UNDERSTANDING CONTEMPORARY GERMANY

£13.99

Understanding Contemporary Germany is a wide-ranging survey of Europe's largest and most powerful country. It examines political, economic and social aspects of post-unification Germany, as well as considering questions relating to German identity.

More specifically, it discusses whether the new Germany is a stable democracy based on solid political and economic foundations. It assesses the extent to which the German people is at ease with itself following the traumas of the country's history.

By looking at a wide range of topics and including a cultural dimension, *Understanding Contemporary Germany* seeks to widen debate on Germany in a way which will be useful to all who study or work in the fields of German or European studies. Its conclusion is that, in contrast to the widespread fears expressed both in the country and outside, the new Germany largely remains a stable and reliable partner in European and world affairs.

Stuart Parkes is Reader in German Literature and Society at the University of Sunderland, and author of *Writers and Politics in West Germany* (1986).

D0412658

UNDERSTANDING CONTEMPORARY GERMANY

Stuart Parkes

London and New York

First published in 1997
by Routledge
11 New Fetter Lane, London EC4P 4EE

Simultaneously published in the USA and Canada
by Routledge
29 West 35th Street, New York, NY 10001

Typeset in Times by Keystroke, Jacaranda Lodge, Wolverhampton
Printed and bound in Great Britain by Redwood Books,
Trowbridge, Wiltshire

British Library Cataloguing in Publication Data
A catalogue record for this book is available from the British Library

Library of Congress Cataloging in Publication Data
Parkes, K. Stuart
Understanding contemporary Germany / Stuart Parkes.
Includes bibliographical references and index.
1. Germany—History—Unification, 1990. 2. Germany
(East)—Politics and government—1989–1990. 3. Germany (West)—
Politics and government—1982–1990. 4. Political culture—Germany.
I. Title
DD290.29.P38   1996
943.087′9—dc20   96–7154 CIP

ISBN 0–415–14123–0
ISBN 0–415–14124–9 (pbk)

For Sara

CONTENTS

vii

CHRONICLE OF POLITICAL EVENTS IN POSTWAR GERMANY

1945

May
Unconditional surrender of German forces. End of Second World War. Germany comes under Allied occupation.

June
Soviet authorities allow resumption of political activity in their zone of occupation. The KPD rejects the imposition of the Soviet model in Germany.

July
Start of Potsdam conference, at which the wartime Allies lay down principles for the future of Germany. Key principles include 'de-nazification' and 'democratisation', while in the economic area Germany is to be treated as a whole. The Oder–Neisse Line is made the eastern frontier of Germany until a final peace treaty and the German population east of these rivers is to be expelled.

August
Political activity resumes in the western zones.

1946

April
The union of the KPD and SPD to form the SED, enforced by the Soviet authorities, takes place in the Soviet Zone.

September
US Secretary of State James F. Byrnes makes a speech in Stuttgart in which he announces American support for the restoration of Germany within the international community.

October
State elections take place in Berlin (where the SED receives only 19.8 per cent of the vote) and in the Soviet Zone. Within the next twelve months state elections take place in all the western *Länder*.

1947

June — In a speech at Harvard, George C. Marshall announces the European Recovery Programme.

June — A conference of *Ministerpräsidenten* from all *Länder* takes place in Munich. When German unity is not put on top of the agenda, the representatives from the Soviet Zone leave.

1948

June — The currency reform (*Währungsreform*) whereby the D-Mark is introduced in the western zones and West Berlin comes into force on 20 June. It is followed four days later by the start of the Berlin Blockade.

September — A parliamentary council (*Parlamentarischer Rat*) made up of representatives from *Landtage* is charged with creating a constitution and an electoral law for the western zones.

1949

May — The *Grundgesetz* is agreed by the *Parlamentarischer Rat*.
End of the Berlin Blockade.

August — First elections to *Bundestag*.

October — Creation of the Deutsche Demokratische Republik.

1950

June — The Federal Republic becomes a member of the Council of Europe.

July — The GDR recognises the Oder–Neisse Line in a treaty with Poland.

1951

April — A treaty to form the European Coal and Steel Community is agreed. The six signatories (France, Italy, the Benelux Countries and the Federal Republic) subsequently become the founder members of the European Economic Community.

September — An agreement on trade between the two German states is signed.

1952

July   Thc SED decides on the 'planned creation of the foundations for socialism'.

September   The Federal government agrees to make restitution to Israel.

1953

May   The *Bundestag* agrees to the creation of a European Defence Community, of which the Federal Republic will be a member. The idea is subsequently rejected by the French parliament.

June   Anti-government uprising in Berlin and other parts of the GDR is suppressed with the aid of Soviet troops.

1954

October   Following the failure of the European Defence Community, the Paris Treaties envisage the creation of a (West) German army within NATO and the restoration of sovereignty to the Federal Republic.

1955

May   The Federal Republic becomes a sovereign state and a member of NATO. In the same month the Warsaw Pact is formed with the GDR as a member.

September   During a visit to Moscow by Konrad Adenauer, the Federal Republic and the Soviet Union agree diplomatic relations. In the same month the GDR is given sovereignty.

November   The first units of the *Bundeswehr* assemble.

1957

January   The Saar is returned to the Federal Republic from French administration and becomes a *Land*.

March   The Federal Republic is a co-signatory of the Treaty of Rome, which provides for the foundation of the EEC the following year.

September   At the hcight of Adenauer's popularity, the CDU/CSU gains an absolute majority in the third federal election.

1958

March   A majority in the *Bundestag* votes for atomic weapons for the *Bundeswehr*. This ambition is never realised.

1959

November   With its Godesberg Programme, the SPD moves away from left-wing economic positions and accepts membership of the western alliances. In this way, the party hopes to become more attractive to middle-class voters.

1961

August   Construction of Berlin Wall and other measures make unauthorised flight from the GDR almost impossible.

1962

October   A raid on the premises of the news magazine *Der Spiegel* and the arrest of its editor Rudolf Augstein lead to the Spiegel Affair. Following mass protests the Defence Minister Franz Josef Strauß is forced to resign.

1963

January   The Franco-German Treaty on greater co-operation between the two states sets the seal on the official reconciliation between the two peoples.

October   Adenauer resigns as *Bundeskanzler* and is replaced by Ludwig Erhard.

1965

May   Diplomatic relations are established between the Federal Republic and Israel.

1966

November   Faced with an economic recession, Erhard resigns as *Bundeskanzler*. The way is open for a Grand Coalition between CDU/CSU and SPD. A former member of the Nazi Party Kurt Georg Kiesinger becomes Chancellor.

1967

June   The shooting by police of a student Benno Ohnesorg
            during a demonstration against the Shah of Iran in
            West Berlin leads to major disturbances.

1968

April   A new 'socialist' constitution comes into force in
            the GDR following a referendum, in which it was
            approved by 94.49 per cent of voters.
            The student leader Rudi Dutschke is shot and
            wounded in West Berlin. This prompts demonstra-
            tions, particularly against the anti-student Springer
            press group, the publisher of the mass circulation
            Bild-Zeitung.
            The extreme right-wing NPD gains 9.8 per cent of
            the vote in the state election in Baden-Württemberg,
            the zenith of its popularity.

August   GDR troops take part in the invasion of
            Czechoslovakia by Warsaw Pact forces led by the
            Soviet Union.

1969

September   The federal election allows the formation of a
            coalition government between the SPD and FDP
            with a nominal majority of twelve. Willy Brandt
            becomes *Bundeskanzler.*

1970

August   As part of the Federal Republic's new *Ostpolitik* the
            Moscow Treaty with the Soviet Union is signed.

December   The Warsaw Treaty between the Federal Republic
            and Poland is signed.

1971

May   Walter Ulbricht is replaced by Erich Honecker as
            the First Secretary of the SED.

September   Four Power Agreement on Berlin is signed by the four
            former occupying powers. Overland access to West
            Berlin is made easier by the provisions of the treaty.

December   Chancellor Brandt is awarded the Nobel Peace Prize
            for his *Ostpolitik.*

xiii

1972

November   Elections called prematurely because the SPD/FDP coalition no longer commands a parliamentary majority result in a clear victory for the ruling parties. Largely as a result of the popularity of the *Ostpolitik* the SPD receives more votes than the CDU/CSU for the only time.

December   The *Grundlagenvertrag* between the Federal Republic and the GDR is signed. The two states have official diplomatic relations for the first time.

1973

September   Both German states are admitted to the United Nations.

1974

May   The discovery of a GDR spy in his immediate entourage leads to the resignation of Willy Brandt. He is replaced as *Bundeskanzler* by Helmut Schmidt.

1977

September   The kidnap of the leading businessman Hanns Martin Schleyer following the murders of a leading lawyer Siegfried Buback and a top banker Jürgen Ponto represents the high point of the terrorist activity of the self-proclaimed Rote Armee Fraktion. As part of the same action a Lufthansa jet is hijacked and lands at Mogadishu where it is stormed by elite commandos from the Federal Republic. After the failure of the hijack and the murder of Schleyer, the three terrorists, Andreas Baader, Gudrun Ensslin and Jan-Carl Raspe, whose release was sought, commit suicide. Increased security and anti-terrorist legislation cause this time to be called *der deutsche Herbst* (the German autumn).

1979

December   The decision of NATO to deploy Cruise and Pershing missiles gives a new impetus to the anti-nuclear movement in the Federal Republic.

1980

January   Die Grünen (the Greens) is formed from a merger of various peace and ecological groups.

1982

October   Helmut Kohl becomes *Bundeskanzler* after the Schmidt government loses its majority as a result of the decision of the FDP to form a coalition with the CDU/CSU.

1983

January   Federal elections confirm the Kohl government in power.

June   A credit of DM 1 billion for the GDR is agreed. The Bavarian CSU politician Franz Josef Strauß is instrumental in this loan to the ideological enemy.

1985

March   Mikhail Gorbachev becomes leader of the Soviet Communist Party.

May   *Bundespräsident* von Weizsäcker in a speech to commemorate the fortieth anniversary of the end of the Second World War describes 8 May 1945 as a 'day of liberation'.

1986

June   In response to public concern a ministry for the environment is created at federal level.

1987

September Erich Honecker makes an official visit to the Federal Republic. This marks the zenith of his career and appears to confirm the status of the GDR.

1988

January   About 150 people are arrested in East Berlin during a demonstration to commemorate the murder of Rosa Luxemburg. Although she was venerated as a socialist in the GDR, the demonstrators' insistence on Luxemburg's dictum – in contrast to the view of Lenin – that freedom must include the freedom of others to hold different opinions was not welcome.

1989

May	Hungary begins to dismantle its frontier with Austria. This leads to large numbers of discontented GDR citizens travelling to Hungary with the hope of reaching the West.
	The blatant rigging of the GDR local elections – the published results claim 98.77 per cent support for the official list of candidates – leads to widespread protests.
June	The SED leadership praises the Chinese government for restoring order in Tiananmen Square.
September	Hungary ceases all measures to stop GDR citizens crossing to Austria.
September/ October	GDR citizens who have taken refuge in the embassies of the Federal Republic in Prague and Warsaw are allowed to leave for the Federal Republic. GDR insistence that all must cross the territory of the GDR on land in order to be officially expelled leads to disturbances in Dresden (5 October), through which the train from Prague has to pass.
October	Mikhail Gorbachev attends the fortieth anniversary celebrations of the GDR, famously warning Honecker, 'He who comes too late is punished by life.' During the celebrations crowds demonstrate asking 'Gorbi' for help.
	Despite deployment of troops, the established Monday anti-government demonstration in Leipzig on 9 October passes without violence. It appears the GDR hierarchy is unable or unwilling to maintain its position.
	Honecker resigns on 18 October to be replaced by his 'crown prince' Egon Krenz.
November	The Berlin Wall is opened on 9 November when crowds gather following ambiguous statements from the GDR leadership about the relaxation of travel restrictions.
	Egon Krenz resigns. The last communist-led government under Hans Modrow acts as a 'caretaker' until free elections can be held.
	Bundeskanzler Kohl publishes a Ten Point Plan for Germany leading to eventual unification.

December   The SED reconstitutes itself as the Partei des demokratischen Sozialismus (PDS). Gregor Gysi becomes party leader.

1990

March   Free elections in the GDR result in a victory for the CDU-led Allianz für Deutschland. Lothar de Maizière (CDU) becomes prime minister and commences talks on unification.

July   As a first step towards unification, monetary, economic and social union comes into force on 1 July.

September   The Two plus Four talks involving the two German states and the four wartime Allies who have residual responsibility in Germany are successfully concluded. United Germany is to be a fully sovereign state.

October   German unity is completed on 3 October. The GDR ceases to exist.

December   The post-unification elections result in a resounding victory for the CDU/CSU/FDP coalition under Helmut Kohl.

1991

June   The *Bundestag* votes to transfer the seat of government to Berlin.

December   Following pressure from the Federal Republic, the EC states decide to recognise the former Yugoslav republics of Croatia and Slovenia as independent states.

1992

April   After almost eighteen years in office Foreign Minister Hans-Dietrich Genscher (FDP), a leading figure in the unification process, resigns.

August   Anti-foreigner riots take place in the ex-GDR city of Rostock. The police response is half-hearted.

November   An arson attack in Mölln (Schleswig-Holstein) leaves three people of Turkish origin dead.

1993

January   The western Greens and the eastern Bündnis 90 party merge to create the party Bündnis 90/Die Grünen.

May   An arson attack in the western town of Solingen causes the death of five people of Turkish origin. Article 16 of the *Grundgesetz* is amended to stem the numbers of those seeking political asylum.

1994

July   The *Bundesverfassungsgericht* rules that 'out of area' operations by the *Bundeswehr* are permitted by the constitution. Each case must, however, be voted on by the *Bundestag*.

October   The ruling coalition scrapes home in the federal election.

1995

June   The *Bundestag* agrees to the deployment of the *Bundeswehr* as part of the NATO operation in former Yugoslavia.

December   The *Bundestag* supports the sending of 4,000 ground troops to take part in the NATO former Yugoslavia operation.

1996

January   Israeli President Ezer Weizman visits the Federal Republic and in a parliamentary address speaks of his inability to forgive the Holocaust.

ACKNOWLEDGEMENTS

I should like to thank the following institutions and individuals for their support. The University of Sunderland and the Nuffield Foundation who provided financial support for visits to Germany; my friend and colleague Dr Ian King who read drafts of the manuscript and provided invaluable advice. In Bonn Barbara Friedl-Stocks of the *Bundeshaus* lived up to her title of research assistant. I would like to thank Professor Martin Greiffenhagen, formerly of the University of Stuttgart, Dr Will Cremer of the *Bundeszentrale für politische Bildung*, whose material was also of major help, the *Deutsches Literaturarchiv* in Marbach, which provides unparalleled facilities for research, the various ministries and officials in Bonn, who patiently answered questions and provided materials and the German Embassy in London, which supplied much useful material.

INTRODUCTION

Although historians and political scientists correctly warn against regarding any state of affairs as permanent, it is reasonable to claim that with the events of 3 October 1990, when the German Democratic Republic (East Germany) ceased to exist and became part of an enlarged Federal Republic of Germany, many problems that have beset German history had been resolved. The newly enlarged Federal Republic of Germany represented the ideal of a nation state within fixed, accepted boundaries more closely than any previous German state.

The idea of Germany as a geographical entity existed long before the creation of a single German state in 1871. The English word Germany originates from the Latin: the area and its people were the subject of a work by the Roman historian Tacitus with the title *De origine et situ Germanorum*, usually referred to as the *Germania*. However, just as there was no single German state prior to 1871, ideas about which area constituted Germany varied over the centuries, particularly as there were no natural geographical boundaries, especially in the east. Accordingly, it remains a matter of dispute to this day whether the astronomer Copernicus should be regarded as a German or a Pole. Given the geographical and ethnic uncertainties, it is small wonder that the greatest German poet, Goethe, spoke of his inability to 'find' the country Germany.

Someone who attempted to 'find' Germany in the period prior to the 1848 Revolution that sought in vain to establish a unified German state was the less exalted poet, Hoffmann von Fallersleben. His 'Deutschlandlied', beginning 'Deutschland, Deutschland über alles', became the national anthem in 1919 at the inception of the Weimar Republic and its third less nationalistic stanza praising unity, justice and liberty fulfils the same function today. He located the frontiers of Germany at the Belt (that is to say at the Baltic Sea around Denmark) in the north and at the Rivers Adige (now Italy), Maas (now Holland, Belgium and France) and Memel (now Lithuania) in the south, west and east respectively. Only briefly, at the height of Hitler's power, was all or nearly all of the territory between these locations in the power of Germany (the exception being the South Tirol area around the Adige that had been ceded by Austria to Italy in 1919 and which Hitler could not demand back from his ally Mussolini).

A few years later, it was the defeat of Hitler that led to Germany's losing a large part of the territory that prior to Nazi expansionism had made up its internationally recognised boundaries. As part of the Potsdam Agreement between the victorious Allies in 1945 it was decided that the frontier between Germany and Poland should be along the Rivers Oder and Neisse, at least until a final peace treaty was signed. After a certain degree of prevarication, this frontier was finally accepted by Chancellor Kohl at the time of unification as the eastern boundary of the new German state. In 1991 an Agreement of Friendship and Co-operation between Poland and Germany was signed, the aim of which was to overcome centuries of emnity between the two peoples. What is significant in this context is that Germany had accepted its own borders which were also the internationally recognised ones. What is more, these borders were not a major issue for the vast majority of the German people. It is true that an initially powerful lobby claiming to represent those Germans who had been expelled from their former homes to the east of the Oder–Neisse line as part of the Potsdam Agreement continued to fight against recognition of postwar realities. However, with the passage of time it had lost its ability to influence events and undoubtedly could have been safely defied earlier. This would have been welcome in the light of previous difficult German–Polish relations, especially as international opinion required a clear statement from the German government. Despite all these difficulties, the Federal Republic of Germany now exists within clear frontiers. The age-old problems of uncertain boundaries and of division have gone.

Just as there has always been the idea of Germany, the concept of a German nation existed in the title 'The Holy Roman Empire of the German Nation'. Despite this title, as a, if not the, major force in Europe throughout the Middle Ages and later, it ruled a population that always consisted of more than Germans. Even as the HRE increasingly lost power prior to its demise in 1806, its subjects still included, among others, Czechs, Hungarians and Poles. The Empire was ruled from Vienna, a German-speaking city, which raises the question of the relationship of Austria to the German nation. For a long time there was no question about it: Austria regarded itself as part of Germany and the plans of the 1848 revolutionaries for a united Germany included Austria. It was, however, the other powerful German state, Prussia, that through the policies of its Chancellor, Otto von Bismarck, forged German unity in 1871 and excluded its rival from the new German Reich. When the Austro-Hungarian Empire, the successor to the Holy Roman Empire, was broken up in 1919 as part of the peace process that ended the First World War, the position of Austria, now reduced to an almost exclusively German-speaking area, became acute once more with many Austrians wanting to join the German state. Indeed, following the proclamation of an Austrian republic in 1918, the Austrian parliament voted to become part of the German Reich. However, under the provisions of the 1919 Treaty of Versailles, any merger between Germany and Austria was ruled out and Austria became – in geographical and political terms – the state it is today. It was of course incorporated into Hitler's Germany between 1938 and 1945, but at the end of that period the Austrians, who at the very least knew that links with Germany were no longer expedient, were happy to return to a separate existence. Austrians no longer felt part of the German nation and, with the exception of a few nationalist extremists, Germans too accepted the existence of an Austrian nation and state. Another problem of history has been resolved. A German nation, albeit one with varied historical and cultural traditions, as will be made clear in Part 3, exists largely within a single state.[1]

The defining of the German nation does not mean that the question, 'who is a German?' has been entirely answered, as will be seen in Chapter 5 with reference to people entering Germany and people of non-German descent living there. What can be said is that there are no longer any groups in the countries bordering Germany, with the possible exception of a small minority in Poland, who claim to be German and would prefer to be part of a German state. By contrast, border disputes, exacerbated by the existence of minorities, were a problem between Germany and Poland and Germany and Czechoslovakia at various times in the interwar years. As for some of the other border areas, the

German-speakers of the French region Alsace-Lorraine, part of Germany between 1871 and 1919 and 1940–4/5, express no wish to return; the same is true of those who found themselves living in Belgium in 1919, when Germany lost the districts of Eupen and Malmedy. Equally, although there are long-established minority groups within Germany's frontiers, Danes in Schleswig-Holstein and the Wendish people known as Sorbs in the former GDR, there is no equivalent to the discontent felt by the Polish minority before 1919, who, in the absence of a Polish state, were forced to be German subjects and during the First World War obliged to fight against fellow Poles whose enforced citizenship was Russian.

Just as there are few if any grounds for animosity or tension based on ethnic and frontier questions between Germany and its neighbours, there is an overwhelming consensus within Germany about the nature of its state organisation. The words federal and republic meet with as good as universal approval. German federalism reflects the traditions of a country in which, given the lateness of unity, regional traditions are strong. Federalism is also seen as an antidote to the centralism of non-democratic rule; both the Nazis and the GDR regime abolished any vestiges of regional authority. The importance of the regional tier of government can be seen from the way that the interim GDR government in the period between the free elections of March 1990 and unification, admittedly in part under the influence of Chancellor Kohl, quickly reinstated the states (*Länder*) that had been abolished in 1952. As for the fact that Germany is a republic, there is no noticeable opposition to this, as there was in the first German republic, the Weimar Republic of 1919 to 1933, when certain conservative forces could not come to terms with the abdication of the emperor. Finally, it can be pointed out that the overall acceptance of the existing state extends to its symbols, its national anthem, although there have been right-wing voices demanding the reinstatement of the first stanza of the 'Deutschlandlied', and its flag. The current black, red and gold flag, which has its origins in the movement for democracy and unity in the first part of the nineteenth century, was first adopted by the Weimar Republic but was replaced in 1933 with a flag incorporating Nazi symbols and the imperial colours of black, white and red.

All of these points suggest that there is now no such thing as the German Question, as the term was understood in the immediate postwar period, when the future of Germany exercised the minds of world statesmen and created tensions among the former war-time Allies. Moreover, the historical roots of the postwar German Question, the open questions of German history, referred to above have largely disappeared. The post-1990 Federal Republic of Germany is an internationally recognised sovereign state within fixed boundaries whose state organisation is almost universally accepted by its citizens. With many countries this might all be taken for granted. Against the background of German history, it is a great advance that there are, to use a metaphor employed during the period of post-1945 division, no more 'open wounds'.

It does not follow from these optimistic statements that all must be well in contemporary Germany. No mention has yet been made of democracy, although the terms federal and republic might be said to imply a democratic system of government. Clearly, creating a functioning democracy has also been one of the main problems of German history, given the only limited democracy of the Reich established in 1871, the problems of Weimar despite its democratic forms and the totalitarian dictatorship of Hitler's Third Reich. Not surprisingly, the stability of (west) Germany's fledgeling democracy was at the centre of many concerns, both internally and externally, in the postwar period. Long before 1990, however, most observers saw the Federal Republic as a healthy democratic state and a reliable partner in international affairs.

This book seeks to examine and explain the current situation in Germany, six years after the reunification process and fifty years after the end of the Second World War. In particular, it addresses the question of whether the promise of 1990 is being fulfilled. Since post-unification Germany cannot be understood without some discussion of the two states that existed before 1990, the first two chapters look at the GDR and the pre-1990 Federal Republic. The GDR may have passed into history but its former citizens, with their distinct biographies and aspirations, represent about a fifth of the approximately 80 million people living in the new Germany. The unified state is in organisational terms essentially a continuation of the old Federal Republic within expanded boundaries. Thus the importance of the pre-1990 state cannot be overemphasised, particularly in the light of the fact that its specific achievements, along with a continuing sense of belonging to a single German nation, were the magnet that made unification an attractive prospect to most of the GDR's citizens.

Part 2 turns to issues relating to post-unification Germany, although many have their origins in the earlier period. The emphasis is on both internal and external affairs, which in many areas interrelate and, given Germany's size and strength, affect Europe and increasingly the whole world.

The third part turns to questions of identity and culture. This is essential because events are influenced not simply by day-to-day material issues but also by ideas and their interpretation. It is hard to believe, for instance, that Hitler could have come to power without there having been intellectual and cultural traditions in Germany to which he could appeal and which he could appropriate, or rather misappropriate. This is not to say that any particular tradition or school of thought led directly to National Socialism, as was claimed by certain British critics who, on the evidence of the art exhibition 'The Romantic Spirit in Germany' held in London in 1994–5, concluded that a link could be established between Romantic painting and Nazism. My only claim is that the battle of ideas can influence the future of German democracy, as well as overtly political factors. Ideas also help to forge the identity of a nation.

There is another major point to consider in the German context. It is extremely difficult, if not impossible, to speak of a distinct German identity rooted in unbroken and accepted traditions of the kind that exist within other nations. Given the discontinuities in the development of Germany, the establishment of such an identity has proved elusive. This becomes clear if the German situation is compared to that of its major allies, the United States, Great Britain and France. British people can, for instance, identify with the monarchy and the long parliamentary tradition; the French with the values of liberty, equality and fraternity, as expressed in the Revolution; and Americans with the democratic ideals of the founding fathers as expressed in the constitution. In Germany there have been few such factors that might contribute to a settled identity. This can be illustrated by reference to the calendar. Whereas the 4 July in the USA and the 14 July in France stand for the start of positive national traditions, there is no comparable date in Germany. This was illustrated at the time of unification when not only an appropriate event to celebrate but also a date for a national day were sought. The date of the fall of the Berlin Wall, 9 November, was impossible because it was also the day of the infamous *Reichskristallnacht* of 1938, when Jewish property was attacked and many Jews imprisoned and killed. It was a relief when a date for unification and in consequence a national day – 3 October – could be found that was free from similar opprobrium. The closest the pre-unification Federal Republic had come to a national day was the 'Day of German Unity', 17 June, that commemorated the anti-government rising in the GDR in 1953. With unification this day had lost its significance.

One reason for the uncertainties of German identity lies in the course of German history. Accordingly, Chapter 7 deals with the legacy of that history. The next chapter traces some of the difficulties Germans, especially writers and intellectuals, have had with conceptions of Germany and the Germans. The third chapter in this part (Chapter 9) is concerned with intellectual disputes since unification. The point at issue throughout is which events and ideas have influenced or might in the future influence an identity that, given historical events, not least those of recent years, is inevitably fluid.

Finally, I would like to point out that this book is written out of a concern and interest in Germany which goes beyond academic objectivity. I do not go as far as the maxim the young Goethe put in the mouth of his Faust, 'Gefühl ist alles' (feeling is all) – I certainly would not compare myself to either the fictional character or his creator but would accept the point made by the poet and essayist Hans Magnus Enzensberger in an interview in early 1995 that the worlds of knowledge and emotion should not be entirely separate (Enzensberger 1995b: 47). Accordingly, I hope that readers will find the subject-matter rewarding, even if they are reading *Understanding Contemporary Germany* as part of an examined course of study primarily for the facts and arguments it contains, and that those who look at it purely out of interest will both maintain that interest and gain more knowledge and understanding of what is the pivotal country within the new, thankfully no longer divided, Europe.

Part I
DIVIDED GERMANY

1

THE GERMAN DEMOCRATIC REPUBLIC
The state that failed

INTRODUCTION

The German Democratic Republic was an entity that was foisted on the inhabitants of the territory it covered. Its existence was based on the wish and the ability of a foreign power, namely the Soviet Union, to sustain it. As soon as that power was willing to relinquish control it was no longer able to survive.

Although it might be possible to dismiss the forty-year existence of the German Democratic Republic with those few words and immediately confine it to the dustbin of history, it would be wrong to do so. The creation of a new, largely unwanted state did not necessarily mean that such a state was condemned to failure. The *alter ego* of the GDR, the Federal Republic of Germany, as constituted in 1949, was, in geographical terms, equally artificial and its frontiers could certainly not have been regarded at the beginning as corresponding to the aspirations of its inhabitants. Forty years later, that had changed. As the next chapter will show, there are good reasons for believing that many citizens of the Federal Republic would have been happy with a continuation of the status quo and embraced the new post-1990 unified Germany with less than wholehearted enthusiasm.

Equally, as was pointed out in the Introduction, the state of Austria, in the form in which it was created at the end of the First World War, was not in accordance with the wishes of the many who wished to be part of a greater German-speaking state, but three-quarters of a century later there is no question of Austria becoming part of Germany. It is therefore wrong to assume the inevitability of the disappearance of the GDR without seeking in more detail the reasons for its demise. Moreover, such a search is

3

not just a raking over of the embers of the past; as will be seen throughout this book, the forty years of the GDR have had a major influence on the new united Germany and will continue to do so for the forseeable future.

PROBLEMS OF NATIONAL LEGITIMACY

Although few European states are nation states in the sense that they contain all those who consider themselves part of a particular nation and do not contain minorities from different nations and cultures, the GDR was an extreme example of a mismatch between state and nation. As long as the inhabitants of the GDR saw themselves as part of a German nation, the greater part of whose people lived in the Federal Republic, and desired to maintain this link, the GDR as a state lacked legitimacy in national terms. Historically, a sense of German nationhood linked to the existence of a unified German state may have been relatively new – it could only have existed since 1871 with the creation of Bismarck's Reich – but it proved to be persistent throughout the existence of the GDR. Such a claim does not invalidate what has already been said about the existence of other forms of identity, older regional ones dating back centuries or even some degree of acceptance of a GDR identity. It can also be argued that Germany could not have been divided without some measure of acquiescence on the part of the inhabitants, who, with the defeat of 1945 and the moral opprobrium heaped on them as the truth about the Nazi regime surfaced, were happy to withdraw or at least conceal their identification with Germany as a whole. Nevertheless, there can be little doubt that the vast majority of GDR citizens continued to regard themselves as Germans and that this factor made acceptance of their state more difficult.

It was also a factor that the GDR leadership had to bear in mind. In the early years of the state's existence, the official line was to stress that Germany had been divided by the western powers. It was possible to advance plausible arguments for this claim given that a single German currency had been abandoned with the introduction of the D-Mark in the western zones in 1948 and that the Federal Republic predated the GDR. Moreover, unification was always presented as an urgent political priority. Thereafter, there was a period in the late 1950s and early 1960s when the idea of a German confederation was advanced as a precursor to

4

eventual unity; subsequently any prospect of unification was seen as impossible until the Federal Republic embraced socialism or at least abandoned its membership of NATO and other western alliances.

Nevertheless, until the coming to power of Erich Honecker in 1971, the idea of a single German nation was maintained in the GDR with the term still being used in the new 'socialist' constitution that came into force in 1968. Six years later, Honecker amended this constitution to remove all such references; it was now claimed that a new socialist nation had grown up that was distinct from the old capitalist nation in the west. A new, casuistic distinction was made between the German words *Nation* and *Nationalität*, with the latter seen as continuing to be German. With a few exceptions, such as the title of the Communist Party newspaper *Neues Deutschland*, the word *'Deutschland'* was expunged from official vocabulary with the result that the GDR national anthem with its references to a single German fatherland could be heard but not sung.[1] It was only in the mid- to late 1980s that Honecker occasionally seemed to hold out the prospect of unity, but again only following a change to socialism in the west. To all intents and purposes the Federal Republic was to be regarded as a foreign country, a development that was matched in the west, not in official circles, but rather among those who equated Germany with the Federal Republic and, for instance during sports commentaries, spoke of 'German' athletes competing against their counterparts from the GDR.

The attempts made to proclaim some kind of national legitimacy for the GDR did not consist solely of a denial of links with the Federal Republic but included attempts to create some kind of national identity. The GDR always saw itself as the inheritor of progressive forces in German history, making great play, for instance, of the Peasants Revolt of 1524–5 and the revolutionary activities at the end of the First World War. Even the spirit of the music of Beethoven was seen as being realised in the GDR when the 200th anniversary of his birth was celebrated in 1970. Later, in the Honecker era, the search for historical legitimacy went far beyond those with whom some form of ideological identification could be sought. The 500th anniversary of the birth of Martin Luther, who had previously been vilified as the enemy of the peasants, was widely celebrated in 1983, while a statue of Frederick II of Prussia, who, despite his policy of military expansionism, again

5

received the accolade 'Frederick the Great', was returned to a position of prominence in Berlin. It is small wonder that GDR intellectuals with genuine left-wing beliefs were irritated by this or that GDR cabaretists dressed up as Luther and Frederick playfully asked what the régime was intending. The ultimate answer has to be that ideological inconsistencies were no longer taboo in pursuit of the establishment of the GDR in the public consciousness as something more than a state without historical roots foisted on its reluctant citizens from outside.

Such attempts had to overcome any sense that the GDR lacked sovereignty and was controlled from the outside by the Soviet Union – an early somewhat unsubtle political joke referred to the telephone between Moscow and Berlin having an earpiece but no mouthpiece at the German end. There can be no doubt that the GDR was in the shadow of Soviet power, not just because of the Soviet troops in the country, who were used to suppress unrest in 1953, but also because of the Brezhnev doctrine of limited sovereignty which justified the 1968 invasion of Czechoslovakia in which GDR troops participated less than thirty years after Hitler's aggression against the same state. This doctrine stated that the socialist countries could intervene in the internal affairs of one of their partners if the political system there was endangered. Given the ideological affinities, at least until the coming to power of Mikhail Gorbachev in 1985, the GDR leadership accepted the dominance of the Soviet Union. Nevertheless, praise of the Soviet Union as the model to be followed in all cases and the establishment of the GDR as an accepted sovereign state at home and abroad was a difficult circle to square. In fact, the events of 1989–90 quickly confirmed that the GDR had failed to achieve the legitimacy required to survive without the support of the Soviet Union. The national ties that had existed before 1945, together with the political lure of the Federal Republic and its self-evident greater prosperity, prevailed.

THE POLITICAL SYSTEM

It was stated at the beginning of this chapter that it is possible for states to gain acceptance and overcome initial resistance to their creation. In the case of Austria, after 1945 there was no further wish to be associated with Germany, either because of the feeling of revulsion about the crimes of the Nazis or, as seems to have

6

been of at least equal importance, because of the realisation that a better future appeared to beckon those who could cast themselves as the victims of tyranny. With the Federal Republic, the starting-point was also favourable. It was not hampered, as the GDR was, by a lack of national legitimacy since, as the larger German state, it could claim to be the successor to the all-German states that had existed previously. Nevertheless, other factors were important for its success too. Without economic prosperity and accepted political institutions it would not have become the state with which so many were happy to be identified despite the exclusion of so many fellow Germans. It is to these areas of economics and politics that one must also look to find reasons for the failure of the GDR to overcome its legitimacy deficits. Neither its political system nor its economic performance provided enough to counter-balance the sense that this was an artificial creation under the tutelage of a foreign power.

It is the political sphere that merits most attention because political considerations were always paramount in the GDR. The influence of politics was all-pervasive, dominating all areas of society, including the economy, education and culture. Only the church, which in the GDR meant largely the Lutheran Church, had some degree of autonomy since it could hardly be 'nationalised', given that it represented a set of beliefs at odds with communist ideology. At the same time, it could not escape the influence and attention of the state, while nevertheless retaining enough independence to become the institutional focus of the protest movement that gathered force in the 1980s and contributed to the sweeping away of the old system in 1989.

To speak of the all-pervasive influence of politics does not mean that everything that happened was totally controlled. There were spheres into which the individual could retreat, not least those of the family and West German television, some of whose pro-grammes could be picked up in most parts of the GDR. It should be remembered that not everything functioned as the state would have wished. Even without allowing for the frailty of all human endeavour, it was impossible to control everything up to and including television preferences without a system of total surveil-lance of Orwellian proportions. Moreover, western television reported the social problems of the Federal Republic, and thus appeared to act as a brake on the desire to leave the GDR. There were proportionately more applications to leave the country from

7

people living in the Dresden area where it could not be received. Nevertheless, given the range of controls to which the citizen was subjected and the attempts to escape them, it became common to talk of the GDR as a 'niche society' (*Nischengesellschaft*), that is to say a society where many citizens sought a niche in which they could retain some degree of autonomy.[2]

It must be pointed out immediately that a niche can only exist where most of the territory is occupied by someone else. In the case of the GDR, this was to a large extent the ruling Communist Party: the Sozialistische Einheitspartei Deutschlands (SED), which was formed in 1946 through a merger between the old communist KPD and the social democratic SPD. Although there were Social Democrats who wanted a merger of the two left-wing parties whose division had contributed to the rise of Hitler during the Weimar Republic, what happened has to be seen as an enforced marriage brought about under the auspices of the Soviet Union. Indeed, some Social Democrats who opposed the merger found themselves imprisoned in the former Nazi concentration camp at Buchenwald which continued to function as a prison until 1950. The subsequent course of events certainly did not conform to the traditions of the SPD. The SED became a party that was modelled on the Soviet Communist Party; power lay not with the ordinary party member but, in accordance with the Leninist system of 'democratic central-ism', with the few functionaries who occupied top positions and in particular with the party leader. By virtue of their office, Walter Ulbricht until 1971 and thereafter Erich Honecker, along with the roughly twenty members of the *Politbüro*, exercised close to absolute power in the GDR, albeit under the watchful eye of the Soviet Union. The task of the ordinary party member was not to seek to influence the way that power was used, but to represent the views the leadership of the party expressed on any given issue.

From the adoption of the 1968 constitution, and *de facto* from the foundation of the state in 1949, the supreme power of the SED was enshrined in the political system of the GDR. Other parties continued to exist but did not challenge the leading role of the SED. They certainly did not compete with it or with each other in elections in the way that political parties do in other countries. They were happy or forced to accept the number of seats allocated to them by the SED in the various representative bodies that existed and to act as transmission belts to the constituencies they purported to represent. The GDR's Christian Democrats in the

CDU, for instance, were supposed to represent citizens with Christian beliefs; in reality, their role was to make SED policy palatable to anybody who might listen. As for the ordinary voters, elections consisted of their affirming the approved list of candidates or drawing attention to themselves by crossing out particular names. Given that citizens were under immense pressure to vote, the result was the 99 per cent plus approval rate common throughout the communist states. When, due to the rising tide of unrest, such results could not be obtained in the local elections of May 1989, the true figures were simply falsified in order that the same level of approval could be claimed.

There were no institutions that might challenge the role of the SED. The national parliament, the People's Chamber (*Volks-kammer*), certainly could not, even if one discounts the point that its members consisted of the SED parliamentary group and its, to a greater or lesser extent, coerced allies in the other parties, along with representatives of various social groups that it controlled, for instance, the Free German Youth (FDJ) which had been founded in 1946 and remained the only legal youth organisation outside the churches. Equally significant was that the *Volkskammer* met only occasionally and then almost exclusively to rubber-stamp legislation. The executive, in the form of the Council of Ministers (*Ministerrat*), was equally subservient to the SED, even though not all its members belonged to that party. Similarly, there was no question of an independent judicial system; judges had to advance party policy in their particular sphere. If one adds the mass media to the list of controlled organisations, then it becomes obvious that the system of government in the GDR bore no resemblance to the ideal of the pluralistic democratic society as propounded and practised with various degrees of (im)perfection in the western world.

It is not difficult to show that the SED exercised supreme power in the GDR or even embodied the GDR; it did not conceal this fact itself, even if it presented itself as the party of the working class and the guardian of its interests.[3] Its claim was, in the words of one of its slogans, that everything was done for the well-being of the people.

What is clear, is that by 1989 the majority of the people saw things differently. It is therefore necessary to ask what was the true nature of SED power. Two points should be made initially. Given the power relationships, the SED, even if it had wished to, could not

9

attempt to do anything that contravened the vital interests of the Soviet Union. In a sense this axiom remained true to the end, although on the surface Gorbachev no longer sought to intervene in the internal affairs of his nominal allies. Honecker's refusal to make concessions to the new mood sweeping central and eastern Europe hastened his own end and that of the GDR whose survival was no longer seen as a vital interest of the Soviet Union. The second point has to do with the corruptive nature of power, and especially absolute power, as formulated by Lord Acton.[4] Even if one assumes initial good intentions on the part of the SED, the absolute power its leaders exercised in the daily running of the GDR within the Soviet sphere of influence was bound to corrupt.

This corruption was undoubtedly most visible in the role played within GDR society by the State Security Service (*Staatssicherheitsdienst*). Beside this the individual corruption of leading party figures, in particular their life of relative luxury away from the gaze of the people in the enclosed compound at Wandlitz north of Berlin, pales into insignificance. It might be possible to argue that the economic espionage conducted by this organisation was in the interests of the state as a whole but its overall function, encapsulated in its definition of itself as the 'sword and shield of the party' (*Schwert und Schild der Partei*), was to defend those in power. To this end, no effort was spared. Anyone who was perceived of as a potential enemy of the system was subject to surveillance at the very least. Even when arbitrary arrest followed by stringent punishment including the death penalty became much more a thing of the past (in the 1980s the death penalty was in fact abolished), intimidation did not cease. Although there may have been limits to Stasi power, in that it would have been impossible to take steps against everyone under surveillance, and the plodding diligence revealed in its files may, with hindsight, seem pathetic, it still remains totally impossible to see the exercise of power by the Stasi as anything other than coercive. Since German unification, it has become clear that the system could not have functioned without the co-operation of large numbers of GDR citizens, put at 109,000 in the 1980s, who were willing to act as unofficial informants (*Inoffizielle Mitarbeiter*) (Weidenfeld and Korte 1993: 116). However, this does not change the overall situation: the Stasi was the epitome of a system where all power was in the hands of a group of people who had internalised Lenin's dictum that control was better than trust.

What did this mean for ordinary citizens? Quite simply, they were unable to exercise civil rights, as these are generally understood. As already stated, voting was a charade, freedom of speech certainly did not extend to the right to criticise the government or party (although apparently criticism of immediate superiors generally brought few repercussions) and freedom of assembly outside the confines of the church was non-existent. Even organisations devoted to such harmless pastimes as stamp-collecting came under the supervision of the Kulturbund, an organisation founded in 1945 by the occupying forces of the Soviet Union to promote 'democratic renewal' in the area of culture. Another restriction that was felt very keenly was the lack of opportunity to travel abroad beyond the frontiers of allied socialist states, and even here problems with the exchange of currency or, in the case of Poland for a time, fears that the ideas of Solidarity might prove infectious imposed limits. It is true that, apart from those who were willing to risk their lives by crossing the heavily guarded frontiers with West Berlin and the Federal Republic, some GDR citizens could reach the west, as visitors whose numbers increased following the signing of the *Grundlagenvertrag* with the Federal Republic in 1972 and as refugees. The purchase of disaffected GDR citizens by West Germany became a regular if unwholesome feature of intra-German relations in the 1970s and 1980s, while the GDR itself increasingly saw the expulsion of dissidents, in particular writers and intellectuals, as a way of stemming discontent. Nevertheless, the restrictions on travel imposed on those under the age of retirement remained a major bone of contention for GDR citizens, many of whom claimed that they wanted to prove their loyalty by returning home after any stay in the west. Of those who felt constrained to leave without official sanction and tried to cross the border to the Federal Republic or West Berlin illegally, over 800 paid with their lives as a result of a frontier regime which demanded that would-be refugees were 'destroyed' if other means of stopping them failed.

To sum up: the normal GDR citizen was excluded from political power. Even membership of the SED did not guarantee influence, given its undemocratic structure. Clearly, some could rise in the hierarchy, but it was only in the higher echelons, the central committee or more significantly the *Politbüro*, that power resided. The ordinary member might use membership to further his or her career but otherwise life in the party meant the duties of attending meetings and supporting the official political line, as expounded in the press and other media, all of which were subject to strict control.

THE ECONOMY

The reasons for the failure of the GDR cannot be sought solely in the political sphere. On coming to power in 1971, Erich Honecker implicitly proposed a kind of pact with the population: the reward for the loss of political rights would be a high material standard of living. That this never materialised, at least not on a comparable level to that attained by the majority in the Federal Republic, can be regarded as the major reason for the failure of the GDR. Favourable comparisons with other Warsaw Pact states did not wash, given the natural fixation with the other German state; indeed awareness of the 'backwardness' of the Soviet Union could only undermine faith in the whole socialist system, whereas the USA for all its problems could remain a positive focus for many West Germans because of its undoubted riches.

Before examining in more detail the reasons for the comparative failure of the GDR economy, it is worth pointing out what can only be regarded as an admission of defeat. Certain items, in particular but not exclusively imports from the west, were frequently only available in a network of shops called Intershop which only accepted convertible western currencies. Not only did this downgrade the country's own currency which could not be freely exchanged, it also created two classes of citizen, those with access to western money, specifically the D-Mark, and those without. Since economic advantage lay with the first group, the lesson about the relative standing of the two economic systems practised in Germany could hardly be ignored. That certain luxury goods were available for GDR marks at highly inflated prices in a chain of shops with the name Exquisit did little to sweeten the pill.

It is possible to advance historical and political reasons for the relative failure of the GDR economy. The GDR occupied a territory lacking raw materials with the exception of lignite; the north of the country in particular had always been a somewhat backward rural area, as illustrated by Bismarck's inspired comment that, if the end of the world were to be announced, he would move to Mecklenburg because everything happened there a hundred years later. The country lacked major ports until the facilities at

12

Rostock were expanded; the overall infrastructure was based on a united Germany where lines of communication ran from east to west rather than, as the geography of the new state demanded, north to south. In terms of politics, the questions to be considered are whether the GDR economy was the victim of discriminatory policies applied towards it in the west and whether it was exploited by its major ally, the Soviet Union. The first was a major claim of GDR propaganda; it was also mirrored in literature, for instance, in Christa Wolf's 1963 novel *Der geteilte Himmel* (*The Divided Sky*), where the production of a new railway carriage is hampered by the sudden refusal of a western firm to continue supplying a particular part. It is true that the west sought to prevent the sale of hi-tech goods to the Soviet Union and its allies by the Co-Com (Co-ordinating Committee for Strategic Exports to the Communist World) system which was based on a list of proscribed exports, efforts the GDR attempted to undermine by covert tactics including industrial espionage. On the other hand, the terms of intra-German trade were favourable to the GDR, which was able to obtain interest-free credit under a system known as Swing. Moreover, intra-German trade arrangements gave the GDR access to the whole of the European Community. From the 1970s, the Federal Republic paid an annual lump sum, in the 1980s around DM 500 million, for the use of the access routes to Berlin and helped to maintain and improve them, not to mention the loans it helped to secure for the GDR in the 1980s, which caused a political sensation at the time because the leading right-wing politician, the Bavarian Franz Josef Strauß, played a major part in negotiations. The arrangement mentioned above whereby the Federal Republic bought the release of GDR political prisoners, to whom were added criminals the GDR felt incapable of reforming, also provided the GDR with substantial funds, totalling DM 3.4 billion.[5]

That the Soviet Union might exploit not just the GDR but all its allies was a taboo subject at an official level, although it was a strong feeling among the population of every partner country. The population of what became the GDR had to witness the ruthless dismantling of industrial plant in the early postwar years by the Soviet authorities, who sought restitution for the immense damage inflicted on the Soviet Union during the war. Subsequently, the system of economic co-operation created by the Council for Mutual Economic Aid (Comecon) that was set up in 1949 in response to the Americans' Marshall Aid (of which the Federal

Republic was a major beneficiary) was dominated by the Soviet Union. However, the Soviet Union helped to sustain its allies by, for instance, selling raw materials at less than world market prices. It was only with the explosion of oil and other raw material prices in 1973 that prices were linked to those on the world market.

The above points show that the GDR did not enter the economic race with the Federal Republic on equal terms; how far this continued to be the case is hard to determine. What cannot be doubted is that the kind of economic policies pursued in the GDR did not help. From the outset, the GDR adopted a planned economy with the result that the SED became, as an article in the magazine *Der Spiegel* once put it, 'the party that distributes chives'. Economic activity was controlled centrally, with production guided by the dictates of the Economic Plan, whose term was usually five years. The problems of the planned economy are well known; they include the arbitrary fixing of prices, the inability to react quickly to customer demand and to changed economic circumstances that render the plan obsolete, along with the lack of criteria by which to judge economic performance. The first point can be illustrated by the way that bread was cheaper than grain in the GDR; accordingly it was frequently fed to poultry with all the waste of effort that involved. The question of criteria can be illustrated by reference to a phenomenon referred to as *Tonnen-ideologie* (tonnage ideology). There were many stories in the early years of the GDR of managers only thinking of the numbers of goods produced, as this was the yardstick by which success was measured within the planned economy. Accordingly it was better to make, for example, large numbers of small-sized shoes than a smaller number in a variety of sizes. The consequences for those with bigger feet are obvious. Even if such tales are partly apocryphal, they illustrate a major point: that the GDR was not able to give consumers what they wanted when they wanted it.

The other point to stress is that the overall direction of the economic policies of the GDR was inappropriate. In accordance with the Soviet model of the time, the initial concern was to develop heavy industry rather than produce consumer goods which only became more of a priority in the Honecker years. This reflected the political control over the economy; virtually all industry and everything else to do with the economy was in the hands of the state. Although at various times consideration was given to allowing individual enterprises more freedom of action,

14

particularly with the New Economic System announced in 1963, nobody could escape the dictates of the central plan. As in politics, control rather than trust was the order of the day. This was amply illustrated by the reversing in 1970 of the movement towards decentralisation that was part of the New Economic System.

The economic system affected the citizens of the GDR in a variety of ways. The workplace was generally free from stress, as shortages of materials frequently limited the time that was productively occupied. After the fall of the Berlin Wall, it was reported that building workers who moved west were amazed that there could be deliveries of materials in the afternoon and that nearly all the working day was spent actually working. Those employed in the service industries often only carried out their tasks when they felt motivated to do so. Irene Böhme, the author of, at the time, a most informative book, *Die da drüben* (*The People over There*) published in 1982, gives some typical examples of this, for instance, closed doors in a housing or similar office behind which the sound of laughter could be heard. Instead of serving the public, the employees might be celebrating a colleague's birthday. Her conclusion was that the American concept of 'time is money' was totally alien to the citizens of the GDR, not least because the general shortage of labour meant that nobody's job was ever endangered. The only example of a dismissal Böhme quotes is the case of a shop assistant who told customers an item was not available if she had to fetch it from the stockroom (Böhme 1982: 20–32).

This anecdote implies the situation of the GDR citizen as consumer. It was accepted as normal that goods might not be available. Although the overall supply improved over the years, it is doubtful whether at any time it came close to matching demand. It certainly did not in the case of motor vehicles where a waiting period as long as fifteen years for a new car was possible. It was not that consumers lacked money – the average amount of savings was high – it was rather that there were not enough goods to spend it on. This was the case, even though the price of most goods, with the exception of highly subsidised basic items and services (the case of bread has already been alluded to) was comparatively high, particularly when wages were taken into consideration. Statistics published by the Federal government show that, whereas in 1979 an average shirt in the west cost about DM 20, the GDR citizen had to pay double in eastern marks and, given the wage levels, work on average more than five times as long as his or her western counterpart to earn the required sum. Although western inflation – inflation did not exist, at least officially, in the GDR – may have eroded the gap over the next decade, it always remained significant. In many areas, too, the equivalent western product was of a higher standard; one needs only compare a Volkswagen with a Trabant, the noisy and polluting but robust vehicle that became known throughout Europe in 1989 as GDR citizens moved west.

There is one other area connected with the economy that should be mentioned as having a direct effect on many GDR citizens, namely the environmental consequences of the economic policies pursued. Whatever economic progress was achieved in the GDR was frequently at the cost of a hideously damaged environment. The chemical town of Bitterfeld, for example, was associated with some of the worst pollution in Europe. It became the subject of Monika Maron's appropriately named novel *Flugasche* (*Flying Ashes*), publication of which proved impossible in the GDR. Equally, the opencast mining of lignite, the GDR's main source of energy, left numerous scars on the landscape, particularly in the Halle and Leipzig area and in the south-east of the country near Cottbus.

The GDR sought to present itself as a modern industrialised country, not least with the aid of falsified statistics. If these frequently misled observers in the west, as recurring overestimates of the GDR's economic performance show, they might even have fooled the GDR leadership as well, as Honecker's claims, made after his fall, that the truth was concealed from him suggest. At all levels, those responsible attempted to put a better gloss on their achievements by what can only be described as 'fiddling the books'. Their superiors were only too happy to receive good news and pass on the message that the plan was being fulfilled until it reached the top. It would be wrong to say that in this case the emperor had no clothes; it would be more accurate to speak of limited low quality clothes. As a producer, the GDR citizen may not have suffered extreme exploitation, unless working in particularly unhealthy surroundings. However, as a consumer, he or she was likely to suffer extreme frustration, not least waiting to be served or even allowed to sit down in a less than busy restaurant where the staff had other priorities.

THE 'ACHIEVEMENTS' OF THE GDR

It was commonplace for official GDR publications to speak of the
socialist achievements (*sozialistische Errungenschaften*) of the
country. Some of these alleged achievements had to do directly
with economic policy and have been hinted at above. The shortage
of labour, occasioned in part by the loss of population in the war
and the flow of refugees prior to the building of the Berlin Wall,
together with the prevailing ideology meant that the GDR enjoyed
full employment. Although this fact should not be overlooked, it
did not mean, as has been shown, that all were sensibly occupied.
(Incidentally, those employed by the police, army and Stasi might
also have come into the category of not being usefully employed.)
That cheap prices too had certain drawbacks has already been
hinted at. This was arguably most obvious in areas relating to
housing. Heating, light and water were supplied so cheaply that
energy conservation was not an issue – excessive heat in a building
generally would be countered by opening a window rather than
switching something off. As rents were kept at prewar levels in
the case of older housing, there was no incentive nor possibility for
owners to carry out improvements. The result was all too often a
depressingly run-down townscape that was as much a reminder of
the problems of the system as the polluted environment. Ironically,
given the nature of the political system, many properties remained
in private hands, as the state had no interest in taking over items
that would only cause it expense. In the case of new housing, a
priority in the Honecker era, monotonous blocks constructed from
prefabricated materials at the lowest possible cost predominated.
Even though, as is now known, some within the SED argued for
increased rents in the interests of quality, the same rigid policies
continued to be pursued in this as in so many areas.

It goes without saying that the achievements of a country rest on
more than economic performance. It is also necessary to consider
other areas, such as social, educational and cultural policy. In all
these the GDR claimed major successes. In the sphere of social
policy there is no doubt that a welfare state existed so that, for
instance, nobody was faced with economic ruin as a result of illness.
On the other hand, the level of provision was sometimes low, not
least in the case of old-age pensions, the basic level of which were
just about sufficient for basic survival. Since this state of affairs
encouraged many to continue working, it also helped to alleviate
labour shortages. Health care showed a mixed pattern. Here there

were undoubtedly major achievements, such as low infant mortality, while the system of out-patient care at *Poliklinken* functioned reasonably well; on the other hand, many hospitals were ill-equipped by modern standards. Nevertheless, since life expectancy was roughly the same as that in the Federal Republic, it would be ridiculous to portray the GDR's health system as totally unsatisfactory, particularly given the resources available.

Education was one area in which the GDR received a great deal of recognition. It was claimed by some in the Federal Republic on the GDR's behalf that the provision of free school textbooks was rightly a more important social priority than, for example, a regular supply of bananas. As in the case of social welfare, the GDR did provide a blanket state system for all: the unified socialist system of education (*Einheitliches sozialistisches Bildungssystem*). Provision started with creches for the very young, something that allowed women to return to work relatively quickly, through kinder-gartens to a basic ten-year school system, after which the majority went into vocational training and a minority continued at school to prepare themselves for higher education. This system had both strengths and weaknesses. On the one hand, all were catered for so that qualifications were almost universally achieved; on the other hand, the system was entirely attuned to perceived economic needs with the inevitable consequence of rigidity. This meant personal hardship for those individuals who were unable to pursue their preferred educational path, something which was particularly visible at the level of higher education. Since it was felt that only a certain number of graduates were required in any given area, selection tended to be rigorous and based on more than academic criteria. Male students stood little chance of entering university at all unless they had volunteered for three years' military service rather than the basic eighteen months, while female students were also expected to take part in paramilitary exercises. Indeed the increasing militarisation of the whole education system, indicted by the author Reiner Kunze in his book *Die wunderbaren Jahre* (*The Wonderful Years*) (1976),[6] led to protests by the church following the introduction of a school subject entitled military education (*Wehrerziehung*). This example underlines the major problem of the GDR education system – the way it was permeated by ideology. Clearly, this was most noticeable in such areas as history and literature, but the central control of syllabuses and textbooks was felt in all areas.

The same could also be said of cultural life. The GDR sought to encourage many areas of cultural activity, hoping to achieve 'world class' in this as in so many other fields, and assuming that even culture could somehow be planned. Along with national recognition, the overall aim, as with education, was to develop socialist consciousness, an ideal reflected in such terms as the 'Socialist National Literature of the GDR' ('Sozialistische Nationalliteratur der DDR'). In reality, this meant censorship and the imposition of cultural norms, in particular the doctrine of 'socialist realism', as developed in the Stalin era in the Soviet Union, to all areas of art. There were times when cultural dogmas were less strenuously applied, primarily when Erich Honecker promised 'no taboos' immediately after his accession to power. At the same time he hedged his bets by saying that art had to remain socialist. In fact, from the late 1970s onwards, starting with the celebrated case of the poet and singer Wolf Biermann, the expulsion of dissident artists to the west, many of whom left reluctantly because their ideal was reform of the GDR from within, became a feature of GDR cultural life.

In that it did not lack talented artists, the GDR can be said to have achieved its cultural aims; however, the most creative ones tended to have the most difficulties with the authorities. It must also be borne in mind that everything printed in the GDR, even the labels on consumer goods, had to go through the censorship process. What this said about the works of writers such as Christa Wolf, Christoph Hein and Volker Braun became a major subject of controversy following the collapse of the GDR, a topic that will be dealt with in Chapter 9. At this point, it is sufficient to draw attention to the parameters imposed on artistic activities. These mean that the claims made about the GDR being, for example, 'a land of books' have to be seen in perspective, however much it may be true that there was a wider interest in culture than in many other countries.

Finally, in this section I will examine the position of women in the GDR, specifically the claim that in the GDR women enjoyed equality and emancipation. It is undoubtedly true that the workplace was as open to women as to men and that women were to some extent represented in areas that might still be seen in many countries as male preserves. However, women continued to dominate the traditional areas of female employment such as retailing and service industries generally. It was also official policy to encourage female education and the number of women gaining qualifications rose rapidly in the 1960s and 1970s. Equally, female participation in political and other areas of public life was a policy priority. However positive these developments were, it is necessary to ask whether women achieved true positions of power in society and whether they suffered from the dual burden of having to work and look after a home. In the case of the upper echelons of political power, the answer is not particularly positive, with one of the few women to achieve power at the highest level being Margot Honecker, the wife of the party leader and an extremely dogmatic minister for education. Women were better represented at other levels, achieving between 30 and 40 per cent of seats in the various local, regional and national parliaments in the 1980s.

The burdens placed on working women are common to all kinds of societies. Attempts to make GDR men share domestic duties more equitably do not seem to have been particularly successful; the ideal of a socialist marriage did not prevent divorce rates that compared with those in capitalist countries. The lot of GDR women may have been harder because of the difficulties resulting from shortages that meant that more time was spent shopping. On the other hand, social provisions, the financial support given to women for twelve months following the birth of a child (*Babyjahr*) and the monthly free day given to women for domestic duties (*Haushaltstag*) provided significant help.

Women were also able to control their fertility, particularly after the granting of abortion rights in 1972, the only worthwhile achievement of the GDR for Monika Maron (1992: 91). That the birthrate was generally low suggests that, despite the help afforded to mothers and families, having children put a strain on GDR women. In this respect, the situation did not differ much from that in the Federal Republic. Nevertheless significant differences from the other German state must be noted. Female participation in all areas of society was encouraged, rather than being merely accepted, in many cases after long struggles. That this occurred partly because of economic necessity rather than simply as a result of idealism does not alter the fact that it happened. The only proviso that has to made is that emancipation was restricted by the limits placed on individuals by the overall political and economic system of the GDR.

This is the major point that has to be borne in mind in any consideration of the achievements of the GDR. Although barriers of class and gender were to a degree swept away, the one omni-present barrier for citizens remained the limits imposed by a rigid, ordered system that penetrated most areas of life. A frequently heard complaint in the GDR was that life was mapped out from birth to grave, from creche to old people's home, that it was entirely predictable where a person would be at any given stage of his or her life. To an extent this is true of any society, although dreams of riches and travel can alleviate grinding reality for those who lack privilege or the ability to exploit the prevailing economic system. In the GDR, it was largely impossible to sink; it was equally impossible for the overwhelming majority to rise, whatever their talents, beyond a modest level of comfort within the frontiers of the one small state. There was no 'GDR dream' which could compensate for society's shortcomings.

This section has sought to show the balance between certain claimed achievements and their limitations. It would be ludicrous to suggest that there were no achievements or that life was universally not worth living. Even where the realms of politics and economics brought frustration to the majority, the private sphere could provide personal happiness, although post unification attempts to conjure up the idyll of a society dominated at a personal level by human warmth that was destroyed by the events of 1989–90 have to be taken with a pinch of salt, given that the human communities referred to might have included a Stasi spy who passed on intimate details of friends or even family members to the state. One example is that of the civil rights activist Vera Lengsfeld (formerly Wollenberger), a member of parliament since 1990, who was informed on by her husband. In fact, the state frequently cast a dark shadow over nearly all aspects of life in the GDR. Even where there appeared to be success, as in the field of sport, there was a price to pay – in this case the widespread use of drugs. This example appears to epitomise much of what at first sight seemed positive about the 'socialist achievements' of the GDR. All too frequently it proved impossible to square the circle: to have, for instance, full employment and productive work, cheap rents and adequate housing.

CONCLUSION

The points outlined above inevitably lead to the conclusion that the GDR used the methods of the totalitarian state to control the lives of its citizens and to exert its power and influence in as many areas of life as possible. What such a conclusion does not mean is that all the efforts and achievements of individual GDR citizens are to be regarded as worthless. The whole question of the relationship between the GDR and its citizens is extremely complex and does not allow for easy categorisation, which either regards the majority as the hapless victims of an evil system or castigates it for acquiescing in its own oppression.

The accusation that most people in the GDR failed to resist political tyranny has frequently been heard since German unification. The implication is that there is a parallel between the behaviour of the majority in the Nazi era and in the GDR. Such a comparison is extremely dubious in as far as it fails to distinguish the two regimes. Whatever its failings, the GDR did not pursue genocide or total war, nor did its leaders fight to the bitter end.[7] Moreover, it is possible to understand a degree of idealistic identification with the GDR, particularly in its early years. The GDR always represented itself as the embodiment of a better Germany, that is to say as an alternative to the unhappy tradition that dominated German history between 1871 and 1945, and which appeared still to be alive in the Federal Republic where former National Socialists continued to enjoy positions of power in economic and political life.[8]

Although in many respects the official anti-fascism of the GDR was a sham, in that it was imposed from above and seemed almost to imply that the territory and people of the GDR had not been under Nazi rule, it was an understandable point of identification for postwar generations. The difficult, if not impossible, question is how quickly it should have been realised that the GDR did not represent an alternative, was not the country where an ideal of democratic socialism could be realised. This was as true in the early years when the SED acted against reformist tendencies in the 1950s as it was in the Gorbachev era when Kurt Hager, the *Politbüro* member with responsibility for ideology, made his infamous comment, when asked about reforms in the Soviet Union, that it was not necessary to wallpaper one's own house just because the neighbour was doing so. This kind of dogmatism, which even led to the banning of reformist Soviet publications in the 1980s, helped to destroy any idealism there was left, particularly among young people and intellectuals who might still have harboured the hope of reform. It is true that those who began the demonstrations in 1989 still hoped for a reformed GDR; once the Wall was breached and unification became a realistic possibility, the ground was taken away from under them.

If it is possible to feel understanding and sympathy for those who nourished the ultimately vain hope of reforming the GDR and in many cases took personal risks in the pursuit of their ideal, what is the appropriate attitude to adopt to those who, despite their dissatisfaction, remained outwardly loyal to the state? It is true that ultimately the GDR could not have functioned without the *Mitläufer*, those who went along with the system. On the other hand, the impossibility of overturning the system as long as the Soviet Union wished to maintain it was plain to see. The suppression of protest in the GDR itself in 1953 by Soviet troops, and subsequently in Hungary in 1956 and Czechoslovakia in 1968, showed the limits of protest. Even in Poland, where mass opposition to the system became visible for all to see with the creation of Solidarity, the form of government could not be changed without Soviet consent. Some degree of acceptance of the inevitable was therefore essential for all but the brave few who were willing to suffer imprisonment for their convictions. Even these were faced with a dilemma: protest might lead to expulsion to the Federal Republic, which was not a solution for those who wanted to reform the GDR.

It is of course possible to argue about the degree of acceptance or compromise. An obvious distinction might seem to be between those who worked directly and enthusiastically within official organisations such as the Stasi, and those who went about their daily business and restricted shows of loyalty to voting and taking part in obligatory parades. The problem with such a distinction is that the influence of the state extended into so many areas: a teacher, for instance, was in most cases not able merely to impart objective knowledge but, as mentioned above, had to teach a curriculum that reflected official ideology. Nevertheless, moral absolutes that would condemn all teachers on the basis of some degree of compromise with the system seem extremely harsh. It is clearly necessary to differentiate between subjects, and even in areas such as history it is known that some teachers were less than rigid. The arguments become even more complicated when the position of those who sought to help fellow citizens at odds with the authorities is considered. This has become clear since unification in the debate about the role played by the current *Ministerpräsident*

23

of the state of Brandenburg, Manfred Stolpe, who was previously an official of the Lutheran Church. In this capacity he inevitably had to deal with the authorities, in particular the Stasi, when, for example, he intervened on behalf of people wishing to leave the GDR. Now the question being asked is whether contact became co-operation, or even collaboration to the point of becoming an *Inoffizieller Mitarbeiter* who put the interests of the Stasi above those of the church and those he was supposedly helping. It is not the details of this individual case that matter here. What it illustrates is the difficulty or rather impossibility of making generalised judgements about the behaviour of GDR citizens. Given the coercive and all-pervading nature of the system, it is wise to speak of guilt or moral failure only in those cases where the actions of individuals harmed others. Otherwise an appreciation of the difficulties faced by GDR citizens is more appropriate.

Some of these difficulties have already been alluded to. There were the material difficulties brought about by an inflexible economy incapable of satisfying more than basic needs and the non-material ones that resulted from a rigid ideology that affected so many areas of life. It is no wonder that, with the fall of the Wall, the majority of GDR citizens sought salvation from what seemed the promised land of the Federal Republic, known to some degree from the watching of western television but distant enough to be lent considerable enchantment. Few were in a mood to follow the cries for a reformed GDR that emanated from those who, particularly to outsiders, enjoyed moral authority because of their history of protest. For most insiders, whose major priority was to share in western prosperity, they were or became, as the influence of the Federal Republic grew, other-worldly idealists who wanted to indulge in another experiment comparable to the one that had gone so wrong over the previous forty years. Given that undoubted failure, the only possible conclusion is that the GDR, in the form that it existed, deserved to disappear from the political map.

2

THE FEDERAL REPUBLIC OF GERMANY (1949–90)

The state that succeeded

BONN STABILITY AND WEIMAR INSTABILITY

In 1956 the political scientist Fritz René Allemann published a book entitled *Bonn ist nicht Weimar*. The implication of this title is that the Federal Republic of Germany, as constituted in 1949 with Bonn as its capital, had attained the stability that had been denied to the post-1919 Weimar Republic. This first attempt to create a democratic republic in Germany collapsed in ignominy on Hitler's coming to power in 1933. Whether Allemann's thesis can now be regarded as proven is a moot point; it depends on whether the unified German state of 1990 is regarded as a new entity whose future, like anything else, cannot be entirely predicted or whether it is merely a continuation of the post-1949 Federal Republic. If, however, the period 1949 to 1990 is regarded as a discrete era, it is self-evident that Allemann's statement has proved to be correct. Not only did the Bonn Republic survive almost three times as long as Weimar (and more than three times as long as Hitler's 'Thousand year Reich'), it proved to be, as its political leaders were wont to point out, the most liberal and democratic state that had ever existed on German soil. Cynics might argue that it had little competition, given its historical predecessors; nevertheless, this chapter hopes to show that the Federal Republic of 1949 to 1990, if not utopia, was a highly successful state and, as the 1970s slogan of the then ruling SPD, *Modell Deutschland*, implied, in many ways exemplary.

It is appropriate to begin with a reference to the failed Weimar Republic because the structures of the Federal Republic were intended from the very beginning to overcome some of the weaknesses of the post-1919 republic. Political life in the Weimar period

25

had been marked by a plethora of unstable coalitions and a series of inconclusive general elections, particularly in its last years. There were general elections in 1928, 1930 and twice in 1932, a year which also saw a presidential election. Another problem of the Weimar system was that executive power was split between the Chancellor and the President, who was able to assume almost dictatorial powers by virtue of Article 48 of the constitution which allowed him to issue emergency decrees. The use of these powers by President Hindenburg in the last years before the Nazi takeover, when successive governments were unable to command, and unwilling to seek, a parliamentary majority, certainly played a part in undermining Weimar democracy.

By contrast, the constitution of the Federal Republic – the *Grundgesetz* – sought to avoid these weaknesses. Executive power was placed firmly in the hands of the Federal Chancellor (*Bundeskanzler*), who occupies a position comparable to that, for example, of a British Prime Minister. This position is confirmed by Article 65 of the *Grundgesetz* which states that the Federal Chancellor 'determines the guidelines of policy'. By contrast, the Federal President (*Bundespräsident*) is reduced to a largely ceremonial role as head of state. One of the few exceptions to this state of affairs is the power of the Federal President to dissolve the lower house of parliament (*Bundestag*) before the end of the fixed four-year legislative period, which was also introduced to avoid the political instability caused by frequent elections, if the government has lost a vote of confidence and the *Bundeskanzler* requests such a dissolution. These powers were used to call 'early' elections in 1972 and 1983. Otherwise the Federal Chancellor can only be removed within the four-year legislative period by a 'constructive vote of no confidence' ('*konstruktives Mißtrauensvotum*'), that is to say a vote in which a named potential successor must gain an absolute majority of members of parliament for the incumbent Chancellor to be dismissed. It was through such a vote that Helmut Kohl gained power in 1982, the only example of its being employed successfully at federal level.

The search for political stability was also reinforced by the requirement, within the modified system of proportional representation adopted in time for the 1953 elections, that a political party should gain 5 per cent of the total vote (or win three constituencies) to be represented in parliament, an arrangement that helped to cut down the number of splinter groups and make the formation of coalitions easier.[1] Measures were also introduced to combat the scourge of political extremism that in the form of National Socialism had directly destroyed Weimar democracy. Article 21 of the Basic Law requires that political parties should embrace the democratic principles of the constitution or face prohibition by the Federal Constitutional Court (*Bundesverfassungsgericht*), a fate that befell two parties in the 1950s. One of these – KPD – had had seats in the *Bundestag* from 1949 to 1953. The neo-Nazi Sozialistische Reichspartei was proscribed in 1952, and in 1956 the same fate befell the KPD, which, in the eyes of some, not only threatened the democracy of Bonn but had also contributed to the collapse of Weimar through its rejection of parliamentary democracy.

However important these structures may be, they are not sufficient to explain the political success of the Federal Republic. Desperadoes like Hitler are hardly likely to be deterred by constitutional niceties. Any consideration of the success of the Federal Republic must pay attention to the processes by which such success was achieved. As was pointed out in the previous chapter, the Federal Republic was as much an artificial creation as the GDR. The population was never asked to agree to its creation, nor was the *Grundgesetz* submitted for popular approval. Indeed, it can be (and has been) described as a constitution that reflects distrust of popular opinion because of the constraints it puts on political activity, some of which have been mentioned above and to which might be added the more or less complete absence of provision for referenda, a form of political participation possible in the Weimar system. At the time of its inception, this was most probably justified, given recent history. Surveys taken in the early years of the Federal Republic suggest a lack of interest in all aspects of politics and specifically a lack of enthusiasm for democracy, to which the authoritarian style of the first Federal Chancellor, Konrad Adenauer, might well have contributed.[2] Because of this, even if the influence of generational change is allowed for, it remains essential to consider in some detail the processes that turned the Federal Republic of 1949 to 1990 into a stable state and made the democratic system acceptable to the vast majority of its citizens.

ECONOMIC FACTORS

It is undeniable that the economic success of the Federal Republic, encapsulated in the expression 'economic miracle' ('Wirtschaftswunder'), played a major role in the increasingly enthusiastic acceptance of its social and political order. Once more it is useful to make a comparison with the ill-fated Weimar Republic. Without the worldwide economic crisis or Great Depression following the collapse of the Wall Street Stock Exchange in 1929 it is unlikely that Hitler would have come to power. By contrast, the Federal Republic was born into an era of economic prosperity when developed countries were recovering from the ravages of the Second World War. The correlation between economic success and political stability in Germany, in particular in the early years of the Federal Republic, can be illustrated by the repercussions of the first, albeit by today's standards, minor economic crisis of 1966–7. This led not only to the collapse of the government of the then *Bundeskanzler* Ludwig Erhard, Adenauer's former economics minister who had been revered as the 'father of the economic miracle', but also to the rapid growth of the extreme right-wing NPD, whose temporary success in *Land* elections, given the historical precedent, raised fears for the future of German democracy. Subsequent economic crises have not had the same political effects, although it probably remains the case that Germans continue to judge their political system by its success, not least in the area of economics.[3] What can no longer be claimed is that democratic structures are secure only in times of economic prosperity.

Notwithstanding the opportunities presented to all developed economies during the postwar years, the success of the economy of the Federal Republic remains remarkable. In the 1950s, the economy grew by an average of 8 per cent annually and by 4 per cent in the following decade. Over roughly the same period unemployment dropped from over 1.5 million in 1949 to 140,000 in 1970, while at the same time almost 2 million foreign workers had been integrated into the labour force. Even if not all sections of the community benefited equally, the growth in average monthly incomes from DM237 to DM856 between 1950 and 1967 was enough to give most citizens a sense of economic well-being.

When speaking of the economy of the Federal Republic, it has become common, on the basis of the economic requirements laid down in the Stability Law (*Stabilitätsgesetz*) of 1967, to refer to a 'magic square', whose sides are inflation, growth, unemployment

28

and balance of payments. The unusual or 'magic' element has been to achieve positive results simultaneously in all four areas, something that has not generally been possible, for instance, in Great Britain. There growth and lower unemployment have generally been accompanied by inflation and balance of payments problems. Efforts to cure these have in turn led to higher unemployment and lower growth. By contrast, between 1951 and 1990 the Federal Republic did not experience inflation above 7.8 per cent, registered growth in all but three years, enjoyed unemployment rates that sank to 0.7 per cent in four years and only rose above 10 per cent in 1951 and recorded a balance of payments surplus for all but five years. Why has the German economy tended to perform so well? Words like 'miracle' or 'magic' are a shorthand way of expressing the success; they do not provide explanations. In seeking answers many factors have to be borne in mind, although it will only be possible here to refer in general terms to those that have widely been seen as contributing to the economic success of the Federal Republic between 1949 and 1990.

The new Federal Republic adopted an economic system known as *soziale Marktwirtschaft* (social market economy). The adoption of a market economy on the western model, as opposed to the dead hand of the planned economy as introduced in the GDR, provided the basis for progress; what was peculiar to the Federal Republic, however, were the features that became associated with the adjective *sozial*. It is important to differentiate between the social and the free market economy in which state intervention is reduced to an absolute minimum. The role of the state in the German model was at least twofold: first, to regulate the market so that optimum conditions for competition and individual enterprise were maintained and not thwarted by the growth of monopolies and cartels; and second, to ensure a social welfare system for those who might have fallen by the wayside in a totally free market system. *Soziale Marktwirtschaft* can thus be seen as an attempt to balance different interests, to create a climate of co-operation rather than confrontation.

This aspect of co-operation is underlined by other features of the economic order of the Federal Republic: partnership or co-determination in industry and the role of the trade unions. Co-determination (*Mitbestimmung*) was introduced into German industry in 1951 when legislation required that representatives of employees should occupy half the seats on the supervisory board

(*Aufsichtsrat*) of companies in the mining and steel industries. As the name implies, the role of the supervisory board is to keep a controlling eye on a company's overall affairs. Additionally, employees' interests were to be represented on the management board (*Vorstand*), responsible for the daily running of such concerns, by the labour director (*Arbeitsdirektor*). Subsequently, employees acquired the right of *Mitbestimmung* in other industries, although not to the extent of full parity, and rights to be consulted at plant level, for instance over working hours, through a works council (*Betriebsrat*) in firms above a certain size. How far these measures represent true industrial democracy is a subject of debate; it is certainly true that the significance of employee influence in the coal and steel sectors declined along with that particular industrial sector. What cannot be doubted is that these systems of co-determination were part of an economic framework that set great store by co-operation. This was even reflected at a linguistic level, with employers and employees referred to as *Sozialpartner*, a term that could hardly have been used in Great Britain during the 1950s and 1960s, given the frequently fractious behaviour of what were, probably correctly, described as the two sides of industry.

Who benefited most from the co-operation within German industry is not the issue here. It is sufficient to point out that structures that favoured co-operation were created, not least within the trade union movement, which, when re-created after 1945, was based on a system of large industrial unions (*Industriegewerkschaften*).[4] In other words, there was, for example, only one union in the railway industry with no distinctions according to a worker's particular status or craft within that industry. Nor were there any ideological distinctions within postwar trade unions. Unlike the situation during the Weimar Republic, unions were not affiliated to any political party or religious grouping. The apparent success of these structures showed itself in the lack of strikes and the economic achievements referred to above. No doubt, too, the experience of military defeat and the overwhelming need to rebuild favoured a conciliatory rather than a confrontational approach within industry and the economy generally. The first priority was to create a cake rather than argue about how it should be divided. And even if it became clear to some that the new cake was not being divided equally, the majority felt replete with their share.

The foundations for *soziale Marktwirtschaft* were laid a year before the foundation of the Federal Republic with the currency reform carried out in the three western zones of occupation in 1948. This introduced the Deutsche Mark (DM) in place of the Reichsmark which had been rendered almost worthless by wartime and postwar inflation, the result of the Nazis' lack of financial prudence. The creation of a stable currency allowed economic activity to resume in an orderly way after the postwar chaos, during which cigarettes had assumed the status of unofficial currency. Subsequently, it has become the symbol of postwar German affluence. What in fact happened was that a kind of virtuous circle began to operate. The D-Mark stabilised the economy, which in turn strengthened the D-Mark. Within this circle, the Central Bank (Deutsche Bundesbank) was given the task of controlling inflation by having the power to control the money supply and interest rates independently of government. Given the trauma of inflation in Germany, with money rendered worthless on two occasions within twenty-five years, during the Weimar Republic in 1923 and in the 1945 to 1948 period, the importance of this role cannot be overestimated. The success can be measured by a tradition of low inflation and the appreciation of the D-Mark from a rate of DM4.20 = $1 in 1949 to one of under DM2 to the dollar at the time of unification. In turn, the health of the currency has inspired a tradition of saving, with the household saving ratio, that is the percentage of household disposal income saved, never falling below 11 per cent in the years 1985 to 1994.

The Bundesbank is not the only bank worthy of mention in any discussion of the economic performance of the Federal Republic. The whole banking system has been geared to the long-term interests of industry, in particular through the establishment of partnerships and networks. Within the *Universalbank* system,[5] major banks such as the Deutsche Bank own large shareholdings in companies, for example, Daimler-Benz, and through representation on the supervisory board influence the conduct of companies. If this means that companies are run in the interests of banks, it is part of the banks' interest as shareholders to ensure that the company prospers through, for example, supporting necessary investment. A greater willingness to invest than in certain competitor countries has remained a feature of the German economy ever since it was necessary to replace machinery lost in the war or as a result of the Allies' postwar dismantling of industry, something that, incidentally, allowed the replacement of older with more modern plant. Gross fixed investment remains at about 20 per cent

31

of GDP, having ranged in the last decade from 19.7 per cent in 1985 to 23.4 per cent in 1992. In the case of smaller companies, the support of a bank, although less likely to be one of the *Universalbanken*, is usually based on a relationship of mutual trust developed over a long period. Particularly worthy of note are the Bank for Reconstruction (Kreditanstalt für Wiederaufbau) formed in 1948, which specialises in favourable loans to smaller firms and the regional banks that can base their judgement on local knowledge. This has meant that small- and medium-sized companies, what is called in German the *Mittelstand*, have prospered and become a central part of the German economy. Across the whole of industry the relationship between banks and companies means that it is not usually necessary for firms to go to the stock exchange to raise capital. Firms not quoted on the stock exchange are not vulnerable to takeover bids (fear of which, in other countries, arguably takes management's attention away from its core task of running the company), and in any case with a system of voting and non-voting shares operating in the Federal Republic, the power of shareholders is less than absolute. The result of all this is that contested takeover bids are almost unheard of, since those whose only interest might be a quick return on their capital are not in a position to influence events. This means a stable climate for business activity in which takeovers certainly take place – enough for some observers to worry about lack of competition in certain areas and complain about the ineffectiveness of the *Bundeskartellamt*, which is charged with preventing the growth of monopolies – but in an orderly, non-acrimonious atmosphere.

The points mentioned above do not constitute an exhaustive list of the factors that influenced the development of the economy of the Federal Republic until 1990. At the outset there was foreign support within the European Recovery Programme (generally known as Marshall Aid) launched by the USA in 1947, which gave the new West German economy an initial impetus. From the beginning too there was a well-educated workforce, supplemented by those expelled from the former German territories that had become part of Poland and until 1961 by refugees from the GDR. Thereafter some of the gaps in the labour market were filled by foreign workers. For most, if not all, of its existence, the pre-unification Federal Republic did not have to devote as many resources to defence spending as did commercial competitors with overseas commitments, for example, Great Britain and France, which meant in turn that more money could be spent on areas such as education and training to the benefit of the economy. Even the insolvency laws were designed to look after the interests of more than creditors. All in all, the German economic system came to be based on the concept of the stakeholder, that is to say the idea that various groups are equally interested in the prosperity of the individual company and the economy as a whole. As has been shown, these include the entrepreneur, the employee and the supplier of finance, not to mention government at both national and regional level. In recent years, especially, regional state governments have sought to encourage industry by supporting research and technology transfer. The results may never have been perfect or, in many eyes, just – between 1950 and 1969 the self-employed enjoyed on average an increase in wealth twenty times that of hourly paid workers – but the overall economic performance of the Federal Republic between 1949 and 1990 was good enough to bring at least modest prosperity to nearly all of its inhabitants, a great degree of material comfort to many and to cause envy in most neighbouring countries, not least the other German state.

THE POLITICAL SYSTEM

Whereas the economic success of the Federal Republic between 1949 and 1990 was built upon an industrial culture that had a long prestigious tradition, not least in the engineering sector – it is well known that the motor car and the diesel engine originated in Germany – politics, especially democratic politics, was never held in such esteem but regarded rather as a 'dirty business' (*'ein schmutziges Geschäft'*). At the time of the First World War, for instance, the writer Thomas Mann prided himself on being non-political, that is to say anti-democratic, as the title of his volume of political writings, *Betrachtungen eines Unpolitischen (Reflections of a Non-Political Man)* (1993), shows. Although there was a democratic tradition in Germany, which Mann himself came to join during the Weimar Republic, it remained weak. Many, especially the middle classes and in particular academics, regarded democracy as something alien to Germany and its people. Accordingly, large sections of the German population rejoiced at the return to authoritarian rule when Hitler came to power. The establishment of democracy was therefore a prime task in the early years of the Federal Republic.

33

As already mentioned, the framework for the political system of the new Federal Republic was provided by the *Grundgesetz*, a term adopted in preference to constitution (*Verfassung*) as it emphasised the provisional nature of the state pending the reunification of Germany. Whereas in the early years this self-classification of the Federal Republic as a *Provisorium* might have militated against popular identification with the new state, by the 1980s at the latest the political system and its constitution enjoyed enough prestige for the term constitutional patriotism (*Verfassungspatriotismus*), with its echoes of the United States, to have entered into political debate.

Why had the *Grundgesetz* achieved such status? It was not simply that traditional more nationalistic articulations of patriotic feeling were rendered more difficult by the German past and by postwar division, but rather that the new constitution incorporated desirable political ideals and provided a framework for effective governance. To do this its provisions had to go far beyond those features already referred to as attempts to avoid some of the pitfalls of the Weimar Republic. Its first nineteen articles contain basic rights, whose affirmation can be seen as a reaction to the contempt for human rights shown by the Nazis. Since they include the inviolability of human dignity, the right to free expression and the right of assembly, they underline the importance of individual liberty within a democratic society. Thereafter, in Article 20 the Federal Republic is defined as 'ein demokratischer und sozialer Rechtsstaat'. *Rechtsstaat* is usually translated as constitutional state and implies a state of affairs where everything is subject to the rule of law. This concept is not new in German constitutional history, going back to the nineteenth century when it was used in connection with the provision of rules within which economic activity could take place; in other words the *Rechtsstaat* was the basis for liberal free-market capitalism. The innovation in 1949 was the addition of the adjective *sozial*, a word whose significance has already been referred to in connection with the social market economy. The importance of a degree of social justice and equality is further underlined in Article 72, which requires a 'uniformity of living conditions' ('*Einheitlichkeit der Lebensverhältnisse*'), that is to say comparable standards of life in all parts of the country. This concept has taken on a new significance with the incorporation of the much less prosperous former GDR into the Federal Republic.

34

There is no doubt that these ideals of the *Grundgesetz* soon began to enter the consciousness of large numbers of citizens of the Federal Republic. This can be seen by the way critics of certain developments in the Federal Republic came to contrast the ideals of the constitution with what they termed 'constitutional reality' (*Verfassungswirklichkeit*). Issues were judged by the yardstick of what were considered the positive provisions of the *Grundgesetz*. Moreover, it can be claimed that in certain major scandals affecting the Federal Republic, during which democratic values appeared to be challenged, the spirit of the constitution prevailed against those who sought to undermine it. One example of this is the Spiegel Affair of 1962 when the editor and journalists of the news magazine *Der Spiegel* were arrested for allegedly betraying state secrets in an article about the state of readiness of the armed forces. In reality, the arrests seemed to be revenge for attacks by the magazine on the government in general and the Defence Minister, Franz Josef Strauß, in particular. After huge public protests, the affair ended with the release of the journalists and the resignation of Strauß.

In this and other cases, the ideals of the Basic Law triumphed. It would, however, be naive to put down the success of the political system of the Federal Republic simply to ideals, however desirable. The Basic Law gained credibility as part of a system that worked effectively, not just politically but, as already shown, most particularly in the economic sphere. At the same time, the role of the political system within the overall success of the state should not be overlooked, with certain factors in particular deserving special attention.

The importance of the federal system is one factor that cannot be overlooked. As stated in the Introduction, federalism reflects the regional traditions of Germany where political unity came so late. Accordingly, most people identify with their region or the *Land* in which they live. However, with exceptions, most particularly Bavaria, these states, especially in the west, do not conform to traditional boundaries but are postwar creations. Even traditional names such as Hessen do not correspond to traditional areas, with, for instance, the wine-growing regions of Rheinhessen now being part of the state of Rheinland-Pfalz (Rhineland-Palatinate). Thus identification with a particular *Land* is part of an overall identification with the federalism established at the inception of the Federal Republic.

The federal states in Germany do not enjoy as much autonomy as, for example, their equivalents in the United States, where such a major issue as the use of the death penalty is decided at state level. It is only in the areas of broadcasting and education that the German states enjoy such powers, as a reaction against the centralised propaganda machine of the Nazis that relied so heavily on these potential means of indoctrination. In general, the states carry out federal legislation at a regional level, their real power lying more in their ability to influence such legislation. This power is executed in the upper house of the federal parliament (*Bundesrat*). Its members represent the governments of each state; thus, if a state government is run by a single party, all its *Bundesrat* representatives come from that particular party, with the number depending on the size of the *Land*. All federal legislation is considered by the *Bundesrat* and a great deal of it, particularly that relating to domestic policy, can only be enacted with its agreement. Otherwise, the *Bundesrat* can be overruled, but if it rejects any piece of legislation by a two-thirds majority, then a two-thirds majority of the *Bundestag* is required for its objections to be overcome.

The power of the *Bundesrat* comes into play when the states feel their interests are being threatened (this can occur especially when it comes to the question of how the federal budget is to be divided between the central government and the *Länder*, although the federal government does have the chance to 'divide and rule' when it comes to the question of how much each individual state receives) or when one party holds sway in the *Bundesrat* and another in the *Bundestag*, the situation during much of the 1970s and at the time of writing in 1995.[6] What is important in both cases is that the upper house can act almost as a second tier of control on government, and given that the government by definition has a majority in the first tier, the *Bundestag*, often potentially a more powerful one. The result is a lesser degree of concentration of power in the hands of the head of government, the *Bundeskanzler*, than in other systems and, as in the case of the economic system, the need for co-operation if the political system is to function. To this end, a feature of parliamentary life is an arbitration committee (*Vermittlungsausschuß*), made up of members of both houses, which has a history of finding compromise solutions to contentious problems. There is also one other institution that can restrain government and parliament, the *Bundesverfassungsgericht*, the legal institution mentioned briefly above as a scrutineer of the democratic credentials of political parties. Its more frequent role is to decide whether any particular piece of legislation conforms to the constitution. It can be asked to adjudicate on such matters by those who feel this not to be the case. At times, for instance with its stance against abortion, the Court has been accused of usurping the legislative role of parliament.[7] The binding nature of its decisions, however controversial, does underline the extent of its powers to curb the executive and the legislature. All in all, the variety of institutions sharing power in the Federal Republic prevents its over-concentration in a few hands, even if, with its members constrained by party discipline, the main legislative assembly, the *Bundestag*, usually follows the wishes of the executive. This is no different from other countries where, however, there might not be a comparable system of checks and balances.

No discussion of the political system of the Federal Republic can restrict itself to institutions. Equally important are the political parties, which were given a special status by the *Grundgesetz*. Article 21 speaks of them as contributing to 'the creation of the political will of the people'. This is a break with the authoritarian German tradition that saw parties as disruptive and divisive, a view reflected in the statement of Kaiser Wilhelm II at the outbreak of the First World War when, noting the almost universal outbreak of patriotic enthusiasm, he declared that he did not recognise any parties any more but only Germans.[8] Hitler of course went one step further by banning all except his own Nazi Party. In the Federal Republic, the parties have come to occupy the same pivotal role as in other democratic states with members of parliament elected primarily as representatives of political parties and the executive consisting of ministers drawn from the parties in power.

It has always been a case of *parties* in power, as the electoral system of proportional representation only once gave an overall majority to one party grouping, the Christlich-Demokratische Union (CDU), along with its Bavarian sister party Christlich-Soziale Union (CSU), in 1957, and even then a coalition was pre-ferred. The need for coalitions was a source of weakness in Weimar, but in the pre-unification Federal Republic it was a source of strength, because, given the small number of parties represented in parliament for most of the time between 1949 and 1990, stable coalitions were usually possible. This also meant that the chances for change and possibly violent and disruptive shifts of policy were extremely limited. This element of stability only developed over time. The composition of the first parliament of 1949 bore some resemblance to the situation in Weimar with eleven parties or groups represented and the first *Bundeskanzler*, Konrad Adenauer, only achieving the constitutional requirement of being confirmed in his position by the *Bundestag* by one vote – his own. By 1953 the number of parties was down to five and by 1961 to three, where it remained until the entry of the Greens in 1983. This development was due in part to the 5 per cent clause mentioned at the beginning of this chapter (p. 26), but also to the ability of the two largest parties, the CDU/CSU and the SPD, to accommodate the majority of voters. The third party, the liberal Freie Demokratische Partei (FDP), whose vote in the eleven elections during the existence of the Federal Republic prior to unity varied between 5.8 and 11.9 per cent, came to have a pivotal role, given the lack of any overall majority for a single party. In effect, the complexion of the government could only change if the FDP changed from supporting one of the major parties to the other (it moved to the SPD for the first time in 1969 and remained its junior partner until 1982) or if the two major parties formed a coalition, as they did with the Grand Coalition (*Große Koalition*) between 1966 and 1969. Neither of these scenarios favoured total shifts of policy; the presence of the FDP in all coalitions except those between 1956 and 1961 and 1966 to 1969 underlines the point. The party constellations that existed for much of the time between 1949 and 1990 allowed for a remarkable mix of democracy and stability. Even excluding the possibility of a Grand Coalition, a change of government was arithmetically usually possible, but not a total change of the type that can occur in a largely two-party system such as the one operating in Great Britain, where one party almost invariably commands an absolute majority.

To work at all effectively a coalition government must be made up of two or more parties with a parliamentary majority. There must be a large area of agreement on matters of policy. It is impossible here to discuss all aspects of the policies pursued by the various parties mentioned, although some broader discussion of current party policies will take place in Chapter 3. What is important here is to draw attention to the degree of consensus that developed after 1949 and enabled the creation of the coalitions referred to above. In the early years of the Federal Republic the SPD did favour traditional left-wing economic policies based on a major role for the state, but in 1959, as part of the many changes of policy within its Godesberg Programme, it largely accepted the social market economy, although stressing the social element more than, in particular, the FDP who set greater store on economic liberalism. For twenty-five years, therefore, until the entry into parliament of the Greens, all parties fully supported the principles that had created the successful economy.

The Godesberg Programme of the SPD was equally significant in the area of foreign policy. In it the party accepted the foreign policy of the Federal government, specifically the integration of the Federal Republic into the western system through membership of such bodies as NATO and the EEC. Previously it had been suspicious of integration as it saw western orientation as standing in the way of reunification. This step also brought it into the mainstream of policy and prepared its path into government. It was particularly in the area of foreign policy that the SPD was able to forge common ground with the FDP during their years in government between 1969 and 1982. Both supported a policy of better relations with the communist states, the *Ostpolitik* that remains associated with the first SPD Chancellor Willy Brandt. This policy has been subject to critical scrutiny since the collapse of communism with the charge being made that, particularly through economic co-operation, it artificially helped to prolong the life of a pernicious political system. The counter-argument is that it helped to open up communism and thus prepared the ground for its collapse. What cannot be denied is that *Ostpolitik* was in keeping with the general policy of *détente* being pursued by the great powers at that time. The Federal Republic was in step with its major ally, the United States, in the same way that it was when Konrad Adenauer was pursuing the policy of integration with the west. Whether Adenauer would have had any choice is an interesting point, given the fact that the Federal Republic remained officially occupied until 1955. Nevertheless his willing acquiescence in western policies helped to restore his country's position in the international order after the humiliation of National Socialism, as will be discussed in Chapter 6. There is also no doubt that this achievement found favour with most of the electorate.

The degree of consensus and co-operation achieved by the political parties and the reduction in the number of parties enjoying enough support to gain representation at a national level reflected a society that had become much less polarised than its predecessors. Divisions between Catholic and Protestant that had beset Germany in previous eras became less and less significant, not just as society, in keeping with developments in other European countries, became more secular but also because of attempts to overcome sectarianism in trade unions and in political life where the CDU, as a postwar foundation, sought to appeal to Christians of all denominations. Other potential threats to consensus in the postwar era were overcome relatively quickly. Particularism raised its head in Bavaria when the state assembly (*Landtag*) refused to accept the Basic Law, something that was referred to in the Introduction (p. 222). Moreover, there was a separatist Bayernpartei which gained seats at the federal level in 1949. However, the clever strategy of the Christian Democrats, creating a separate party in Bavaria in the form of the CSU, whose elected members at the federal level then join with the CDU to form a single parliamentary group, together with effective, if dubious to the point of criminal, tactics for eliminating the Bayernpartei helped to remove the threat. Another threat to consensus that manifested itself in the creation of a separate party – the Bund der Heimatvertriebenen und Entrechteten (BHE) was formed to defend the interests of the Germans expelled from their previous homes – was quickly overcome by the remarkable integration of such groups into society that accompanied the 'economic miracle'. However, the BHE did enjoy parliamentary representation between 1953 and 1957. Its voters, along with those of another right-wing party, the Deutsche Partei (DP), which was in coalition with the CDU/CSU from 1957 to 1961, eventually found a political home in the CDU/CSU. With growing prosperity, the sense of class distinction also declined, even if wealth was far from evenly distributed and differences within the educational system prevailed. Theories about the Federal Republic being a levelled out middle-class society (*nivellierte Mittelstandsgesellschaft*) were wide of the mark in this respect, but did possibly reflect aspirations and a subjective sense of achievement reflected at least in the widespread acquisition of material possessions.[9] For the overwhelming majority radical change was not on the agenda; after the turmoil of the first half of the twentieth century, most citizens wanted security and stability – and the new political system appeared to provide it.

To sum up: the years 1949 to 1990 were marked by substantial political achievements in the Federal Republic. A democratic and liberal political system was established on the basis of a much respected constitution. Policies were pursued that helped to create prosperity at home and respect abroad. Stability was proved by peaceful changes of government, while the population seemed well satisfied with the idea of democracy and the way it worked. Whatever blemishes there may have been – in addition to the Spiegel Affair, it would have been possible to mention controversies over rearmament in the 1950s, the student demonstrations in the 1960s, terrorism in the 1970s and scandals over the financing of political parties in the 1980s – the democratic substance of the state was never undermined. If the example of the student movement is taken, it can be claimed that its demands for reform were met in part after 1969 with only the disaffected few turning to terrorism. Terrorism certainly provoked draconian responses in the 1970s, in particular a series of laws that, for instance, restricted contact between lawyers and accused and made it an offence to glorify violence. This second law proved worthless and was rescinded in 1980. The most controversial measure, however, was undoubtedly the policy of excluding political extremists from public service, which made the word *Berufsverbot* (professional disqualification) known beyond Germany and evoked memories of the Nazi practice of excluding certain groups, especially Jews, from many professions. Since the public service, in particular the status of *Beamter*, was not just restricted to civil servants and teachers but also included postal and railway workers at that time, the measures frequently did appear draconian, as such groups could hardly threaten the security of the state. Over the years this policy, known as the *Radikalenerlaß* (radicals decree), generally fell into disuse, as it was realised how blunt an instrument it was. In recent times, debates over amnesties for imprisoned terrorists suggest growing awareness that draconian punishments are not always the appropriate response to extremism and terrorism. Seen as a whole, therefore, the political record of the Federal Republic prior to unification was largely positive.

FROM *OHNE MICH* TO *DER MÜNDIGE BÜRGER*: PROTEST AND PARTICIPATION IN THE DEMOCRATIC PROCESS

This section will discuss questions of political culture, specifically developments in the history of the Federal Republic that indicate an increasing involvement and identification of its citizens with political and social issues. Clearly this would not be the only way of indicating political interest; factors such as party membership and electoral participation are also important. If the numbers taking part in elections are taken as the only guide, then there was never a problem. In 1949 78.5 per cent of the electorate voted; the figure peaked at 91.1 per cent in 1972 before declining to 84.3 per cent in the last pre-unification election in 1987. All these figures stand comparison with other democracies and are way above the figures achieved in the United States. However, participation in elections cannot be the sole yardstick, as voting is not an everyday occurrence, even where a federal system, like the German one, allows more opportunities to vote than elsewhere; it is also possible to claim that some voters turn out more from a sense of duty than out of the desire to exercise a democratic right. More reliable are figures for party membership. These increased in the Federal Republic as political interest grew, peaking in the late 1970s and early 1980s. In 1977 the SPD had more than a million members and in 1982 the combined total for the CDU and CSU was almost 900,000. That the numbers declined thereafter (at the end of 1994 the SPD had 836,000 members and the CDU 670,000, compared with 719,000 in 1982) probably had something to do with the different kinds of political participation that began to develop at this time.

In an essay entitled 'Zwölf Fragen' ('Twelve Questions'), published in 1961, the novelist Paul Schallück stated that the political system of the Federal Republic provided many opportunities for the citizen but nobody made use of them (Schallück 1961: 105). If this was true at that time, it had certainly ceased to be so by the end of the decade. As the student movement underlined, a remarkable degree of politicisation had taken place, for which writers and intellectuals, as leaders and articulators of public opinion could take some of the credit.

Although they had always been concerned with political questions, young postwar writers and intellectuals, mindful of the dangers of the non-political tradition embraced in 1914 by Thomas Mann and anxious to prevent a repetition of the recent past, did not greet the foundation of the Federal Republic with enthusiasm. After the war, they had hoped for a united, democratic Germany within a united Europe and generally entertained aspirations of a new different Germany that had broken with its past, as will be seen in more detail in Chapter 8. As a product of division and the Cold War, the Federal Republic did not match these ideals; even its democratic credentials seemed endangered by the ease with which former Nazis appeared to be able to regain leading positions. With hindsight, given the large numbers of people who had been members of the Nazi Party, this might be viewed as the successful integration into society of a potentially difficult group; for those, such as the writer Heinrich Böll, who saw the issue in moral terms, it was a despicable state of affairs.

The distance writers felt towards the Federal Republic was matched by other members of the young generation, described by the sociologist Helmut Schelsky as the 'sceptical generation'. A group whose youth had been betrayed by National Socialism was in no mood to embrace any other ideology or even to take much part in politics at all. Moreover, in the circumstances prevailing in the early years of the Federal Republic there were other, more pressing, priorities of an economic nature. In his 1955 book on the burgeoning economy, *Mainsprings of the German Revival*, the American economist H.C. Wallich noted: 'The Germans themselves, indeed, have since the war paid attention to little but economic pursuits' (Wallich 1955: 20). There was certainly no desire among the majority for prolonged introspection about the Nazi era.

Where mass political activity did take place, it did not reflect identification with the state. When German rearmament was mooted within a decade of the ignominious collapse of the German military tradition, many, including writers and intellectuals, were prepared to protest – their slogan *ohne mich* (literally 'without me', but 'count me out' is a better equivalent) also encapsulating very clearly their scepticism towards the political process. Although polls showed a majority against rearmament, it duly occurred with the formation of the *Bundeswehr* in 1955, leaving the protesters to lick their wounds. Subsequent protests against the possibility of the army acquiring nuclear weapons were more successful, as the Federal Republic remained a non-nuclear power. However, this was probably more due to Germany's status as a defeated nation and the attitudes of the western allies than to the effectiveness of the protest movements.

Disillusioned with previous failures, in the 1960s writers and intellectuals became more involved with mainstream politics. At the 1961 and 1965 elections many, including most notably Günter Grass, declared their support for the SPD. At the next election in 1969, Grass was prepared to go a step further by co-founding the

Sozialdemokratische Wählerinitiative (The voters' action group for the Social Democrats). This was an attempt to involve citizens – especially from the middle classes – who were not party members in the SPD's electoral campaign. Its success as a new form of political participation can be seen by the way it was copied by other parties. In addition, its inception coincided with SPD electoral advance; the efforts of writers and intellectuals to change the political climate of the Federal Republic had apparently been rewarded.

In addition to the issues of the continuing role of former National Socialists and of rearmament (it is significant that the most famous political novel of the early years of the Federal Republic, Wolfgang Koeppen's 1953 work *Das Treibhaus* (*The Hothouse*) (Koeppen 1982), ends with a disillusioned member of parliament committing suicide primarily over the issue of rearmament) writers and intellectuals were concerned with the continuing authoritarian climate in the Federal Republic, encapsulated in the influence of the Catholic Church in social and moral questions and the personality of the first Chancellor Konrad Adenauer. The atmosphere changed with the student movement of the late 1960s. Although there is little doubt that intellectual protest helped to develop this movement, its actions and demands for revolutionary change went much further than anything that had occurred before. Looking back in 1995, the writer Hans Magnus Enzensberger, who at the time had appeared to lend his support to some of the students' most outlandish political demands, described the main achievement of the student movement as the way it swept away the ethos of the authoritarian state, which had previously manifested itself throughout society. For instance, relations between pupil and teacher, doctor and patient became more humane and equal (Enzensberger 1995b: 47).[10]

The students also spawned a wider willingness among citizens to engage with political issues. The 1970s were the era of Citizens' Action Groups (*Bürgerinitiativen*), many of which related to environmental issues, especially nuclear power. The women's movement and the peace movement also developed, spurred on by the decision of NATO to deploy Cruise and Pershing missiles. Even if, with hindsight, some protests may seem misguided and certain actions shared the fate of earlier protests against rearmament – the million or so who demonstrated in Bonn against nuclear weapons in 1983 achieved little tangible success – the increase in citizen participation cannot be doubted. Writers and intellectuals were no longer on their own; they tended to withdraw from direct political involvement, in certain cases feeling themselves superfluous.

One exception to this development was writers' misgivings about the anti-terrorist legislation passed in the 1970s to combat the activities of the Rote Armee Fraktion. The title of a book on this subject that appeared in 1977 is significant: *Briefe zur Verteidigung der Republik* (*Letters in Defence of the Republic*) (Duve *et al.* 1977). Such a title shows that concerns about the new legislation were being expressed by writers and intellectuals on the basis of their overall identification with the Federal Republic. Similarly, when the movements of the 1970s led to the formation of the new green party, Die Grünen, and its entry into parliamentary politics, some degree of accommodation with the political system took place, even if the new party claimed to be (and indeed initially was) very different from its established competitors. By making sure that half of their elected representatives were women, Die Grünen certainly advanced female emancipation in other parties; equally, issues such as the environment entered the mainstream of politics as other parties now felt obliged to respond to the new challenge. By contrast, the idea that parliamentarians should only serve for two years and then be replaced, what was called the *Rotationsprinzip*, the aim of which was to prevent individuals becoming 'professional politicians' and therefore open to corrupting influences, found no favour; it was also dropped by Die Grünen when it recognised that continuity and expertise were in fact necessary for effective participation in the political process.

It is not being claimed that the ideas expressed by intellectuals and protest groups coincided with those of the majority; if this had been the case, most election results would have been different. What can be said is that the spread of such activity reflected a growing desire to make use of the opportunities for participation afforded by the political system and also helped in many cases to make the Federal Republic a more liberal and tolerant society, something from which many more members of society benefited than merely those who took an active part in promoting any particular cause. Tolerance and liberality were by no means universal – political extremism, manifesting itself in terrorism and hostility to foreigners, was, and since unification has continued to be, a major problem – but, in general, the Federal Republic can be said to have developed into an open society. The ideal of the *mündiger Bürger*, a term made popular by Federal President Scheel in the 1970s and expressing the idea of a citizen who has achieved maturity and is an active member of society, had moved closer to reality.

Given this, it is not surprising that the prospect of a largely positive era coming to an end in 1990 caused some concern, especially to those who were of the generation that had grown up after 1949 and had therefore no recollection of a united Germany. An example of such concern is an essay that appeared in *Der Spiegel* shortly before unification with the title 'Deutschland, eine Midlife-crisis' written by Patrick Süskind, the author of a rare German international bestseller *Das Parfum* (*Perfume*), who was born in the year of the foundation of the Federal Republic. Süskind begins by expressing how his pleasure at the unexpected fall of the Berlin Wall turned into surprise when this event was followed by an upsurge in nationalistic sentiment. Whereas an emotional response might be understandable among an older generation with memories of a single German state and among younger people who long to keep abreast with the latest developments, Süskind sees his own generation as post-nationalist. He himself claims to have developed a greater attachment to other parts of Europe, including such distant places as Crete and the Outer Hebrides, than to the areas that made up the GDR. Moreover, the apparently permanent division of Germany and Europe, while not good in itself given the lack of human rights in the GDR and elsewhere in the eastern bloc, was mitigated by the advantages of life in the Federal Republic: 'This state had proved itself in a thoroughly unprovisionally good way, it was liberal, democratic, useful and run on the basis of law – and it was exactly as young or old as we were and therefore in a sense our state' (Süskind 1990: 123). Süskind's valedictory comments capture the mood of many at the time.

CONCLUSION

Although many citizens of the Federal Republic, like Patrick Süskind, did not greet German unification with any feeling of euphoria, they largely accepted it as inevitable, as the SPD, whose candidate for the post of Chancellor in the post-unification election of 1990, Oskar Lafontaine, appeared less than even lukewarm about unity, found out to its cost when its share of the vote dropped to 33.5 per cent overall and to 35.9 per cent in the former Federal

Republic. At least there was the comfort that proven institutions were being largely maintained in the new situation, since unification consisted in essence of an enlargement of the Federal Republic rather than a merger of the two post-1949 German states to create an entirely new entity.

In his inauguration speech on being elected Federal President in 1969, Gustav Heinemann, the only Social Democrat to hold that office prior to unification, stated: 'There are difficult fatherlands. One of them is Germany.' This formulation, 'a difficult fatherland', provided the title for an authoritative book on the political culture of the Federal Republic that appeared first in 1979, *Ein schwieriges Vaterland* by Martin and Sylvia Greiffenhagen (see Greiffenhagen and Greiffenhagen 1981). They also gave this part of Heinemann's speech pride of place by putting it at the beginning of their work. What Heinemann was primarily thinking of was no doubt the heavy legacy of the Nazi past and the shadow it cast over the Federal Republic, the state which saw itself, in legal terms, as the successor to the Third Reich. This chapter has attempted to show how and why, despite its difficult beginnings, the Federal Republic developed into a, by most standards, successful state both politically and economically. Only passing reference has been made to some of the problems that had to be confronted, for example, the attitude to former National Socialists in the new democratic state and various political scandals. The treatment of foreigners, in particular those who were euphemistically called guest workers (*Gastarbeiter*) has hardly been mentioned.[11] It was this kind of problem that led the Greiffenhagens to conclude, thirty years after its foundation, that the Federal Republic was in many respects a success, but to reflect a number of worries, particularly about an atmosphere of aggression and hysteria in society perceived by a number of observers (Greiffenhagen and Greiffenhagen 1981: 13–17).[12] It is not only the positive points about the pre-unification Federal Republic that have been inherited by the post-1990 state. The next sections will turn, among other things, to the question of how far the relatively effective methods of the years 1949 to 1990 can be equally successful in the new situation when, in addition to the new problems of unification, existing problems might well have been exacerbated at a time of major social and economic change.

Part II

FACING THE FUTURE

2

THE POLITICAL SYSTEM: STABILITY IN DANGER?

CONTINUITY AND CHANGE

Besides setting the framework for political life in the Federal Republic, the Basic Law of 1949 set great store on the achievement of German unity. The Preamble called on the German people to complete 'the unity and liberty of Germany in free self-determination'. Article 23 spoke of the extension of its provisions to other areas of Germany, while Article 146 spoke of its being superseded when the German people decided freely on a new constitution, by implication the time of unification.

For a long time the provisions of the Basic Law appeared to hinder the search for better relations with the GDR. When within the framework of the *Ostpolitik* the *Grundlagenvertrag* between the Federal Republic and the GDR was agreed in 1972, it was referred to the Constitutional Court by the CSU who claimed that it implied a degree of recognition of the GDR that contradicted the unity provisions of the *Grundgesetz*. Although the Court accepted the treaty, it put strict limits on further diplomatic dealings with the GDR, imposing conditions which to many at the time seemed like an anachronistic straitjacket given the apparent permanence of the division. How far this constitutional insistence on the concept of German unity helped to reinforce the demands for unity made in 1989–90 it is difficult to judge; what is beyond doubt is that a legal framework existed that enabled the coming together of the GDR and the Federal Republic.

Two alternatives appeared to present themselves: either the provisions of the Basic Law were to be extended to the territory of the GDR, in accordance with Article 23, or the unification process was to be completed by the creation of a new constitution

51

for what was a new political entity: the implication of Article 146. In the event, unification took place under Article 23, the provisions of which allowed the process of unification to take place in a rapid and neat manner, although constitutional reform was put on the agenda by the creation of a commission made up of sixty-four members, half chosen by the *Bundestag* and half by the *Bundesrat* charged with suggesting possible changes to the *Grundgesetz*.

In the event so few suggestions for change were made by the commission that in a 1994 issue of the magazine *German Politics* devoted to constitutional developments, the editors Klaus Goetz and Peter Cullen expressed their sympathies with those who asked 'whether the energy invested in the Commission had not been wasted' (*German Politics* 1994, 3, 3: 1). Indeed, the incorporation of the Maastricht Treaty on closer European unity into German law appears to have had greater constitutional consequences than the work of the commission. In particular, disappointment has been expressed by those who feel that the opportunity has been missed to make the Basic Law more directly 'democratic'. It was pointed out at the beginning of Chapter 2 (p. 27) that originally its provisions gave the impression of having been inspired by a distrust of the people who had all too willingly followed the blandishments of the Nazis. Now, it was felt by many that the people should be given a direct voice more frequently, for example, through referenda or the direct election of the Federal President.[1] For the present, such hopes are likely to remain unfulfilled. Continuity in the area of the constitution at least is the order of the day.

Another argument against unification on the basis of Article 23 was that it would create or enhance a sense among former citizens of the GDR that they had been simply swallowed up by their larger neighbour. In other words, they had been the object of a take-over rather than being partners in a merger in which their active participation was required. The question of how widespread such a feeling is, and what consequences it has, will be a major topic in this part of this book. As will be seen, discontent among former GDR citizens has its roots in social and economic problems; what can be pointed out here is that the way unification was carried through provides an argument to support the case of those who stress its negative consequences.

If the lack of constitutional change emphasises continuity between the Federal Republic as it existed before 1990 and the present, one decision made in 1991 implies a change: parliamentary approval of the plan to move the seat of government from Bonn to Berlin. Although it was never at issue that Berlin was the capital city of the unified Federal Republic, the question of the location of parliament and government took on a symbolic significance that brought major issues into focus. A decision to remain in Bonn would have emphasised the status quo, the decision to move to Berlin raised questions about the changing role of the new German state and, given the spectres of the past, gave rise to worries about the future. These questions are at the heart of the rest of this volume. It is worthwhile here to repeat some of the arguments made during the *Hauptstadtdebatte* (capital city debate) as they foreshadow the issues that will be discussed later in this book.

Those in favour of Bonn pointed to the success of the pre-1990 Federal Republic, seeing in Bonn the symbol of a new respected Germany that had broken with its past. Bonn symbolised a Germany that looked westwards and had accepted western democratic values, whereas Berlin invoked the old nationalism and the non-democratic spirit of Prussia. (Against this it was pointed out that prior to their gaining power in 1933 support for the Nazis had been below average in Berlin.) At a different level, the expense of the move to Berlin was stressed, particularly as great commitments had only recently been undertaken to make Bonn into something more like a capital city given its apparent permanence until the sudden changes of 1989. Naturally, too, material interests were a part of the argument; politicians from the state of North Rhine-Westphalia to which Bonn belongs, along with those from the nearby Rhineland-Palatinate, feared the consequences of any move from Bonn for the local economy.

One of the doyens of the case for Berlin was Willy Brandt, who had been the governing mayor of West Berlin at the time of the building of the Wall and who had greeted the prospect of German unity at a special SPD party congress in Berlin in late 1989 with the resonant phrase: 'Jetzt wächst zusammen, was zusammengehört' ('What belongs together, is now growing together'). In the parliamentary debate over the future seat of government he demanded a capital that was not just 'for cocktail parties'. He was voicing the view that a capital city should be a metropolis in which 'real life' took place, not just a centre for politicians, the *Raumschiff Bonn* (spaceship Bonn) as it had been dubbed by many, including self-deprecatingly some politicians. (In the 1950s, Bonn had been scorned as the *Bundeshauptdorf* (federal capital village). In fact it had been chosen in preference to Frankfurt partly because it could not rival Berlin and offer any semblance of permanence.) The other major argument for Berlin was that its rejection would compound disenchantment with unification in the former GDR; by contrast Berlin as capital city could invigorate the economy of the surrounding region.

When the vote was taken there was a majority of eighteen for Berlin. The votes of the members of parliament from the PDS, the successor party to the SED, who were otherwise almost parliamentary outcasts, ironically proved decisive since they split seventeen to one in favour of Berlin. The two major parties were more evenly split.[2] Another interesting point was that 67 per cent of Catholic members voted for Bonn, 64 per cent of Protestants for Berlin, which suggested that cultural divisions could still be important in connection with this kind of issue.[3] That the CSU voted almost exclusively for Bonn was in keeping with the cultural and historical traditions referred to in the Introduction (see p. xxii); the protestant Prussian ethos of Berlin had always been particularly unpopular in Bavaria.

The vote for Berlin implied that something had changed because of the events of 1989–90, even if the state was still called the Federal Republic of Germany and its constitution had remained largely unchanged. Clearly, the Federal Republic of Germany was now larger and had a bigger population than any partner in the European Community. It is inevitable that these changes will have consequences; what matters is how far these will be positive or negative within Germany and outside. The political and economic aspects of the Berlin debate discussed above raised such points as whether the new Federal Republic was looking less towards its western partners, was overstretching itself financially and economically and whether, given the closeness of the vote, it was no longer characterised by a stable and effective political system.[4]

DISILLUSIONMENT WITH POLITICS?

The question of whether the political system of the Federal Republic was losing its prestige became a major question in the early 1990s when the term *Politikverdrossenheit* (disenchantment with politics) became fashionable in political debate. Even the Federal President, the much respected Richard von Weizsäcker, criticised politicians in 1992 for having as their only special talent the ability to criticise others. The politician was in his words the 'generalist with the special knowledge of how to fight political opponents' (Unseld 1993: 25). In as far as such criticisms recall both political failure in earlier German history and the non-political tradition in Germany they are worthy of some consideration.

In any discussion of this perceived phenomenon of *Politikverdrossenheit*, it is important, as it is in so many areas, to distinguish between the situation in east and west. In the former GDR it is understandable that there is a widespread reluctance to become involved at all in politics. This is because, as was stated in Chapter 1, so many aspects of life were politicised in that state and because participation in political life – or at least political ritual – was obligatory. It was, for instance, as good as compulsory to vote in the pseudo-elections that took place and to take part in the 1 May demonstrations. Once that obligation was removed, it was a natural reaction that many would not be willing take part in political life. This phenomenon can be seen in the declining membership of those parties which had a forerunner in the GDR. In 1990 the CDU had 145,069 members in the east, the vast majority taken over from the GDR CDU; by 1994 the figure had slumped to 92,548. Initially in 1990 the FDP, having swallowed the LDPD and NDPD, had more members in the east than the west. By the end of 1994 it had less than half. Accordingly, it has been hard for parties to find candidates, certainly at local level, where material rewards are few. This is especially true in the case of the SPD which has had to build up its organisation from nothing and by the end of 1994 had achieved a grand total of 27,275 members. Another sign of lack of political interest is that participation in elections has been lower than in the western *Länder* with 73.7 per cent of the electorate voting in the 1994 federal election, as opposed to 80.7 per cent in the west. This was a drop of 1.8 per cent as compared to the 1990 elections, although this is perhaps not too worrying since 1990 was special for former GDR citizens as it represented their first chance to vote in all-German elections. There is also the historical precedent of the post-1949 Federal Republic, where, as stated in Chapter 2, it took time for participation in elections to grow. If a sense of success and well-being develops in the former GDR as it did in the Federal Republic, then identification with the political system is likely to grow.

The special factors affecting the east do not mean that people there do not share the criticisms expressed more forcibly in the west.

There *Politikverdrossenheit* has arisen from a sense that politicians are more devoted to furthering their own interests and careers than to the good of society. In 1992 Erwin and Ute Scheuch published a volume entitled *Cliquen, Klüngel und Karrieren* (*Cliques, Intrigues and Careers*) which immediately became a bestseller (Scheuch and Scheuch 1992). What had begun as academic research sponsored by the CDU into the type of candidate standing at elections became a wider indictment of politicians and political parties. The Scheuchs were able to show examples of local politicians gaining well-paid positions in municipal enterprises (Stadtwerke),[5] as well as of scandals involving the higher echelons of political life. They also pointed out that in a system of proportional representation those in positions of power, who occupied a high position on the list, were largely immune from the wrath of voters, as there were always likely to be enough votes for them to be elected. The core of their criticism was that a caste of professional politicians without any area of expertise outside politics was increasingly separating itself from the rest of society and enjoying unjustified material privileges.

The criticisms of another academic, Hans Herbert von Armin, which attracted similar attention at around the same time, concentrated on the material aspects, particularly payments made by the state to political parties and the salaries and allowances of politicians (von Arnim 1991 and 1993). As early as 1959 the state began making direct payments to political parties to help them in their 'work of political education' (*politische Bildungsarbeit*). However, in 1966 this system was ruled to be unconstitutional by the *Bundesverfassungsgericht*, which has generally looked sceptically at legislation relating to parties and their funding, declaring, for instance, in 1992 that the 1988 Party Law was unconstitutional. After 1966 a system by which the state defrayed parties' election expenses was introduced, whereby a party gaining at least 0.5 per cent of the vote received a sum of money per vote cast. After the 1984 Party Law was passed, this sum reached DM5 per voter, but has now been reduced to DM1 or (for the first 5 million votes) 1–30. The 1994 law also restricted total state funding of parties to DM230 million annually with increases not to exceed the rate of inflation. In addition, this law seeks to tackle the question that has frequently exercised the *Bundesverfassungsgericht*: the tax rules relating to individual donations to parties. As for salaries, in 1996 a member of the *Bundestag* enjoyed a monthly salary of DM11,300; together

56

with a DM6,100 non-taxable allowance and a sum of DM14,175 for secretarial and other assistance. The salary is less than that of a university professor. However, it is the allowances, including free travel, that have led to much of the controversy. How sensitive the issue remains was illustrated in 1995 when an attempt was made, supported by both CDU/CSU and SPD, to link parliamentarians' salaries automatically with those of senior judges. Such a step would have required the approval of the *Bundesrat* because it involved changing the constitution. In the event the upper house rejected the plan, moved no doubt in part by popular opposition, but possibly also by the serious point that this was not the issue through which to bring about something as momentous as a change to the *Grundgesetz*. Earlier in the decade various schemes in individual *Länder* whereby state politicians gave themselves or planned to give themselves incredibly generous pension provisions had caused controversy. For example, in Hamburg in 1991 when three and a half years service in, for instance, the position of speaker or parliamentary group leader (*Fraktionsvorsitzender*) was to lead to a pension from the age of 55 amounting to 62 per cent of the previous salary for the job.

Given the high rate of participation in the 1994 federal election – 79.1 per cent as opposed to 77.8 per cent in 1990 – previous talk of *Politikverdrossenheit* seems to have been misguided. Clearly it is normal that expressions of dissatisfaction with politicians arise in the period between elections when, especially given the absence of by-elections in the German system (a member who dies or leaves parliament for any reason is replaced by the next name on the party's previous electoral list), the electorate feels powerless. What should be remembered in connection with Germany in the early 1990s is that the government was trying to deal with major problems such as the economic crisis and an influx of foreigners who were using the provisions of Article 16 of the Basic Law to ask for political asylum. This provision which baldly stated: 'Those suffering political persecution enjoy the right to asylum' had been designed for those few dissidents from the communist countries who might manage to reach the west. However, it had become a means of enabling large numbers of people from Third World countries to enter the Federal Republic. This is not to say that claims of persecution were bogus in all, or in a majority of cases; nevertheless, before the Federal government, with SPD support, took action in 1993 to amend the Basic Law, the issue had reached such a pitch that popular discontent demanded some action. In 1992 438,000 people had asked for asylum; the number dropped by two-thirds following the new legislation, whereupon the issue largely disappeared.

Whereas the word *Politikverdrossenheit* may have passed from the headlines with the end of the economic crisis and the measures taken against asylum seekers, it still seems that the German electorate expects its politicians to take quick and effective action in all circumstances, something that might put the system under strain if easy solutions are not available. It is also suspicious of anything that looks like an attempt at self-enrichment. In this case, it must be admitted, some of the resentment undoubtedly springs from populistic anti-political attitudes that have their roots in the German past.

PARTIES AND ELECTIONS

As was seen in Chapter 2, the political system of the Federal Republic developed around a small core of political parties (in the 1960s and 1970s just three) whose ability to attract the vast majority of voters provided a framework of stability for the governance of the country at both federal and state levels. Of particular importance were the two major parties, CDU/CSU and SPD, who together between 1957 and 1987 always managed to attract at least 80 per cent of the votes cast at federal level. Another feature of voting patterns was that each party enjoyed the support of a large number of committed voters (*Stammwähler*), who invariably remained loyal to their party. What must be considered now is whether the conditions that promoted this situation and the stability it provided are likely to remain, particularly when unification has meant a large number of new voters with no experience of a democratic system.

The success of the CDU/CSU and the SPD in the pre-1990 Federal Republic rested on their ability to establish themselves as *Volksparteien*, a term that is usually translated as 'catch-all parties', although this sounds more negative than the original German which implies that these parties are attractive for all people rather than that the parties go out to lure any voters they can get. From its inception in 1945 the CDU/CSU set out to be inclusive rather than exclusive. First, as the word Christian implies, it sought, as was pointed out in Chapter 2 (p. 40), to offer a political home to people from all denominations. This was a lesson from the Weimar Republic and earlier, when the Zentrum, which had been founded at the time of the *Kulturkampf*, was almost entirely a party for Catholics and therefore reflected potentially harmful social divisions. The second important point to bear in mind about the CDU, rather more than the CSU, is that its origins were left of centre, with its 1947 Ahlen Programme, for instance, condeming the 'capitalist search for power and profit'. Clearly, it has moved to the right subsequently, although it is still as well to remember the differences between *soziale Marktwirtschaft* as embraced by the CDU/CSU and the purely free market system favoured by right-wing parties in other countries. Trade unionists, whose background is the non-ideological system set up after 1945, still have a place in the CDU/CSU.[6] That is not to say that active trade unionists make up the majority of the voters. They tend to be white-collar workers, farmers or professionals, in other words groups that are normally attracted to right of centre parties. More old people and people living in smaller communities also tend to vote CDU/CSU, as do those who maintain a traditional lifestyle based on the church and the family. The decline in support for the CDU is not due to its losing support among its traditional voters; it is simply that the number of such people has declined in a rapidly changing society. The particular contribution of the CSU is that it has managed to link itself with the continuing sense of Bavarian identity; just as, for example, a Scot can only support one national football team, a majority of Bavarians – in the 1994 federal elections it was 51.2 per cent (admittedly a drop from 59.5 per cent in 1983) – can only think of supporting one party.

How has the position changed since unification? As was mentioned in Chapter 1, a satellite party bearing the name CDU existed in the GDR. After a certain degree of heart-searching, the western party decided to take this organisation under its wing. Although this left it open to accusations that it was associating with those who had danced to the communist tune,[7] the influx of members and party infrastructure provided a basic organisation for political operations in the east. The other advantage the CDU enjoyed was that it was seen as the party of German unity, which had been forged by its leader Chancellor Kohl. It therefore attracted the support of those who either hoped to gain from unity or had been particularly disadvantaged in the GDR. In many cases, these were the same people, not least blue-collar workers, who hoped for material improvement through unification. They were certainly among the major supporters of the CDU in the east in 1990 and remained so in 1994, when, according to polls, they attracted 40.6 per cent of the blue-collar vote, as opposed to the SPD's 35.1 per cent. This somewhat unusual state of affairs, which may well not be permanent, has clearly helped to maintain the pre-eminent position of the CDU/CSU following unification. Although its share of the vote in 1994 dropped to 41.5 per cent from the 43.8 per cent it achieved in 1990, it remained 5.1 per cent ahead of its nearest rival, the SPD.

The development of the SPD into a *Volkspartei* following the Godesberg Programme has been traced in Chapter 2. During the course of the 1960s, the SPD became more attractive to the middle class in general and academics in particular, as well as to women and Catholics, because, with society becoming more secular, religious affiliation became less of a political factor. After the 1972 election, however, when the popularity of the *Ostpolitik* helped to lift it above the CDU for the only time at federal level, the SPD began to lose votes. Initially, its losses were among the groups mentioned above whose allegiance it had only recently gained, but much more importantly in the 1980s it lost the support of mainly young left-wingers, who, initially disillusioned by the policies being pursued by Chancellor Schmidt, moved to the Greens. With some skilled workers and white-collar workers in the growing service sector (groups that because of their growing material aspirations have tended to move to the right in many countries) also deserting it, it had lost its power to integrate various sections of society in the manner of the classic *Volkspartei*. Specifically there is tension between traditional working-class Social Democrats and middle-class academics, whose incomprehensible discourse (characterised by imported foreign words) and post-materialist values are alien to the first group. Equally worrying for a reformist party is that only 18 per cent of the membership are under 30 (which is at least better than the 14 per cent in the case of the CDU/CSU), whereas 34 per cent of Bündnis 90/Die Grünen members fall into that age group. Elections since the arrival of the Greens have shown that over 40 per cent of voters are willing to give their votes to left of centre parties that originated in the pre-1990 Federal Republic, but these votes are now split between two parties. The one exception to this was the post-unification election of 1990, when, as already mentioned, the SPD suffered for its apparent lack of enthusiasm for unity and the Greens were also negatively affected by the same phenomenon.

German unity also had a negative effect on the SPD because, as mentioned earlier, it had no basis on which to build in the former GDR (even the party name had disappeared in the enforced merger with the SED). Following its disastrous 24.3 per cent share of the vote in the east in the 1990 elections it did manage to pull up to 31.9 per cent in 1994 but remains in a relatively weak position, not least because it has not yet attracted what might be regarded as potential supporters. The case of blue-collar workers has already been alluded to; there is also the problem of a rival party. In the east this is less the Greens than the PDS, the former communists. If, however, the party makes overtures in that direction it stands to lose the support both of those in the east who support it because it is totally untainted by a GDR past and those in the west who, given their Cold War socialisation, still react violently to any sign of rapprochement with communism. In the west the SPD also suffers, like comparable parties in other countries, from the discrediting of all left-wing parties brought about by the bankruptcy of communism and by changes in social structure that have reduced the number of blue-collar workers whose support was largely axiomatic. There has also been the lack of a leadership figure who might rival Chancellor Kohl. Although Rudolf Scharping, the candidate for the office of Federal Chancellor in 1994, did not make mistakes on the same level as those of Oskar Lafontaine in 1990, his campaign was not without flaws. His reputation for economic competence suffered, for example, when in a discussion on taxes he appeared not to understand the difference between net and gross. As long as its major rival holds together right of centre forces, the SPD seems destined to lag behind.

The pivotal importance of the FDP within the pre-1990 party system was also described in Chapter 2. It has managed to hold that position with some difficulty following unification, particularly in 1994 when the CDU/CSU–FDP coalition only achieved a majority of ten, and this largely due to *Überhangmandate*.[8] Its own share of the vote dropped from 11 to 6.9 per cent with the loss in the east being as high as 8.5 per cent. In the post-unification election it had benefited from the status enjoyed by its best-known figurehead, the then Foreign Minister Hans-Dietrich Genscher, who could not only take credit for unification but was also a native of the former GDR city of Halle. His successor in the role of Foreign Minister, Klaus

61

Kinkel, enjoyed no such prestige; he also had many problems as party leader of the FDP, which led to his resignation in that role in 1995. In fact, the success of the FDP in crossing the 5 per cent hurdle in 1994 can largely be attributed to CDU supporters giving their second vote to it to ensure the continuation of the coalition. By 1994, the FDP as the party of German liberalism had largely lost its substance. Whether it can regain a healthy position within the party spectrum remains a matter of conjecture. At the time of writing, however, there seems good reason to be sceptical.

The specific identity of the party, which had lacked the same core of *Stammwähler* as the CDU/CSU and the SPD, had to a degree always been a problem prior to 1990. One reason can be found in the history of liberalism in Germany which has also been marked by splits, in particular between more rightist national liberals and reformists. The foundation of the FDP after the Second World War had been an attempt to overcome the divisons that had helped to weaken the Weimar Republic because liberal votes had been split between two parties. In the earlier years of the Federal Republic the national liberals held sway when coalition with the CDU/CSU was based on common acceptance of the market economy. At the same time, the party's secularism acted as an antidote to what was perceived in certain quarters as the narrow clericalism of the CDU/CSU, which manifested itself in the wish to impose rigid moral standards in many areas of society. In the 1960s, it was particularly the reluctance of the CDU/CSU to accept the new mood for *détente* that brought the FDP closer to the SPD and to the joint development of *Ostpolitik* following the formation of the coalition between the two parties in 1969. This change of direction by the FDP brought it perilously close to the 5 per cent barrier; in 1969 it gained only 5.8 per cent of the vote. Thereafter, it was able to consolidate, being able to profit from the success of the new foreign policy, while also presenting itself as a bulwark in the economic field against any possible socialistic experiments on the part of the SPD.

It was disagreements over economic policy that led to the collapse of the SPD/FDP coalition in 1982. It was also felt by the then party leader Hans-Dietrich Genscher that it was dangerous to remain tied to one party for too long. Nevertheless, the renewed coalition with the CDU/CSU again created tensions in the party. These were overcome in time by Genscher's success as Foreign Minister and the development of a middle-class clientele, for example, public servants (*Beamte*) and entrepreneurs whose interests the party sought to champion. This basis declined rapidly in the 1990s. The loss of Genscher, the unwillingness to contemplate a change of coalition at federal level, even if election results had made that feasible, the abandonment of what had previously been regarded as liberal positions in such areas as environmental protection and civil liberties – after initial protests the FDP always appeared to give way, as, for example, over the replacement of the traditional identity card with one that could be read by a computer, a development that was perceived as enhancing police powers – all contributed to a sense that the party no longer had a distinct identity. The result was devastating losses in state elections, particularly in the year of elections 1994 (*Superwahljahr*), when the party failed to reach 5 per cent in eight attempts and, as stated above, only gained readmission to the *Bundestag* with the aid of its partners. In the east, where the FDP failed to reach 5 per cent in any of the state elections and in the federal elections, the party's difficulties were compounded by the social structure of the population; in the four years after unification an entrepreneurial class that might have supported the party had yet to establish itself. Whether a major swing to the right, as advocated by certain sections of its membership, particularly in Berlin, would help the FDP can only be a matter for speculation.

The abandonment of 'progressive' positions by the FDP helped the Greens in the 1990s, as, following the turmoil of the first decade of their existence, they settled down into the role of a relatively normal political party. Initially, as their name suggests, they were concerned with environmental issues, as well as with defence questions, demanding the removal of nuclear weapons and the withdrawal of the Federal Republic from NATO. They also championed the rights of women and minorities but paid little heed to such workaday matters as the economy and social security. In terms of their organisation (or lack of it) they sought to differentiate themselves from the established parties by internal democracy and a distrust of any cult of individual personalities. When certain members saw the limits of this approach, there was an internal power struggle between the pragmatic wing (their name *Realos* is self-explanatory) and those who wished to remain in fundamental opposition to the established political order (*Fundis*). The triumph of the first group has meant that the Greens have been willing to enter coalitions at *Land* level on a regular basis. What was a sensational new development in 1985, when the Greens entered into what proved to be a short-lived coalition with the SPD in the state of Hessen, has now turned out to be commonplace with Greens having participated at various times in state governments in eight *Länder*, the latest example being the SPD–Green coalition in Schleswig-Holstein in 1996. Its role in the political spectrum, at least at *Land* level, is becoming reminiscent of the pre-unification FDP. Its voters are now less those who long for an alternative society than an educated middle class with an awareness of environmental and other worldwide problems.

This is not to say that the pathway has always been smooth. In the 1990 federal election, the social issues with which the Greens are still most closely identified were not at the top of the agenda and in the western states the party failed to gain any seats.[9] There have also been problems in the former GDR. Although the post-unification merger with their eastern allies – the grouping Bündnis 90 that grew out of parts of the civil rights movements – led to a new name for the party, Bündnis 90/Die Grünen, the strength of the party in 1994 lay in the west with the party's overall result of 7.3 per cent depressed by failure to achieve 5 per cent in any of the ex-GDR *Länder* (excluding Berlin). Given the nature of the economic problems in the east – especially unemployment – environmental issues continue to take a back seat, despite the legacy of pollution from the industrial policies of the GDR.

In contrast to the Greens, whose electoral strength lies in the west, the only other party to gain admittance to the *Bundestag* following the 1994 election was the almost entirely eastern-based Partei des Demokratischen Sozialismus, the successor to the SED. It achieved a 17.6 per cent share of the votes in the east but only 4.4 per cent overall; its entry into parliament being assured through its winning four parliamentary constituencies in east Berlin. That the party won the constituencies in east Berlin says something about its voters; they are the people who were successful in the former GDR and were therefore likely to live in its centre of power. This does not mean that they all wish a return to the GDR system, rather that they have lost status or a sense of their previous GDR-based identity since the collapse of that state. In conventional sociological terms, they are not the typical voters for a left-wing party. People with academic qualifications (who in many cases may have lost their positions in the purge of GDR academics that took place after unification) and the self-employed (in some cases those whose past in the GDR closes other avenues of employment) are very much to the fore.

Whether the PDS is a communist party under another name is a matter of much debate. One grouping within the party, the *Kommunistische Plattform*, openly demands the restoration of communism, but remains of limited influence. Equally controversial are the Stasi links of its most charismatic politician, Gregor Gysi. Regardless of the merits of the arguments in this debate, for the other parties the PDS is a phenomenon to be kept at arm's length, certainly at the federal level.[10] Parties with a strong base in the west fear unpopularity if they are seen consorting with former communists, whether reformed or not. What is equally important here is to point out that the PDS represents the voice of discontent in the eastern states. As long as this feeling continues, the party looks set to survive, and for much longer than was thought likely in 1990. The other theoretical route to survival, the establishment of the PDS throughout the country, seems less likely; in 1994 it only gained more than 2 per cent of the vote in the city states of Hamburg and Bremen and failed in the Bremen state election of 1995.

What the 1994 federal election shows is that there are two party systems within the new Federal Republic. In the west there is a four-party system, one of whose members is hanging on by the skin of its teeth. In the east only three parties appear to count, with one of these not represented in the west and largely spurned by the other two. Moreover, given the brief history of democracy, it is impossible to speak of *Stammwähler* in the east, where the influence of individual personalities appears much greater. The case of Manfred Stolpe was mentioned in Chapter 1 (p. 24); the CDU equivalent is Kurt Biedenkopf in Saxony. Although a westerner, he can rely, in addition to his other considerable talents, on his history of conflict with Chancellor Kohl which does not make him appear like an unwanted 'western import'. How far the fluid position in the east, along with sociological changes in the west, in particular the decreasing importance of class and milieu and the resulting decline of traditional party loyalties, threatens the stability of the democratic system will be considered in the conclusion to this chapter.

POLITICAL EXTREMISM

Given recent German history, it is inevitable that the health of German democracy will be judged by the extent political extremism manifests itself and the efforts made by those in authority to combat it. Especially if a right-wing extremist party gains some small measure of electoral success, voices are raised, not least abroad, pointing out that the Nazi Party too began its rise to power from initially modest electoral successes in the mid-1920s.

Throughout the history of the pre-unification Federal Republic, right-wing extremists enjoyed periods of success, at least at the level of *Land* elections. Following the decline of the NPD in the 1970s, it was the Republikaner who began to make the running in the 1980s. It achieved 7.5 per cent of the vote in the West Berlin elections in 1989 and 7.1 per cent in the European elections in the same year. Incidentally, both these elections took place before the unrest in the GDR began in the autumn of that year. Since unification, there has been success for the party in Baden-Württemberg where it achieved 10.9 per cent of the vote in 1992, while another group, the Deutsche Volksunion (German People's Union), which is associated with Gerhard Frey the right-wing publisher of the unspeakable *National-Zeitung*, whose extreme nationalism and worse once notoriously manifested itself in the headline 'Criminal state of Israel wishes to teach us morality', managed to gain seats in the state parliaments of Bremen and Schleswig-Holstein in 1991 and 1992 respectively. At the 1994 federal election, however, the Republikaner could only manage 1.9 per cent of the votes cast.

Before considering whether these intermittent successes for far right parties represent any threat to German democracy, it is necessary to consider whether such parties can be classified as neo-Nazi. In their public discourse they generally try to avoid direct adulation of the Nazis, while at the same time using nationalist rhetoric that is reminiscent of Nazi propaganda in its demands that 'German interests' should have top priority. Thus there are claims that Germany is swamped by foreigners, whose main priority is criminal activity, that Germany kowtows to foreigners in international organisations, while German soldiers in the Second World War are to be regarded as heroic defenders of the fatherland against communism. Even if it would be wrong to conclude that all those who vote for extreme right-wing parties are unrepentant neo-Nazis, there is enough that is distasteful in their rhetoric to make any protracted success they might enjoy a genuine source of worry. Fortunately, throughout the history of the Federal Republic, such successes have been confined to periods between federal elections and can therefore be seen as resulting to a large degree from protest votes. There has also been the tendency for right-wing parties to be riven by internecine strife, which has not helped their electoral prospects.

The other manifestation of right-wing extremism that has attracted attention throughout the world has been attacks on foreigners, not least in the former GDR, although two of the worst incidents, the burning down with fatal consequences of houses occupied by Turkish residents, took place in the west, in Mölln and Solingen in 1992 and 1993 respectively. Altogether, it is estimated that there were more than 10,000 offences committed with an extreme right-wing motive in 1993. Equally horrendous have been attacks on disabled people, who, in accordance with the worst depths of Nazi ideology, are regarded by their assailants as 'unfit to live'. Nevertheless, it was the events in the east, the attacks on homes accommodating asylum seekers that took place in Hoyerswerda in 1991 and in Rostock a year later, that initially aroused horror, not least because it appeared that the perpetrators enjoyed the support of large sections of the local population. Although electoral support for far-right parties remains low in the east, which suggests that organised political activity is less established there, there is no doubt that there are many people, disoriented by the collapse of communism, who seek refuge in the over-simplifications of extreme nationalism. It is particularly worrying that many of these are young men of low educational achievement, the group most likely in any society to express its frustration through physical violence.

Attacks on members of other races are common in many countries. One of the factors that always needs to be considered is the reaction to them, at all levels of society. In Germany, there have been reasons to worry about official attitudes. The fact that among the voters for the Republikaner in West Berlin in 1989 there were many members of the police force does not inspire confidence, nor does the behaviour of the police in Rostock and Hoyerswerda, who, in as far as they are former members of the *Volkspolizei*, are in any case finding it difficult to adopt to their changed role in a democratic society. Despite the heavy sentences given to the Solingen arsonists, the judiciary too has at times behaved scandalously, in particular the judge Rainer Orlet, who, in 1994, saw fit to describe the NPD leader Günter Deckert as a man of honour and revived memories of the worst traditions of the German judiciary in the Weimar and Nazi periods. Even more worrying were initial reactions among leading politicians, who were reluctant to identify with the victims of right-wing attacks at a symbolic level by, for example, attending the funerals of victims, leaving the field, after the Mölln tragedy, to intellectuals such as the writer Günter Grass. At least, after Solingen, *Bundespräsident* Weizsäcker chose to attend the funerals. Many politicians were also reluctant to take part in the torch-light parades organised by outraged citizens. Admittedly these were controversial because they used a method of political activity previously favoured by the extreme right. Subsequently executive measures have been taken with the outlawing of certain small ultra-extremist groups whose anti-democratic, neo-Nazi leanings are beyond dispute. Although such administrative measures are unlikely to destroy right-wing extremism, they are a sign that the problem is being taken seriously.

The federal government invariably speaks of the need to combat the extremism of the left and the right in the same breath. An example of this is the comment made by the Federal Minister of the Interior Manfred Kanther when the neo-Nazi Freie Deutsche Arbeiterpartei (Free German Workers Party) was banned in 1995. He was quoted as saying: 'We must fight extremism from the right as well as the left with determination' (*Guardian* 25 February 1995: 13). In the pre-unification Federal Republic this equating of both political extremes had its roots in the anti-communism of the Cold War and an interpretation of German history that held both the Nazis and the communists responsible for the collapse of the Weimar Republic. Although the Weimar KPD was anything but an exemplary democratic party, this interpretation of history over-looks the basic point that it was the Nazis who came to power in 1933 with the active help of traditional conservative forces. Nevertheless, there was left-wing extremism in the 1970s and 1980s in the form of the Baader–Meinhof Group/Red Army Faction and its various successors. Since unification, such activity, with the sad exception of the murder of the head of the Treuhand privatisation agency, Detlev Rohwedder, in 1991, has all but ceased, with much greater interest being aroused by questions relating to the prose-cution and punishment or alternatively rehabilitation of former left-wing terrorists, in particular those who were allowed to settle in the GDR, a policy which shows that the professed anti-terrorist stance of that state was a sham. For some, the PDS represents left-wing extremism, but it seems unlikely that it will be referred to the Constitutional Court as a non-democratic party. Moreover, it does not advocate violence; the major issue facing the Federal Republic remains right-wing extremism.

It is clear that there are many German citizens who are willing to show their abhorrence of right-wing extremism actively by taking part in some form of political demonstration. The government too is willing to take action, although it has not always been clear and decisive. Any electoral success of extreme right-wing parties continues to be short-lived. Despite the number of acts of violence, there is therefore reason not to fall into despair on this issue. Nevertheless, there are related issues which give rise to concern, in particular policy towards foreigners in the Federal Republic and the possible re-emergence of non-democratic, rightist ideas among intellectuals. These will discussed later in Chapters 5 and 9.

CONCLUSION

Most of what has been said in this chapter invites the conclusion that the democracy of the Federal Republic remains healthy. Disillusionment with politics, which appeared to be rife in the early 1990s, was not reflected in the 1994 federal election. This also produced a result that allowed the continuation of coalition government with a working majority, while a potentially powerful opposition remained in place.[11] As for right-wing extremism, however unwholesome and violent it might be, there are powerful forces prepared to combat its worst manifestations.

To conclude the discussion at this point could invite a charge of complacency, not least when it comes to interpreting election results. A less positive view would be that the narrow victory of the ruling coalition parties in the federal election of 1994 showed how precarious the system had become, being only due to a little-known provision of the electoral law (*Überhangmandate*) which is being challenged. Moreover, one of the coalition parties (FDP) is on the fringe of oblivion.[12] Given that one of the four parties in the *Bundestag*, the PDS, has pariah status, the only alternative would have been a Grand Coalition, a phenomenon that might encourage political extremism, as it would appear to have done in Austria with

69

the rise of the charismatic Jörg Haider and his right-wing Freedom Party.

The problem with such an argument is that it only takes into account one election and ignores the workings of the parliamentary system of the Federal Republic. Over the past decade there have been major changes in the pattern of *Land* elections. For a long time these were a reflection of federal elections, providing a similarly stable pattern of results. It was only in 1985 with the victory of the SPD in the Saarland that a change of state government took place on the basis of an election result rather than a change of coalition. Thereafter changes of government have been very frequent, generally made necessary by changes in voting behaviour. The result of this is that a variety of coalitions exist or have existed at *Land* level: Grand Coalitions, SPD–Green, SPD–FDP and so-called traffic-light coalitions (*Ampelkoalition*), the name coming from the colours associated with the three parties, SPD, FDP and Greens, while at local level a few CDU–Green coalitions have proved possible. The changes have also meant that SPD-led governments have a majority in the *Bundesrat*, the importance of which remains undiminished since unification. It might be concluded from these developments that the German voter is an increasingly sophisticated political animal who differentiates clearly between different kinds of elections and knows the consequences of his/her choice for the political system as a whole, even if, according to polls, the relative significance of first and second votes remains a mystery to a majority of electors. On the basis of such an argument, the 1994 federal election result can be seen as more than a lucky chance. The voters have given one group of parties power at one level, while putting a brake on this power through the second chamber of parliament. Again it might be possible to speak of a felicitous combination of stability and flexibility. What is not in doubt is that the German people, possibly still mindful of the events of the first half of the century, remain reluctant to indulge in any kind of untested political experiment.

Given that political life is never static – it is usual to talk of the democratic process – it is hard to draw conclusions for all times. What is clear is that the political system of the Federal Republic remains intact; its institutions are still accepted, while the party system centred on the two large *Volksparteien*, despite the shock of unification, has survived much better than in other European countries, most notably Italy where one comparable party, the DC

(Christian Democrats), has been all but wiped out. Despite some evidence of fragmentation, in comparison to other states Germany remains a beacon of stability, and fears for the future of democracy based on the imminent danger of political instability are exaggerated. Whether the existing stability will be an effective basis for dealing with the economic and social problems facing the Federal Republic, not to mention the establishment of a clear role in European and world affairs, is another question. Whether the current position, which is in some ways a de facto Grand Coalition given the relative powers of *Bundestag* and *Bundesrat*, might lead to sclerosis is a question that underlies the next three chapters.

4

THE GERMAN ECONOMY: THE END OF THE 'MIRACLE'?

STANDORT DEUTSCHLAND AND EURO-SCLEROSIS

In the 1980s, observers of developments in the European Community, as it was then called, particularly those fired with enthusiasm for the free market policies being pursued with apparent success by Ronald Reagan in the USA and Margaret Thatcher in Great Britain, observed a phenomenon they described as 'Euro-sclerosis', the failure of continental European economies to grow at an adequate rate to conquer such major problems as unemployment. This state of affairs was put down to an economic culture that had the effect of stifling innovation and enterprise through excessive costs and burdensome regulation. Nowhere was this thought to be more the case than in the Federal Republic of Germany, the leading economy within the European Community, where a debate started about the future of *Standort Deutschland*. The question being asked was whether the Federal Republic was likely to remain an attractive location – location being the usual translation for *Standort* in most contexts – for economic activity, given the high costs of labour (wage costs and the associated costs for health and social security) and the necessity of complying with environmental and other regulations. Furthermore, it was claimed, German industry was subject to punitive taxes on its profits. In particular, the future of manufacturing industry, the backbone of the German economy (in 1993 it accounted for 36.4 per cent of GNP in the 'old' Federal Republic and slightly less in the new *Länder*), rather than financial services or other service industries, was felt to be at risk.

These perceived threats were a source of concern, at least to

experts, within the Federal Republic, not least because the ability
to maintain competitiveness in export markets played such an
important part in the country's overall economic performance. One
side of the 'magic square' referred to in Chapter 2 was the surplus
in balance of payments. This was due to the success of German
exports, which, given, for example, the amount of money spent by
German tourists abroad, had far to exceed imports if equilibrium in
the balance of payments was to be maintained. If exports were to
be threatened by a lack of competitiveness, then the consequences
would be catastrophic and not only for the balance of payments.
Quite simply, millions of jobs depended directly on exports; it
was estimated, for instance, that in 1991 50 per cent of employees
in German industry were involved in export production (Owen-
Smith 1994: 501). In these circumstances, the Federal Republic
was a keen participant in EC attempts to stimulate growth by the
creation of the Single European Market which came into force in
1993. The aim was to stimulate trade and economic growth by the
abolition of customs and other barriers that had hampered the free
movement of goods and services.

By the late 1980s, the problem of low growth, at least in the
Federal Republic, appeared to have been overcome. Following
growth rates of below 2 per cent in the mid-1980s, a rapid improvement took place with growth of 5.7 per cent being achieved in
1990, due to a great extent to the boom created by unification.
Consumers in the GDR spent part of their new D-Marks on the
goods of which they had previously been deprived. In these propi-
tious circumstances, it is small wonder that the question of *Standort
Deutschland* largely disappeared from the agenda. When, however,
the post-unification boom came to a halt and the economy, along
with those of most other European countries, slid into recession
(1993 saw negative growth of –1.7 per cent) the issue returned with
a vengeance, not least because another factor had entered the
equation, namely the costs incurred by the takeover of the GDR.
Rather than being a contributor to boom, the east, because of the
massive costs being incurred, seemed more like the cause of bust.

This chapter will seek to explain the position of the German
economy, in particular whether the competitive advantage that
made the 'economic miracle' possible has been lost and whether
the country faces a less prosperous future. First, it will be necessary
to examine those factors that are regarded as having a debilitating
effect, before any more positive aspects are considered.

THE PRICE OF UNIFICATION

As was seen in Chapter 1, a major motive for the population of the GDR in seeking unity was the wish to enjoy the undoubted material prosperity that existed in the Federal Republic. This desire was reinforced by the promises of Chancellor Kohl who saw 'blossoming landscapes' (*blühende Landschaften*) in the east and prophesied that nobody would be worse off and many would be better off. If these statements contributed to electoral success by creating the feeling of optimism that was music to the ears of most people in the ex-GDR, particularly in comparison with the Cassandra-like statements of the SPD's Oskar Lafontaine, they stood in contrast with the underlying economic problems and the costs of putting them right.

The first problem was the strength, or rather lack of it, of the GDR economy. As stated in Chapter 1, the GDR's own propaganda about its economic prowess had had some success, not least in other countries; even the West German secret service had been unable to provide an adequate assessment. The truth quickly came to light when the unification process got under way in early 1990. In reality the economy of the GDR was characterised by inferior products that could largely only be sold in other communist countries, and by low rates of productivity. Even in 1994, four years after unification, productivity was only at 40 per cent of western levels. Moreover, with the collapse of communism, the former captive markets in the east no longer existed, either because the new democracies could now choose superior goods on the world market or because, especially in the case of Russia, they were unable to buy on the same scale, if at all. The markets in the east collapsed to a quarter of their previous strength.

Where an economy is weak in this way, two ways it can help itself, at least in the short term, are by devaluation and by keeping labour costs down. The exact opposite happened in the GDR in 1990. One of the major attractions of unification for the citizens of the GDR was the all-powerful D-Mark; when a currency union loomed, the question arose of the rate of exchange between the GDR-Mark and the D-Mark. The decision reached was that the rate should be 1:1 for wages and savings up to 5,000 Marks; thereafter a rate of 1 D-Mark for 2 East Marks applied, as it did in other areas of the economy. Given the low productivity of the GDR economy, this meant that the cost of products rose dramatically, which led in turn to a loss of competitiveness. Many parts of GDR industry were damaged beyond repair.

The decision to go for a 1:1/1:2 exchange rate was a political one, as a more unfavourable rate would undoubtedly have alienated voters in the east. It led to the resignation of Bundesbank chairman Karl Otto Pöhl in 1991 who, in accordance with his position, only saw things in economic terms. It was partly political considerations too that led to the acceptance of a policy of convergence in wages between east and west, something that also increased costs in the east. The popular argument that, for example, a bus driver or a policeman should receive the same wages for doing the same job in both parts of Berlin proved irresistible, particularly when the subsidies that had kept basic goods and services cheap in the GDR began to disappear and living costs approached equal levels in both parts of the country. In any case, the western trade unions, who were now negotiating on behalf of eastern workers, were not interested in cut-price competitors who might have threatened the jobs of their western members. The same could also be said about employers' representatives from the west. It may well be that, in the light of political considerations, the decisions reached were inevitable, but seen from a purely economic perspective they were not good for GDR industry. The extent of the problem was again underlined in 1993 when the employers cancelled the wages agreement in the engineering industry.

The weakness of GDR industry became apparent when the process of privatisation of what had been almost exclusively a system of state-run enterprises began. In early 1990 the last communist-led government under Hans Modrow established the Treuhand agency to oversee the transformation of GDR industry. At the time the assets that came under the control of the Treuhand were valued by Modrow at about DM1,000 billion. This figure was revised by Detlev Rohwedder to DM600 billion, although this was to prove an equally wildly optimistic estimate. By the time the Treuhand ceased to exist as planned at the end of 1994, losses of DM230 billion had been accumulated. These had arisen primarily from the operation of loss-making firms that remained in its hands and from grants paid to firms willing to take on troubled companies that could not have been sold otherwise.[1] To set against this, there were receipts from the sale of enterprises that more readily found a buyer. All in all, around 14,000 enterprises and parts of enterprises were sold, along with 22,000 hotels, restaurants and shops and 41,000 plots of land (excluding agricultural land). In some cases, receipts might have been less than could otherwise have been expected because of criminal collusion between purchasers and Treuhand officials, but there can be no doubt that, given the state of GDR industry, the privatisation process was bound to take place at a loss.

Again, political factors played a part. It was always part of the brief of the Treuhand to close down enterprises that had no hope of ever being profitable. Such decisions were inevitably politically damaging as the Treuhand could be portrayed as a western institution that was destroying jobs. This was the thesis of the play *Wessis in Weimar* (*Westerners in Weimar*) written by the often controversial (western) dramatist Rolf Hochhuth (1993), which caused a stir in many quarters because it was seen as condoning the murder of Detlev Rohwedder.

As a result of the problems, Chancellor Kohl promised that industrial core areas would be preserved – he was thinking particularly of the chemical industry in the Halle and Bitterfeld areas. Such priorities help to explain why 140 unsold companies remained in the hands of the agency's successors at the end of 1994, two of which, the chemical industry complexes at Schkopau near Halle and Böhlen (Saxony), were due to receive further subsidies of DM700 million. When the sale of the Buna complex at Schkopau to the USA firm Dow Chemicals was agreed in 1995, the Federal government promised DM3 billion in investment subsidies to help save around 3,000 jobs at a firm that had once employed 20,000 and whose losses over the years 1992 to 1994 had amounted to over DM1 billion.

The costs incurred by the operation of the Treuhand only make up part of the subsidies to the east paid after unification. In total, around DM640 billion (including 20 billion from the EC/EU) had been transferred by the end of 1994, a sum that was set to increase. Part of this was for adjusting the social insurance system in the east and for job creation and retraining, but the majority was spent on infrastructure and regional development, in particular the programme of regional development and investment support known as *Aufschwung Ost* (Eastern Renewal/Upswing) which took up 60 per cent of funds.

In early 1995 this programme, or at least its misuse, was under attack in parliament and in the media. The news magazine *Der Spiegel* devoted the cover story of its 13 February edition to tales of personal enrichment and senseless investment made possible by funds from the *Aufschwung Ost* programme (*Der Spiegel* 7, 1995: 46–73). Typical were reports of sewage works with far too much capacity for the districts they were built to serve and industrial parks in areas that were unlikely to attract investment. Also interpolated within the story was the financial plight of the town of Weimar whose current expenditure was said to be a quarter above its income, a situation more or less repeated in many other eastern municipalities.

Is one to conclude from this that, on strict financial and economic terms, unification has proved to be a disaster? This would be a gross exaggeration. Following the collapse of many core GDR industries and the shrinking of the workforce from 10 million to around 7.3 million in 1994, there has been growth in many areas, not least building, which in 1994 achieved growth rates of up to 20 per cent. This is not surprising given the advanced state of delapidation that characterised much of the GDR in this area. Nor, in as far as such activity is made possible by transfers from the west is it to be regarded as lost money. Since western firms are involved in most major projects, part of the sums involved find their way back to the west. In a few areas the east is competitive, for example, in agriculture, where larger holdings, a result of the GDR's collectivisation policies and the quickly acquired entrepreneurial skills of their former managers, mean more efficient production. Generally, however, the undoubted economic improvement in the east has been bought at the price of huge subsidies from the west.

COSTS, SUBSIDIES AND REGULATION

One way ordinary citizens of the Federal Republic felt the price of supporting the former GDR in a very tangible form was from 1 January 1995, when a supplementary income tax and levy on dividends (*Solidaritätszuschlag*) of 7.5 per cent was imposed to pay for subsidies to the east. The same tax had previously been imposed in 1991 and 1992. This state of affairs led the magazine *Wirtschaftswoche*, in its 19 January 1995 edition, to produce a variety of tables to show the burden on the individual citizen (*Wirtschaftswoche* 4 1995: 14–23). The burden of direct and indirect taxation, including social welfare insurance, was presented as having risen from 27.38 per cent of income in 1960 to 44.06 per cent in 1993 with rises to 47.40 per cent and 48.50 per cent predicted for

1995 and 1997 respectively. In addition to the *Solidaritätszuschlag* a further new tax came into force in 1995 – care insurance (*Pflegeversicherung*), an obligatory insurance to be taken out against the possibility of needing care in later life. The initial contribution rate was 1 per cent of earnings shared between employer and employee, but this rose to 1.7 per cent in 1996 when the scheme began to cover residential and nursing home care, rather than just care in the patient's home. Previous years had seen VAT increased to 15 per cent and rises in fuel duties. Such increases can be seen as contributing to demands for higher wages and salaries with the potential consequences for industrial costs, as well as a possible disincentive to achievement.

Besides individuals, 72 per cent of whom, according to *Wirtschaftswoche* (1995) felt that their tax burden was too high, as opposed to 54 per cent in 1990, it is also industry that complains about its taxes. Tax changes in 1990 set the rate of corporation tax at 50 per cent, a reduction compared to the previous situation. Nevertheless, industrialists still make unfavourable comparisons with other countries, although it must be pointed out that international comparisons are difficult because of different systems of allowances that can be set against tax Whatever the truth of its claims – in his seminal study *The German Economy* Eric Owen-Smith suggests there are reasons to believe that many have been 'crying wolf' (Owen-Smith 1994: 100) – industry has continued to lobby against certain taxes. For instance, the *Gewerbesteuer* (trade tax), a levy based on profits that is paid to local authorities, was due for abolition following pressure from the FDP. At present, however, any such step is being blocked by the SPD majority in the *Bundesrat*. Whatever happens, demands from industrialists for lower taxation are likely to continue.

Taxation is only one cost burden about which industry is quick to voice its worries. It complains that in Germany some of the highest wages in the world are paid and that workers enjoy some of the longest holidays while working a comparatively short number of hours per week. Between 1972 and 1992, in the area of the old Federal Republic the average working week declined from 42 to 37.7 hours. On 1 October 1995 workers in the engineering industry achieved their long-held ambition of the 35-hour week. At the end of 1992 71 per cent of those whose conditions were regulated by fixed contracts of wages and employment (*Tarifverträge*), another feature of German industrial relations that is felt

78

by some to reduce the flexibility and dynamism of the economy, enjoyed (again in the western states) a minimum of six weeks' holiday. What these figures ignore is the factor of productivity; what ultimately counts are unit labour costs – how much the production of an item costs. In simple terms this means that if certain workers are twice as productive as workers in another company or country, it does not matter if they are paid considerably more. This is a question that will be returned to later. It is not sufficient to say that it is more economical to produce in country X because workers are paid less there or simply to point out that, for instance, average wage costs in 1994 in the German car industry were DM56.9 per hour as opposed to 29.7 in France or 26.7 in Great Britain.

The other area in which German industry sees its costs as above those in other countries has to do with regulation: the sense that excessive regulation imposes burdens on its competitiveness and efficiency.[2] One area where this is felt to be the case is that of environmental protection, with the Federal Republic having, for instance, strict rules on emissions from power stations. In general, standards of environmental protection tend to be based on strict legal limits in keeping with the principles of the *Rechtsstaat*, which make for a juridification of this kind of issue. Within this tradition, individuals have the right to go to court, in this case to the administrative court (*Verwaltungsgericht*), if they feel that environmental standards are not being enforced. There have been cases where work in progress on a major project has been, at least temporarily, stopped. In this climate, industry complains that planning processes can take far too long, although attempts have been made to speed them up in the east where it is felt that rebuilding should not be held up by unnecessary bureaucracy.[3]

It is certainly true that some regulations in the Federal Republic do not appear at first sight to make a great deal of sense, even if not all of them seem to have a direct impact on international competitiveness. A prime example is the *Ladenschlußgesetz* (law relating to shop closing hours), which ordains that with few exceptions, such as in airports and railway stations, shops must close at 6.30 p.m. on weekdays, except on Thursdays, and on Saturday afternoons, except on the first Saturday of the month and for four weeks before Christmas, and Sundays. Thursday evening opening is a relatively new phenomenon but is balanced by shorter Saturday opening than previously. It is argued that such restrictive

79

regulations, which exist to protect shopworkers, prevent the creation of new jobs in the retailing sector at a time of high unemployment. The number of jobs in this area fell in relative terms (expressed as a proportion of those having or capable of employment) between 1960 and 1992, whereas it rose, for example, in the USA.

More significant, in international terms, might be the tradition of regulation in the area of telecommunications, universally deemed to be a significant industry for the future. The nationalised Deutsche Bundespost has continued to enjoy an almost monopolistic position, although its internal structures were reformed in 1990 with separate arms created for postal services, banking and telecommunications. Privatisation is due to begin in 1996 and a free market in telecommunications is due to start in 1998. As early as 1995, however, the renamed Deutsche Post AG was producing a glossy brochure announcing *Die neue Lust am Wettbewerb* (the new joy in competition), as several new firms prepared to enter the telecommunications market in particular. Deregulation is certainly on the agenda in the Federal Republic. In some areas, for example broadcasting, its results can be seen – a plethora of new radio and television stations may have created jobs but not improved quality. Here, too, though there are complaints that restrictions on advertising are blocking expansion.

Regulation forms part of a German legal tradition in which norms enforcible in law take precedence over self-regulation of the type favoured in some other countries. This in turn has to do with the tradition of the state which in Germany – and its most important predecessor Prussia – was never content to take a back seat in economic or social affairs, as the introduction of the beginnings of a welfare system by Bismarck shows. The role of the state within *soziale Marktwirtschaft* was discussed in Chapter 2; it is now time to consider another aspect of state intervention in economic affairs which has direct financial consequences: the willingness to pay subsidies in many areas, something that goes far beyond the help to the former GDR already described.

The amount of help given to particular industries can be illustrated from the examples of coal and the railways. As in other western European countries, the coal industry began to decline in the 1960s in the Federal Republic. At the time of the Grand Coalition rationalisation took place, with state encouragement, which led, in the main coal-mining area of the Ruhr, to the creation of a single mining company, the Ruhrkohle AG. Currently, the coal industry is kept alive by subsidies and agreements with the electricity generation and steel industries to use German coal. Subsidies have risen from under DM6 billion in 1984 to over 10 billion in 1994. The railways, like the post office, were run in the manner of traditional nationalised industries until, after unification, the merger of the separate eastern and western systems, Deutsche Reichsbahn and Deutsche Bundesbahn, brought about reform, again comparable to that in the area of the post, with the creation of the Deutsche Bahn AG. Prior to the reform the railways had accumulated debts of DM70 billion. To some extent, the reform allowed a new start and the railways proudly announced a modest profit of around DM88 million for 1994. However, this figure does not take into account the annual subsidy of DM15 billion now paid to *Land* governments to support local services and DM33 billion committed for infrastructure programmes.

Financial support for the regions has also a long tradition in the Federal Republic, although support previously given to West Berlin and areas close to the former GDR border has been phased out. It would almost be possible to call Germany a land of subsidies, not all of which can be listed here. One area that is worthy of note is that of culture, with public expenditure in 1990 amounting to DM9 billion. The theatre is particularly highly subsidised (in the case of the opera in Bonn this amounts to DM260 per seat per performance), while the film industry, despite its failure to produce attractive films, enjoyed subsidies of DM15.1 million, along with DM1 million to mark a hundred years of films, from the Federal government in 1995. In a related area, the Goethe Institute and the German Academic Exchange Service, both dedicated to the advancement of German language and culture abroad, each enjoys support to the tune of over DM300 million. The subsidies for the theatre and opera have to do with the esteem in which traditional culture is held in Germany, along with a decentralised cultural landscape that offers top quality in many centres, while expenditure on German culture abroad was generally linked in the early postwar period to the need to restore the country's prestige abroad. It is not being argued here that all such expenditure is wrong, nor that it might not have indirect economic benefit if a country is held in high esteem abroad, a point argued strongly by Hans Magnus Enzensberger in a 1995 critique of aspects of German cultural policy abroad (Enzensberger 1995a). Nevertheless, all such costs have to be paid for or accounted for. What is undeniable is that the expenditure referred to in this section has helped to create a massive debt burden for the German state. At the end of 1994 the total debts of public authorities amounted, according to the Bundesbank, to DM1,654,742 million. At *Land* level the amount of debt was most marked in the case of the small city states. The debts of Bremen, Hamburg and Berlin stood (early 1995) at DM17,147, 23,031 and 26,880 million respectively, that is DM25,220, 13,430 and 7,690 per head of population. These represent burdens that will affect the economic well-being of future generations. They could also distort the credit market with potentially harmful effects for industry if enough credit ceases to be available for its needs.

The other area worthy of mention where costs affect both individuals and companies is social welfare. Reference has already been made to the introduction of *Pflegeversicherung*. Both employees and employers contribute to this, but the effects for employers were cushioned by the abolition of a bank holiday, except in Saxony where the holiday remains but the employers do not contribute. In general health and social security are areas where costs and contributions have risen. From January 1996 employees paid 9.6 per cent of gross wages for pensions insurance and they also pay over 6 per cent (to a maximum of DM780 per month) for compulsory health insurance provided by bodies known as *Krankenkassen*, unless they are free to take out private insurance on account of a salary of over DM5,800 per month. The same level of payments is also made by the employer which means that, on average, in the summer of 1995 health costs amounted to 13.2 per cent of wages and salaries.

Unemployment and increased poverty have contributed to a rise in the costs of *Sozialhilfe*, the welfare money that is paid to the worst placed members of society, from around DM1 billion in 1963 to around DM18 billion in 1993. The number of recipients increased from under a million to just under 4 million in the same period. These sums and numbers can only be explained to a limited extent by problems caused by unification; in any case they do not include people living in homes and similar institutions. With an ageing and longer living population, the cost of pensions continues to rise, particularly because pensions are paid for by the contributions of those in employment at a given time rather than from an individual's own contributions, a system referred to as the 'contract between generations' ('*Generationenvertrag*'). With the current low birthrate giving rise to predictions of a ratio of approximately one pensioner per employed person in 2030, as opposed to the 1993 ratio of approximately 1:2.5, there is cause for concern. One area of pension provision that is particularly worrying is that for public servants (*Beamte*).[4] The numbers of public service pensioners are expected to rise from just over 800,000 in 1995 to over 1.2 million by the year 2015. The cost of these pensioners is predicted to reach over 2 per cent of GNP. In the light of such figures, some kind of reform seems to be necessary.

THE FAILURE OF REFORM?

Although the Kohl government did not set out as one inspired by reforming zeal, unlike, for instance, the post-1979 Thatcher governments in Great Britain, new legislation has been enacted over the years which has been presented as major reform. It is intended in this section to look in more detail at three areas – tax, health and the environment – where reforms have been enacted to see whether changes have been beneficial, not least in financial and economic terms.

The tax changes introduced by Federal Finance Minister Theo Waigel in 1990 were presented as a major reform of taxation (*Steuerreform*), although in certain quarters they were not seen as socially just. As part of the package lower and higher rate bands of income tax were reduced, the latter pegged at 53 per cent, while allowances were raised. It was not long, however, before the post-1990 tax regime fell foul of the *Bundesverfassungsgericht*, which has ruled that the basic sum needed for survival should be free from tax. This has been set at around DM12,000 per annum for 1996 if the new plans prove acceptable.

The arrangements made are, however, far from straightforward,[5] which perhaps highlights a major fault of the tax system. The true meaning of nominal rates is affected by a system that allows all kinds of claims to be set against tax. These include allowances to encourage home ownership and tax relief if someone has a study at home. Whereas it would be possible to advance arguments for this kind of provision, it might remain unclear to many, except golf fanatics, why it should be possible to set a gift of DM5,000 to a golf club against tax, a sum planned to rise to DM8,000, or why public liability insurance taken out by dog-owners in case their pets should cause an accident should enjoy the same privilege when children who pay for residential care for their parents can claim nothing. If some of these allowances were to be removed it might make not only for social justice but a lower rate of taxation.

As already indicated, expenditure on health insurance is high in the Federal Republic. The growth of health care can be illustrated by the fact that the number of doctors rose by 98 per cent between 1970 and 1992 (figures for Germany as a whole) and dentists by 46 per cent over the same period. Total spending rose from DM69.6 billion to DM336.6 billion over the years 1970 to 1991. Only in the early 1980s and particularly 1988, when the Kohl government implemented its first set of reforms, did the rate of growth slow down markedly. By 1991 health care amounted to 9.6 per cent of GNP as opposed to 6.5 per cent in 1970. Clearly there was not a comparable, almost 50 per cent, increase in life expectancy or, one suspects, general good health. A subsequent reform in 1992 attempted to limit overall spending on health, but by 1994 costs were again rising inexorably, with the total expenditure of the *Krankenkassen* amounting to DM190.6 billion in mid-1994 and further attempts to cut costs pending, especially as many of the *Krankenkassen* were beginning to make losses. Although health care clearly creates jobs, if one looks solely at the area of costs it is clear that the government has not achieved its aims and that its reforms must be regarded as a failure.

A major change in the area of environmental policy was the introduction of the Dual System in 1991, designed to encourage the recycling of packaging material. Producers pay for their packaging to be awarded the mark, *der grüne Punkt* (the green dot), which indicates that the material is suitable for recycling. The costs involved are generally passed on to consumers, who, it is hoped, will be environmentally conscious enough to accept the added charge. The material, once used, is placed in a separate dustbin, which is collected by the Duales System Deutschland (DSD), the company set up by industry to manage the whole process, including the giving of licences to use the green dot. The initial results have been less than encouraging. Of the packaging made from synthetic material (*Kunststoff*) collected in 1994 55 per cent was exported, mainly to India and China, while much of the rest was burnt (in certain cases this can also be classed, somewhat incredibly, as re-cycling). The target of ending exports by 1997 therefore seems ambitious. The DSD has also incurred great losses which have already resulted in one bankruptcy. The same would have occurred again in 1994 if creditors had not foregone loan repayments. The result of all this is that both the consumer and the taxpayer lose, through higher prices and subsidies, while the pressure on the environment is at most marginally reduced. The major beneficiary is industry, which is not required to mend its profligate ways. Could it be that the policies pursued by the Kohl government are not as harmful to industry as is sometimes claimed?

THE POSITIVE SIDE OF THE COIN

Against the various points discussed above that are seen as being detrimental to the economic life of the Federal Republic, it is possible to mention a number of areas that can be said to provide competitive advantage. Although levels of taxation for both individuals and companies may be high and public funds may be misused on occasions, there can be little doubt that taxpayers do get a certain degree of value for their money in terms of, for example, a highly developed infrastructure, for instance, a dense motorway network and a railway system that is developing a new network of tracks for high-speed trains. Nor has the kind of support for industry described in Chapter 2, favourable lending by banks and systems of technology transfer, stopped with unification. If it is true, as was claimed in an article by Edward Balls in his 'World View' column in the *Guardian* on 6 February 1995, that capital flows will 'flock to countries offering high quality infrastructure, innovation and a skilled workforce', then Germany is well placed in comparison with many of its European partners.

It is especially in the field of education that Germany can claim to have an advantage over many other states. Education was always a distinct part of the national project in Prussia and the German Reich, with teachers, by virtue of the *Beamter* status they enjoyed, representing the authority of the state. One consequence of this is that state education has, at least until very recently, carried the most prestige in Germany. Private schools, on the other hand, unless they embody a distinctive educational philosophy such as that of the *Waldorf-Schulen* founded by Rudolf Steiner, have often been seen as repositories for the not particularly gifted offspring of the rich. It is true that in recent years private schools have become more popular, as their school-day, unlike that of state schools, often extends into the afternoon, an important criterion for working parents. At the same time, private schools are usually keen to point out that they are 'recognised by the state' (*staatlich anerkannt*), whereas in Great Britain, for example, they are more keen to express their independence from the state. This is not to say that the ideal of *Bildung* (education) developed in Germany in the nineteenth century was without flaws in political terms. It is significant that Thomas Mann should have chosen a schoolmaster steeped in the humanistic traditions of the educated German bourgeoisie to narrate *Doktor Faustus*, his novel of the German tragedy, as the bombs of Allied air-raids fall around him.

What is more relevant in the economic context is that the education system that grew up in Germany did not neglect the technical and the vocational. As attempts were made to catch up with Britain, the first industrialised country, it was felt that there was no possibility of following the British *laissez-faire* approach; the resources of the state had to be used to make good the time lost. A separate institution for advanced technical education was founded, the *Technische Hochschule* (now generally incorporated into the university sector), and a system of vocational education developed to replace the traditional guilds. What is particularly remarkable is that technical and vocational education came to enjoy equal prestige. This can be seen at a linguistic level in the use of the word *Ingenieur* in German as compared to the equivalent term in English. An engineer in Germany is a highly qualified person who enjoys considerable status, not a broad term that can be used for people working on the shop-floor as well as for trained professionals.

In terms of vocational education today, what this tradition means is that when young people leave school in Germany and do not intend to continue full-time education they normally seek an apprenticeship. Training takes place partly within the firm and partly within one of the various types of vocational school. This 'dual' system is supported by industry, not only by the offer of apprenticeships but also by the role of Chambers of Trade and Commerce (*Industrie- und Handelskammern*) and other professional bodies in running the system of vocational examinations. Within this system, the aim is to produce young people with qualifications in a specific area; in this sense those who are qualified have a job or profession (*Beruf*) which gives them a clear status, along with skills that are known and recognised. In 1992 there were 376 such recognised *Berufe* that required vocational training. Any lack of flexibility that results from compartmentalisation is compensated for by the way the system at its best produces a highly skilled and trained workforce. This is not to say that everything always works perfectly; an apprenticeship does not always lead to a job and not everybody finds an apprenticeship. This is particularly true in the ex-GDR states, where, despite subsidies, there was an expected shortfall in apprenticeships of 50 per cent in 1995. By contrast, in the west, numerically supply exceeded demand, although by less than in previous years. It must also be borne in mind that bald statistics hide regional variations and ignore the individual aspirations of the young people themselves. In general terms, however, it is possible to speak of a system of vocational education that produces an effective workforce and benefits the economy accordingly, even if there are currently worries about the declining numbers being trained overall.

It is not being claimed here that the sole purpose of education is to impart the skills needed by a country's workforce, nor that all parts of the German educational system do or seek to do that. In certain areas, not least the university sector, it might seem that increasingly unfavourable conditions are not helping the economy at all. German universities are currently characterised by increasing student numbers, high failure rates, longer individual study times (there being generally no fixed limit on periods of study) and by failure of graduates to obtain suitable employment. Traditionally, German universities trained students for careers working as *Beamte* in the public sector, hence the qualification *Staatsexamen* (state examination) in the humanities and law. Now that student numbers have expanded beyond the demands of the state, there is a need for a redefinition of this role, at least in certain subject areas. With the exception of times of recession, graduates in economics and business subjects, as well as in scientific and technical disciplines, have remained in demand, while other institutions of higher education, in particular *Fachhochschulen* with their emphasis on applied knowledge and shorter courses, have developed a good record of employment for their graduates, so that the figure of 45,921 unemployed graduates of *Fachhochschulen* in September 1993 stood comparison with the figures for universities. Even in the universities, it has been argued that students, who because of diminishing state support are increasingly forced to take up part-time employment, add a flexible, lower-paid element to the workforce that helps to counterbalance some of the negative cost factors mentioned above. More importantly, the universities and other institutions ostensibly less concerned with vocational training are

87

part of a national culture that sets great store on learning and education. Where education is held in respect, the positive effects are felt in all areas, not least in the institutions specifically devoted to imparting skills that are of more direct benefit to the economy.

THE GERMAN ECONOMY SINCE UNIFICATION

The global recession of the late 1980s and early 1990s, the impact of which was delayed in Germany by the unification boom, made itself felt particularly in the labour market. For the first time since the war, Daimler-Benz, the maker of Mercedes cars, was forced to introduce compulsory redundancies. In total 134,000 jobs were lost during the recession in the motor vehicle industry. Unemployment rose above the 2 million mark in the area of the pre-unification Federal Republic, back to where it had been throughout much of the 1980s. The balance of payments moved into the red, while higher inflation rates than in other European countries forced the Bundesbank, in accordance with its statutory duty to maintain stability, to keep interest rates at very high levels until 1994, when a series of rate reductions arguably helped the Kohl government to its narrow victory. It is small wonder that the debate over *Standort Deutschland* came to a head once more, with many of the apparently negative factors discussed above receiving a good deal of attention.

With hindsight, there were never any grounds for panic. In the years of recession the German share of world exports generally held up, while the currency remained strong. It was Great Britain that was forced to pull out of the EC Exchange Rate Mechanism and accept a substantial devaluation in September 1992 when it became impossible to sustain the pound at something close to the chosen exchange rate of £1: DM2.78–2.95. When recession began to ease in the mid-1990s, the German economy began to look much more healthy again. Growth amounted to 2.3 per cent in 1994, while the balance of trade also improved. Gross fixed investment, which had dropped by 4.5 per cent in 1993, rose again by 4.3 per cent in 1994, when it was 22.9 per cent of GDP, while an increase in stocks of DM8 billion suggested renewed confidence in the future. Most significantly, in 1995 the average German worker was backed by US$4,700 capital per head, whereas British counterparts had to make do with US$3,000.

The years of recession also revealed that flexibility was possible despite all the claims to the contrary. At Volkswagen, for instance, it was agreed during the recession by management and unions that rather than mass dismissals it would be more sensible for workers to be put on a four-day week, a plan that aimed to improve the financial health of the company while preserving jobs. In 1995 at the same company, following a brief industrial dispute, the compromise struck allowed for the working week to be extended to 38.8 hours without overtime payments during times of high demand. The extra time worked is put into a kind of 'time-bank' which can be drawn upon later by the employee. Other parts of the car industry, in particular BMW and Opel, had already shown that the demands for a shorter working week, pressed for by trade unions in the 1980s, could be reconciled with industry's need to keep machines working longer by a pattern of four 9-hour shifts per week including weekend working. The new plants set up in the east are also marked by flexible working patterns. In fact, the traditional five-day week, achieved following a campaign in the late 1950s by the trade unions with slogans such as 'samstags gehört Vati mir' ('on Saturdays daddy belongs to me') backed by appropriate pictures of children, is gradually disappearing in many areas. Other factors to be borne in mind are increases in productivity (4.5 per cent in 1994) and the subsequent decline in unit labour costs, a key factor in international competitiveness. These costs declined in Germany in 1994, whereas they rose considerably in Japan.

CONCLUSION

There are reasons to draw parallels between the economic and the political situations of the post-unification Federal Republic. Although there are reasons for concern (in the economic sphere, for example, high levels of public debt and high unemployment), outright pessimism would be totally misplaced. Most Germans continue to enjoy an extremely high standard of living, as can be seen by the numbers taking holidays abroad. Some 44 million such holidays were taken in 1994. The turnover of the package holiday industry more than doubled between 1986 and 1994, helped no doubt by the people in the east enjoying their new freedom of movement. Such growth in travel shows that substantial numbers in the former GDR, too, have enjoyed an economic boost since unification. That car ownership figures have risen from 640,000 to 6.4 million is a sign of affluence, even if the figures from GDR days are distorted by the suppression of demand caused by long waiting lists for new vehicles and high prices.

The main question nevertheless remains that of international competitiveness in a world market which, all experts agree, is undergoing considerable change. In most areas, not least information technology, industry is no longer bound to a specific location, as it used to be by the proximity of raw materials such as coal or iron-ore, but can settle in the most favourable area, basing its decision on costs and the available labour force. This phenomenon of 'globalisation', it is claimed, especially by adherents of free market economics, is bound to affect Germany negatively given its high costs.[6]

What is beyond doubt is that production of low quality goods by untrained workers in labour-intensive industries is never likely to be competitive. Wages in Germany will never sink to the level of the, in comparative terms, pittances paid elsewhere. In any case, the export success of the pre-unification Federal Republic was based to a large degree on quality; in this case the comparison between the Volkswagen and, if not the Trabant, the products of other European car-makers are relevant. What is at issue is whether Germany can maintain its quality advantage in such areas as vehicle production and machine-tools, which, along with chemicals, have been the mainstays of its export success. Until now there are few grounds for panic; it is possible to agree with David Head's conclusion in a 1994 essay '"Made in Germany" in the 1990s' that fears about German industry 'have not been borne out' (Head 1995: 177). It is also important that Germany is represented in the areas that are felt to be significant for the future, not least the computer industry, in which, like most of its European partners, it lags behind the USA and Japan. All in all, *Der Spiegel* concluded, in a piece in its 20 February 1995 edition entitled 'Wir wollen Geld sehen' ('We want to see money'), that there was no shortage of money to invest but of innovative ideas in which it might be invested (*Der Spiegel* 8, 1995: 100–2).

The other key, and partially related, factor is unemployment. If increasing efficiency and information technology destroy many existing jobs, will it be possible to find positions for those displaced? If it is assumed that new areas of technological innovation will not create enough new jobs, then the only alternative might seem to be service industries, although the introduction of new technology here too, for example, shoppers adding up their own bills in supermarkets and bank automation, might lead to a reduction in the number of jobs. Nevertheless, it is still claimed that deregulation in this area, the demise of the *Ladenschlußgesetz*, for instance, would alleviate unemployment. The creation of low-paid, part-time employment in this kind of area is, however, only likely to have a marginal effect in helping those whose standard of living is depressed by unemployment, not to mention the social consequences for families of one or both parents working 'unsocial hours'.

In the present circumstances, it would only seem to add to existing problems if, as proponents of the free market demand, subsidies and regulation were to be cut away. Negative social consequences can be alleviated if decline in employment in such areas as coal and the railways is carefully managed. Moreover, regulation can promote new industry; it is not a coincidence that Germany leads in goods that help to reduce environmental pollution. It is interesting to note that an, admittedly small, organisation representing businesses committed to ecological principles, the *Verband Unternehmensgrün*, has come into existence as a rival to traditional chambers of commerce.

To sum up: the German economy retains many strengths. Its leading position in Europe has been underlined in recent years by takeovers such as those of Skoda by Volkswagen and Rover by BMW. In financial services and insurance, too, German companies are increasingly present in such important markets as London. It is of course free market economists, often critical of the German economy, who set great store on markets as perfect indicators of relative strengths and weaknesses. When during the currency turmoil of early 1995 the money markets turned, among all the other currencies, to the D-Mark, this, given their belief in markets, should indicate to free marketeers that their critique of the Germany economy is substantially wrong. There is no reason to cast aside the model of *soziale Marktwirtschaft* that served the Federal Republic so well between 1949 and 1990.

The validity of this conclusion was underlined by the OECD (Organisation of Economic Co-operation and Development) report on the German economy published in 1995. It suggested some adjustments, for example, a greater role for the stock market, 'but not the abandonment of the German model of economic governance' (OECD 1995: 125). At about the same time a report published by the Swiss-based World Economic Forum placed

91

Germany sixth in a 'league table' of global competitiveness that also took into account such factors as infrastructure and the environment, behind the United States, Singapore, Hong Kong, Japan and Switzerland but well ahead of European partner states France and Great Britain who occupied seventeenth and eighteenth positions respectively. Less positively, according to government estimates, the Federal Republic failed in 1995, because of its debt burden, to meet the financial criteria agreed at Maastricht for a country to enter a Single European Currency. Moreover, surveys published in the spring of 1996 suggested a loss of competitiveness. Nevertheless, there is no reason to lapse into undue fear for the Germany economy. Some reform of the welfare system may well be due, but just as worrying are the social consequences of the changes of recent years, such as unemployment and homelessness. The former stood at 2,576,000 (8.3 per cent) in the west and at 1,031,000 (13.8 per cent) in the east in August 1995, with the prospect of the total reaching four million in 1996 all too real (in fact the 4 million mark was passed in January 1996), while in 1991–2 homelessness was the highest in the then EC countries. It is this kind of problem that will be examined in the next chapter.

5

GERMAN SOCIETY: THE END OF CONSENSUS?

OSSI **AND** *WESSI*

As was pointed out in Chapter 2, the society of the pre-unification Federal Republic, although by no means classless, was marked by a consensus that was remarkable by the standards of some other western European countries. That there were limits on social mobility – most leading positions in society remained in the hands of the same elite groups was largely concealed by the general increase in prosperity. In the GDR, too, while there were clear differences between the privileged way of life enjoyed by top party functionaries and that of the masses they claimed to represent, the prevailing ideology meant that social differences based on wealth and, for example, educational privilege remained relatively insignificant. This chapter will consider whether, in post-unification Germany, the tradition of consensus prevails or whether social cleavages are beginning to threaten cohesion and stability.

The first question that must be considered is the relationship between the citizens of the two former states. That all is not well is already suggested by the nicknames the two groups have acquired, *Ossis* and *Wessis*, which indicate a sense of separation and opposition. When these two terms are expanded to *Jammer-Ossis* (moaning easterners) and *Besser-Wessis* (a play on the word *Besserwisser* which translates as know-all), then the core of the mutual recriminations becomes clearer. Westerners accuse the former GDR citizens of complaining too much about their fate since unification, while easterners accuse west Germans of the arrogance of colonial rulers as the system of the old Federal Republic is extended into the east, in part through the agency of westerner *Beamte* whose job it is to introduce the western system and who enjoy financial privileges for their pains. That these extra payments have been dubbed a 'jungle bonus' (*'Dschungelzulage'*) also suggests, for all the humour of the term, that the east is not universally regarded as the ideal place to work.

To a large extent, unification does not impinge upon the daily lives of those western citizens who live far away from the former intra-German border. Many have also limited curiosity about the territory of the former GDR, being less than anxious to sacrifice their holidays abroad for exploratory visits to an area that was for so long largely out of bounds. The one respect in which such people directly experience unification is in their pockets, specifically the loss of income caused by the tax rises referred to in the previous chapter. It is hardly surprising that this gives rise to a feeling of resentment, especially when it seems that the recipients of their largesse are ungrateful. There are also complaints that the Germans in the east want prosperity handed to them on a plate, whereas in the west affluence was only gained through many years of hard work, a view that overlooks the role of Marshall Aid in the development of the Federal Republic. Such resentment expresses itself in the perception of their eastern fellow citizens as lazy or, given the technological backwardness of the GDR, stupid, a feeling expressed in post-unification cartoons in which easterners appear not to know the difference between a television and an automatic washing-machine or jokes in which Turks appear to have a better command of the German language than the Germans from the ex-GDR.[1]

By contrast, east Germans cannot overlook the changes that have overtaken them. They are likely to read a different newspaper, shop in different shops, as much that was once familiar, for good or ill, disappears. Turning the title of Christa Wolf's controversial post-unification story *Was bleibt* (*Something Remains*) (1990) into a question, they ask what remains of the GDR, with some coming to the conclusion that the only thing to survive (and even spread to the west) might be the green arrow that in the GDR allowed traffic to ignore a red light and turn right at traffic-lights, if the way was clear. The sense that the familiar and, in certain areas such as health care, not entirely negative is being swept away and something new and unknown imposed in its place is bound to cause worry, especially to older people. Accordingly, it is not surprising that a sense of alienation develops, even if radical change was once desired and few want a return to the previous state of affairs in most areas of their life.

When concrete causes for unhappiness in the east are sought, the economic changes are undoubtedly the first factor to come into mind. The shake-out of GDR industry described in the previous chapter has led to massive increases in unemployment in a society where the phenomenon was as good as unknown. Moreover, the official figures for unemployment mask the true extent of the problem, as they do not take into account those on job-creation schemes and those, especially women, who have dropped out of the labour force. From being an integral part of the GDR labour force, women have found themselves increasingly disadvantaged, not least through the reduction in child care facilities that has taken place. In a speech at a women's gathering in July 1995, the Minister for the Family, Old People and Women, Claudia Nolte, herself from the east, outlined the scale of the problem. From the pre-unification figure of 90 per cent, the percentage of women working had dropped by 1993 to 73. Nolte also pointed out that two-thirds of the un-employed in the east were women and periods of unemployment were also longer in the case of women. With unemployment in certain regions running well above the average, it is no wonder that public opinion surveys have consistently shown that for most easterners it is the major political issue.

The other related economic issue is privatisation. It is not simply a case of a perceived equation that privatisation, as practised by the Treuhand agency, equals unemployment, but the sense that privatisation has handed over the economy to people from the west. Eighty per cent of firms privatised by the end of 1994 did, in fact, end up in western hands; what is more many eastern firms felt themselves to have been disadvantaged by the ruthless competitive methods used by western rivals. The number of insolvencies in the former GDR (the figures rose from 1,092 in 1992 to 3,911 in 1994 and to as many as 5,874 in 1995) suggests in itself that life in a market economy has proved difficult for many. Where closure of a firm has followed a western takeover, there have been suspicions that the aim has been to remove a potential rival. This was certainly the feeling of the potassium miners of Bischofferode in the west of the former GDR, who went on hunger strike in 1993 when the new owners announced the closure of mines that had once employed almost 4,000 people. Another perceived example of western discrimination is the fate of the optical and precision engineering company Carl Zeiss Jena, now called Jenoptik. Its position was made difficult by the existence of a firm with the name of Zeiss in

95

the west, which had been founded after the war by people from the original Jena company and which, on unification, naturally did not relish a new competitor. In 1995 there were 2,400 people working for Jenoptik where once there had been 23,000 jobs.

It has not just been the ownership of companies that has been a major matter of concern for people in the east, but also the ownership of land and property. Many people who once owned real estate in the GDR had it confiscated by the state; following unification, the rights of such people, the majority of whom now resided in the west, became an important issue. The decision of the Federal government was that in principle a policy of restitution rather than compensation should apply.[2] The result of this is that many in the east fear losing the roof over their head and that disputes over ownership are blocking investment. Nobody will invest and no bank will lend money when the project is linked to land and property whose ownership is unclear. Despite amendments to the original decision, ownership difficulties remain a barrier to investment; changes that do take place are likely to disadvantage former GDR citizens who find that their property suddenly belongs to someone else.

Legal disputes over property are not the only area in which the use of the law has been controversial in the former GDR. Fired with a zeal that was remarkably absent when it came to the crimes committed in the Nazi era, particularly where there was a case against those in the legal profession responsible for outrageous death sentences for minor offences, the legal authorities in the Federal Republic have been comparatively quick to pursue former GDR citizens accused of offences related to the political system of that country. One major example is the successful prosecution of former borderguards whose finger was on the trigger when people attempting to flee to the west were shot dead. The issues raised are less to do with the immoral nature of the offences committed – there can be little doubt that in many areas the GDR operated a morally reprehensible repressive system within which the risk of death for anybody attempting to escape its jurisdiction without official sanction played a major part in maintaining the survival of the state – than with the legal basis of any prosecutions and the ability of the courts to pursue those most responsible for the worst aspects of the regime.

A principle of a state based on the rule of law is that there can be no punishment of actions that are not illegal at the time committed.

This means that the Federal government is unable to introduce legislation that would brand vast areas of what was normal in the GDR as illegal and try those in authority retrospectively. All that is possible is that alleged offenders are tried under the provisions of GDR law, as it existed at the time the offences were committed. It was clearly an offence under GDR law to kill somebody who had abandoned an attempt to escape and surrendered to the border authorities – there is at least one case where this is alleged to have happened – or to leave someone who had been wounded to bleed to death, as happened to the would-be refugee Peter Fechter in 1962, but the position is much less clear when it comes to border-guards who followed the command to shoot those bent on escape. In such cases, the prosecuting authorities have to fall back on the obligations made by the GDR in international law, for example, its acceptance of the UN Charter of Human Rights, to help their arguments. It remains to be seen whether it will be possible on this kind of basis to convict Egon Krenz and other leading GDR politicians whose trial commenced in late 1995.

In certain cases, the attempts to find a legal basis for prosecution runs in the face of what appears to be common sense; why, for instance, should the former GDR spymaster Markus Wolf be tried for espionage against the Federal Republic when his western counterparts who were engaged in similar activities against the GDR face no sanctions? This appeared to be recognised in part by a Constitutional Court ruling in May 1995 which demanded leniency towards former GDR spies, especially if they had not been active on the territory of the pre-1990 Federal Republic. Similar considerations apply to the prosecution of the East Berlin lawyer Wolfgang Vogel, who acted as an intermediary between the governments of the GDR and the Federal Republic and took on the cases of GDR citizens wishing to leave for the west. At the time of unification, Chancellor Kohl was reported to be considering honouring him for his humanitarian efforts; in January 1996 he was fined DM92,000 and given a two years' suspended sentence for blackmail, perjury and false certification on the basis of his involvement in the sale of would-be refugees' assets at what, from today's standpoint, were knockdown prices.

More than legal niceties relating to prosecutions that have taken place or are pending, it is probably the failure to prosecute those who were really responsible for the worst misdeeds of the GDR regime or prosecutions relating to only minor offences that concerns former GDR citizens most. The trial of Erich Honecker was stopped for medical reasons, while the conviction secured against the head of the Stasi, Erich Mielke, had to do with a murder of two policemen he was involved in as a young communist in 1931. The head of the GDR trade unions (and as such a leading functionary of the regime, since trade unions enjoyed no independent existence), Harry Tisch, received an eighteen months' suspended sentence for financial irregularities. Such anomalies have not helped to create a belief in the judicial system of the Federal Republic among former GDR citizens.

This leaves the question of what should be done. There are increasing demands for an amnesty, particularly for those who only held minor offices within the GDR system and whose alleged offences were part of normal behaviour in that country. The group most opposed to such an amnesty, the advocates of which claim that it would help in the integration of the two parts of the country, are former dissidents who experienced repression at first hand. In strictly moral terms, it is hard to deny their claims; it is a practical political decision whether they should be sacrificed to pragmatic considerations – the need to make many former GDR citizens feel that they are not the victims of a legal system that imposes its own standards from outside.[3]

The overall sense among people in the east that they have been the victims of procedures and processes imposed from outside is encapsulated in the word *Abwicklung*. This term is taken from the world of business where it is used to describe the way an order is processed within a firm from the time it is received until the finished product is dispatched. It contains, therefore, in the GDR context the idea that various elements of society, for example, the economy, the legal system (although it appears that some of those responsible for harsh sentences have been treated leniently by their western peers), the system of health care and not least the education system, were subjected to a calculated process of review and alteration with the predetermined aim of destroying what had existed before. This can be illustrated by what happened in the university sector, where the position of teaching staff was reassessed in the light of previous ideological pronouncements. Anyone with close links to Marxism–Leninism was liable to dismissal – it has to be remembered that philosophy, history and large parts of the social sciences were dominated by this ideology – while leading managerial functions were frequently taken over by western academics, often on a part-time basis. It was this kind of change in so many areas that created tensions; whereas the need for change was recognised, imposed change was less welcome, particularly when it seemed that the change was imposed on the basis of arrogant condescension rather than diplomatic tact. The overall result was a sense among former GDR citizens that they were second-class citizens in the new Germany, a view endorsed by 76 per cent in an opinion poll carried out shortly before the 1994 federal election.

The question that has to be asked is whether the feelings of alienation experienced in the former GDR are a cause for worry. Are the hopes expressed by politicians that the internal unity of the Federal Republic might soon be completed anything more than pious clichés? It would not seem to matter too much that people flock to parties in rooms decorated with GDR memorabilia, in particular the previously ubiquitous portraits of Erich Honecker, and indulge in what has been dubbed *Ostalgie*. That some consumers, having sampled western delights, have returned to food and household products manufactured in the east is arguably good for the regional economy. What does seem worrying is that in Berlin, where it might be expected that the preconditions for unity are most favourable, there is little evidence of mixing between citizens from the two parts of the city. Of the marriages that took place in the city in 1994, only 527 out of 15,730 were between partners from east and west.

The real reason for worry is if discontent in the east continues to express itself in political extremism. The success of the PDS is in many eyes one manifestation of such extremism, although its potentially disruptive role within the party system might partly be the result of the reactions of other parties. Undoubtedly more worrying would be any further growth of right-wing violence that would damage both society at home and Germany's name abroad. One explanation of such violence is, as was suggested in Chapter 3, that the doctrines presented to the young people in their childhood under communism have proved so worthless that the resulting sense of disorientation leaves them vulnerable to extremism. To combat this feeling it is not enough to wait for economic progress to overcome or alleviate the sense of disadvantage in the east. People in the GDR understandably do not relish the idea that their previous life was worthless and has, as the writer Stefan Heym put it, to be 'thrown away' (Heym 1991). Whereas it is inevitable that the integration of two groups of people who were separated both physically and ideologically for over forty years will take time, there is a responsibility on politicians and other opinion formers to try to make unity more than the formal process completed on 3 October 1990.

What cannot be denied is the extent of the changes that the years 1989–90 brought. Figures published in *Die Zeit* in its 30 June 1995 edition about developments in the town of Brandenburg west of Berlin over the years 1990–4 underline how much these changes affected people's lives. The number of births decreased from 1,492 to 575 and the number of marriages from 547 to 306; clearly there was a reluctance to enter into long-term commitments. That divorces increased from forty-five to 212 also suggests turmoil, although one might suspect the optimism of 1990 may have depressed the number of divorces in that year (*Die Zeit* 27, 1995: 10). However, there are also tones of optimism to be heard about the future. The magazine *Der Spiegel* ended its cover story on the ex-GDR in its 4 September 1995 edition with the suggestion that skills learned in the GDR, for example, the ability to create networks and to deal with chaotic situations at work, along with the sense of togetherness, might be a better preparation for a future in which greater flexibility is required than a western upbringing (*Der Spiegel* 36, 1995: 118–39). There are also signs that the east is catching up in the key area of incomes. Whereas in 1991 76 per cent of eastern households were in receipt of a net income of DM2,500 or less (as opposed to 39 per cent in the west), the figure had dropped to 47 per cent in 1994, only 12 per cent above that for western households.

PROBLEMS OF MIGRATION

Throughout its history as an industrial country Germany has always had problems connected with a shortage of labour. Even before the creation of a unified German state, Brandenburg/ Prussia, in its attempts to build itself up into a major power, was happy to accept outsiders such as the Protestant refugees from France known as the Huguenots.[4] In the late nineteenth century, the major group of immigrants were Poles who came to work in the heavy industry of the Ruhr and whose legacy survives not just in names but in dialect words, such as the Polish word for hammer, *młotek*. As the postwar 'economic miracle' gathered steam, workers were hired from southern countries with the largest group coming from Turkey. That the efforts of foreign workers in boosting the economy, particularly when the flow from the east was stemmed by the building of the Berlin Wall in 1961, were appreciated in official quarters is indicated by the gift of a moped in 1964 to the millionth such worker, a man from Portugal.

The postwar influx of workers rested on two major assumptions: that the foreign workers were temporary residents, guest workers (*Gastarbeiter*), and that economic growth would continue. Neither proved to be the case. The so-called guests increasingly settled, brought their families to Germany or founded families, in short took on the characteristics of other immigrant communities in, for example, Great Britain and France. When, in the 1970s, full employment gave way to recession, the stage was set for the at times grudging acceptance of outsiders, whose different habits were balanced by their important economic role, to give way to resentment about unemployment and other social ills. Moreover, it is possible to argue that the resentment faced is in part attributable to the peculiar legal position in which this group of people has always found itself.

Comparisons with immigrant populations in other countries of the type just made are partially invalid because those entering the Federal Republic to work, and more importantly their descendants in the second and by now third generation, have never been automatically eligible for citizenship and the civil rights citizenship bestows. This is because German law – on the basis of a statute that dates back to 1913 – determines nationality on the basis of blood – the Latin legal term is *jus sanguinis* – and not on the basis of place of birth: *jus soli*. What this means quite simply is that people born on German soil of non-German parents do not have an automatic right to German citizenship. They remain, therefore, at least in political terms, second-class citizens, disenfranchised unless they have a passport from another EU country that allows participation in European elections. At the other end of the scale, suggestions that participation in local elections should be extended to foreign residents are doomed because of the current legal position, which reflects an untenable fiction that there are no immigrants in the Federal Republic, only temporary foreign residents. The unsustainability of the idea was underlined by the failure of many Turks, who were encouraged to return in the mid-1980s by the newly elected Kohl government, to settle in their former homeland and the subsequent decision of many of their fellow countrymen and women to regard Germany as their permanent home.

The unfortunate position of *Gastarbeiter* and their descendants has been exacerbated by the way the government of the Federal Republic has always been willing to regard other groups as German and grant them full civil rights. What is meant by this is not the citizens of the GDR prior to 1990, when the refusal of the Federal Republic to accept a separate GDR citizenship caused tension with the other German state, but groups living in the (former) communist states to the east known as ethnic Germans (*Volksdeutsche*). As was mentioned in the Introduction, the redrawing of boundaries in 1945 and the less than complete expulsion of German populations left behind minorities who continued to regard themselves as German; part of the Brandt government's *Ostpolitik* was aimed at helping these groups, not least by making immigration to the Federal Republic easier. Much more tenuous was the position of German minorities in the Soviet Union and Romania whose forbears had left Germany centuries earlier, in the case of the Volga Germans to settle land conquered in the eighteenth century by Catherine the Great of Russia. They were removed from there to Central Asia (today's independent state of Kazakhstan) by Stalin who doubted their loyalty in the Second World War, something which admittedly does imply that they were clearly regarded as Germans in the Soviet Union. With the collapse of the Soviet Union and the end of the Ceauçescu regime in Romania, these groups were free to travel to the Federal Republic[5] and immediately acquire German citizenship, even if, as was especially the case with the younger generation from the Soviet Union, the individuals concerned no longer spoke German. The numbers entering Germany on the basis of ethnicity were large, with figures reaching 377,055 in 1989 and 397,095 in 1990. Subsequently figures for this group, generally known as *Aussiedler*, have declined, to 220,530 in 1992. Their privileged position appeared even more incongruous, when compared to that of a third-generation member of a family of *Gastarbeiter*, as it emerged that some claims to German blood were based on Nazi policies which, as part of the overall racial ideology, had assigned certain individuals to the German race and, in a few cases, the service of a grandfather in the SS. By contrast, the emigration to Germany of Jewish citizens of the former Soviet Union, even if on a small scale, is a development that gives grounds for optimism. The Jewish community in 1995 was put at some 60,000, an increase of about 20,000 over two years.

The situation at the time of unification was complicated even further by a third group: asylum seekers or as they were disparagingly called in German, *Asylanten*. How their presence became a political issue in the early 1990s has already been considered in Chapter 3. The pressure put on the Federal government at that time is indicative of the conduct of the debate over many years. Great stress has been laid on numbers with the implication that the indigenous Germans were in danger of being swamped by large numbers of outsiders. In fact, in 1994 there were 6.8 million foreigners resident in the Federal Republic, well under 10 per cent of the population. In that 75 per cent of these had lived in Germany for more than ten years and that 1.5 million had been born there, the bare figure hides the reality of a more complex situation. For many though, simplification is the order of the day; in addition to creating unemployment, foreigners are held largely responsible for crime, housing problems, increasing drug abuse, prostitution and every other imaginable social problem. The reality that foreigners live in poor housing, do the most menial jobs, benefit least from the education system – the standards achieved in all these areas by foreigners are one-half of the national average – is frequently lost in a debate inspired more by prejudice than any other consideration. Although opinion polls have shown that many Germans are able to distinguish between the various groups entering the country and generally accept that long-term residents deserve more rights, it would be difficult to claim that a climate of perfect acceptance and tolerance exists. Violent physical attacks are only the outward sign of a widespread problem.

In this situation, it is interesting to consider how far there are forces in society which do speak up for the interests of foreigners and immigrants. One group, the *Aussiedler*, do have official support in that they automatically enjoy civil rights, and because of their official status as Germans they are also less likely to be singled out by right-wing propagandists, the group most vocal in anti-immigrant propaganda. Most in fact vote CDU or CSU, no doubt out of gratitude for being allowed to resettle. Others are more dependent on less structured systems of support, although it is true that the embassies of the countries of origin of foreign citizens, as well as the home governments, do continue to take an interest in their citizens who live in the Federal Republic, even if in certain cases, particularly with asylum seekers, that interest is far from benevolent.

Among Germans, understanding and support comes from certain groups of intellectuals and from parts of the media. It has, for instance, been pointed out on television political magazine programmes that foreign workers make a positive contribution to the economy by doing essential menial jobs that would otherwise be hard to fill (it is a gross simplification to claim that unemployed Germans, who in many cases are well qualified, could or would take over the unskilled and sometimes dangerous work done by foreigners) and by paying into the social security system. Given the strains on this system, caused not least by an ageing population, the higher birthrate among foreigners, often a souce of resentment, can be seen as a positive advantage. In 1992 out of 809,000 births, 100,000 were to foreign parents. The role of intellectuals in drawing attention to the plight of foreigners has already been mentioned in Chapter 2 in connection with Günter Wallraff's *Ganz unten*. More recently, certain writers responded to the attacks on asylum seekers by organising readings in hostels. Increasingly, too, German literature reflects the multi-ethnicity of German society. Whereas the Italian worker in Max von der Grün's 1963 novel *Irrlicht und Feuer* (*Will o' the Wisp and Fire*) (Grün 1967) belongs with his excitable temperament totally in the realm of cliché, Sten Nadolny's 1990 *Selim oder Die Gabe der Rede* (*Selim or the Gift of Oratory*) presents a much more differentiated picture of the friendship between a German and a Turk.

Another interesting development of recent years has been the growth of a literature written in German by writers of Turkish and other non-German origins. It can of course be argued with some justification that this kind of literature and even serious television programmes are only likely to reach those who already hold tolerant attitudes and are prepared, for instance, to take part in anti-racist demonstrations. On the other hand, this group does have some political influence; it is a sign of progress that Bündnis 90/Die Grünen, the party most likely to be associated primarily with the educated middle class, chose as a candidate and had elected the first member of the Federal parliament of Turkish origin, Cem Özdemir, in the election of 1994.

It is in fact politicians who are most challenged by the issue of immigration. The record shows that they have been most decisive when taking measures to limit numbers. A general stop on recruitment of foreign labour – the process of medical examination and other formalities at the German embassy in Turkey is described in Nadolny's novel – was introduced with the first oil crisis as long ago as 1973 by the SPD/FDP government; since then it has largely been a case of foreign workers being joined by members of their families.

In the case of the contract workers (*Vertragsarbeiter*) hired by the GDR, where the shortage of labour led the government to recruit workers on short-term contracts, principally from Vietnam and Mozambique which had ideologically compatible regimes,[6] after unification every effort was made to expedite their return home with contracts only being extended if employment and a fixed place of residence could be proved. In most cases, the foreign workers were the first victims of the wave of unemployment to hit GDR industry with two-thirds unemployed even before the end of the GDR's separate existence.

The alteration of Article 16 of the Basic Law to stem the tide of asylum seekers was referred to in Chapter 3. Essentially the changes meant that any asylum seeker reaching the Federal Republic from a country that was deemed to operate a system for such people which corresponded to democratic principles could be turned back. The list included not just partners in the European Union but most of the new democracies in the east, whose co-operation was purchased in part by financial aid. Additionally, deportation was made easier and the processing of asylum applications speeded up. Previously, although few applications were granted (between 1988 and 1993 the figure never reached 10 per cent), many had been allowed to stay.

It would be unfair to say that all government action has been concerned with restricting numbers. Official bodies have been set up at *Land* and local levels to concern themselves with the interests of foreign residents, in particular the office of *Ausländerbeauftragter* (commissioner for foreigners). The law of 1991 relating to foreigners (*Ausländergesetz*), while laying emphasis on the restriction of numbers and very controversially requiring, for instance, schools and doctors to pass on information to the relevant authorities about foreigners, did stress integration, which remains the official policy of the Federal government. Subsequently there has been discussion about making it easier for people of foreign descent to acquire German citizenship (current figures of about 40,000 per annum are very low) and permitting those born in

Germany to choose German nationality at the age of 18.[7] However, the general rejection of dual nationality (about 25,000 out of 1.9 million Turks enjoy this privilege with certain *Länder* being more generous than others) makes even this difficult, as there is a frequent reluctance among prospective applicants to break entirely with their country of origin. Without that happening, it is hard to see how integration, whatever that term may mean in detail, can take place. However assiduous and sympathetic *Ausländer-beauftragte* may be in working in the interests of those they serve, they cannot be a substitute for those concerned expressing their own interests as citizens who enjoy equal rights.

It is not being claimed that the granting of civil rights and associated legislation can act as a panacea, although the enforced disappearance of signs and advertisements displaying the words *keine Ausländer* (no foreigners) would be welcome. Nor can it be argued that numbers are entirely irrelevant – no country can take in all the world's victims of injustice and experience in many European countries has shown that levels of tolerance decrease with increased immigration. This latter point underlines the fact that in many respects the situation in the Federal Republic is not unique, with polls indicating that society is not significantly less tolerant there than elsewhere. This does not mean that there is not room for improvement[8] and that, specifically in the Federal Republic, there are no concrete steps in the area of citizenship that can be taken. It ought, for instance, be possible to accommodate the interests of both *Aussiedler* and those of non-Germans. Furthermore, especially as there is absolutely no chance of all people of foreign origin leaving the Federal Republic, greater tolerance or at the very least measures, be they penal or educational, to reduce violence against those perceived as outsiders are an imperative for a degree of social harmony, not to mention the obligations placed on the Federal Republic by the Nazi past never to relapse into organised racism.[9]

POVERTY AND DISADVANTAGE

Except for the sight of the occasional beggar in a pedestrian precinct, whose appearance invariably contrasts with the affluent surroundings and whose own description of his or her unhappy lot on a scrap of paper or cardboard may in any case not always be genuine, the visitor to Germany, especially to those areas that

106

made up the pre-1990 Federal Republic, may gain the impression that, given the clearly visible level of prosperity, poverty cannot exist in this society. It is true that in all or nearly all cases absolute poverty of the type found in the Third World does not exist in today's Federal Republic, where any discussion of poverty must centre on relative poverty, that is to say the way that certain people are deprived of what is considered normal in other areas of society. Even if not life-threatening, such relative poverty is highly disturbing and distressing, not least for children who are denied what their peers enjoy. That this deprivation might include not having material objects, such as a supply of the latest computer games, the moral and educational value of which may not be obvious, is irrelevant in this context. If children feel unhappy and parents feel stress because of relative poverty, it is pointless to deny that real deprivation exists.

One set of figures quoted in the previous chapter, the increasing sums being spent on *Sozialhilfe*, shows that more people are having to rely on the state to attain the level of income deemed necessary for survival. Other figures contained in the volume *Armut in Deutschland (Poverty in Germany)* show that in 1992 3.6 per cent of households had 40 per cent or less of average household incomes, 7.8 per cent had 50 per cent or less and 15.2 per cent had 60 per cent or less (Hanesch *et al.* 1994: 138). In the period 1990–2, the percentages in the west had remained more or less constant, while those in the east had declined, reflecting the increases in wages and allowances as western standards were introduced. That there were no percentage changes in the west, despite recession, suggests that the social security system provides a safety net for many, albeit, as has been seen, at a price.

It goes without saying that the major cause of relative poverty is likely to be unemployment, particularly long-term unemployment when benefits cease to be as generous. In September 1994 the number of those who had been unemployed for a year or more was more than a million, with women, as seen above, being particularly affected in the east.[10] At this time the Federal government announced a scheme, *Aktion Beschäftigungshilfen* (action to aid employment), to help this group. Under this scheme the government would pay 80 per cent of the labour costs for six months, thereafter 60 per cent for six months to firms taking on someone who had been unemployed for three years and smaller percentages (70 falling to 50, 60 falling to 40) for those who had been unemployed for two years or one year respectively. This underlines the willingness of the Federal government to take specific measures to increase employment beyond the obligation to conduct the national economy in a responsible manner. In fact, the creation of jobs through *Arbeitsbeschaffungsmaßnahmen* has been a feature of recent years not just in the former GDR. By contrast, employers argue that the overall high wage levels in the Federal Republic, bolstered by the system of nationally agreed wage levels (*Tarifverträge*), causes unemployment. Whereas it is true that low-paid jobs may improve the unemployment statistics, they will not end demands on the state for support, while the economic benefit of employing badly motivated low-wage earners in an economy dependent on a high level of skills in many sectors may not be very high.

More important in combating unemployment and the poverty that goes with it would be an improvement in educational achievement. Within the area of the pre-1990 Federal Republic, those without a school-leaving qualification had (on the basis of the survey in *Armut in Deutschland*) in 1992 a 14.9 per cent greater chance of living in relative poverty (50 per cent of the average household income) than other groups (Hanesch *et al.* 1994: 175), while there was also a marked correlation between lack of vocational qualification and unemployment.[11] It would be in the national interest if more people benefited from the educational system. This raises questions about why certain people do not, specifically the much-discussed educational question of whether failures lack potential or do not have their potential developed. The arguments in such a debate which generally relate to questions of intelligence and standards are not specific to Germany and go beyond the scope of the present discussion, although certain groups who do less well within the education system will be mentioned later in this chapter (pp. 110–11).

Other areas that are linked to poverty and deprivation are inadequate housing and poor health. An increasing number of people have no home at all; figures for homelessness are estimated at about 200,000 with a further 800,000 people in temporary, unsuitable accommodation. Other statistics relating to housing are difficult to interpret because of unification. A lack of investment in the older housing stock in the GDR meant that many homes lacked modern facilities, such as a separate bathroom and WC, a situation that is now being remedied.

In the area of the pre-1990 Federal Republic, and increasingly the former GDR too, the housing market in the rented sector has come to be increasingly subject to market forces. This is of major significance, as some 60 per cent of homes are rented (or were in the old Federal Republic in 1987 when the last census was carried out). In the postwar years rent controls operated, while a system of subsidised housing encapsulated in the word *Sozialwohnung* (social dwelling) provided accommodation at a lower rent for the less well-off, although with increasing prosperity many *Sozial-wohnungen* had tenants who no longer came into that category. In the 1980s the Kohl government stopped the building of such dwellings – at a time when it was thought that there was no longer any housing shortage. Subsequent developments would appear to prove that such a view was wrong; the overall housing shortage is estimated by the main tenants' association (*Deutscher Mieterbund*) to amount to 3 million dwellings. This has resulted in the average rent rising (following 10 per cent rent increases in every year from 1988 to 1992) to 24 per cent of net income in the west and 17 per cent in the east in 1994.

What continues to be needed is reasonably priced accommodation for those with lower incomes, particularly families with two or more children. Again those without educational and professional qualifications are more likely to be in unsuitable accommodation, although skilled workers too are being affected. In the field of health it has already been noted (p. 84) that costs have risen. Given such factors as increased longevity, extra expenditure may not mean that people are less well, rather the opposite. Nevertheless, subjective assessments of poor health, surveys of which show a correlation between this and unemployment and other areas of deprivation, are likely to lead to increased demands on medical services and increased costs for the state (Hanesch *et al.* 1994: 171).

The major question that remains to be asked is who is likely to be affected by poverty and the linked phenomena of poor educational, housing and health standards. One area known to be increasingly under pressure is the institution of the family. It cannot be claimed that certain changes affecting family life in many countries, for example, the increasing divorce rate, are due entirely to material deprivation, but, on the other hand, such factors are not irrelevant. Despite politicians' idealisation of the family and the requirement to foster it contained in Article 6 of the Basic Law that states that marriage and the family enjoy the protection of the state, child benefit was not increased for seventeen years prior to 1992. Cuts in state support for students have also not helped families. Since it has been estimated that it costs up to DM250,000 to bring up a child, it is small wonder that the birthrate is dropping. Those with large families, unless they enjoy the privileges of *Beamter* status, are likely to be under financial pressure. Around 13 per cent of families with three or more children are in receipt of *Sozialhilfe*.

Besides the collective institution of the family, there are specific groups of individuals frequently associated with aspects of social deprivation whose position has to be considered: women, the old, members of certain social groups and foreigners. Women, as those most likely to be left with any children in the event of family break-up, continue to be most affected by pressures on the family and the estimated shortage of 800,000 nursery places. Whilst, as was seen in Chapter 1, the proclaimed equality of the GDR was less than perfect, in the pre-1990 Federal Republic women were under-represented in top areas of employment, politics and, in the area of higher education, as students of scientific and technological subjects, the fields that have generally led to secure, well-paid employment. This situation is likely to continue for some time post unification, although efforts to increase female representation in politics through quotas have borne fruit. As already mentioned in Chapter 3, the Greens have always worked on a basis of strict equality, while in 1988 the SPD introduced a system of quotas (due over ten years to rise to 40 per cent) for party positions and parliamentary and council seats.[12] Despite such progress, in the leading article in the 1 September 1995 edition of *Die Zeit*, which coincided with the United Nations Women's Conference in Beijing, Susanne Mayer was able to produce some damning statistics. Although in 1995 over 40 per cent of university students were women and women were gaining a third of all doctorates, only 8.5 per cent of top civil servants and judges and only 5.7 per cent of university professors were women (*Die Zeit* 36, 1995: 1).

In the case of older people, this is an area where in certain respects people living in the former GDR are better off. With the increase in pensions towards western levels, the fact that most GDR citizens had worked throughout their adult lives gave them the right to an income above *Sozialhilfe* levels, although access to this form of support has been less available than in the west because of different rules. In the west 7.1 per cent of those aged 65 and over received *Sozialhilfe* in 1991, as opposed to 5.8 per cent of the whole population in this part of Germany. Although this shows some over-representation, it is minor in comparison with the figures for young people in the west – in 1992 well over a million young people aged under 18 lived in households receiving this form of aid. Poverty and homelessness are an increasing problem for young Germans.

In terms of educational achievements, one group that was always under-represented in the pre-unification Federal Republic was the children of foreign workers. That a shortage of skills often means poverty and the associated problems with employment and housing has already been pointed out. Nowhere is this more obvious than in the case of *Gastarbeiter*, the group of people, who with few exceptions came to Germany to take on menial tasks. This pattern of immigration contrasts starkly with, for example, that of the USA where in recent years it has been well-qualified people who have been encouraged to settle. More than a third of foreign workers are likely to suffer two or more forms of underprovision in the areas of income, housing, education and the labour market (Hanesch *et al.* 1994: 175). Even before cultural factors are taken into account, a young female from non German origins is likely to be among the most underprivileged members of society.

YOUNG PEOPLE IN THE FEDERAL REPUBLIC

At the time of the student movement in the late 1960s the idea of a generation gap entered public consciousness in the Federal Republic. The older generation was represented by the stereotype of an authoritarian father-figure tainted by involvement with National Socialism, while the younger generation was presented as consisting of unkempt adherents of political rebelliousness, free love and any other imaginable form of wayward social behaviour. What is undeniably true, behind these clichés, is that the rapid changes German society underwent in the decades following 1945 led to new attitudes and values establishing themselves among young people. This can be seen from the results of a Europe-wide survey of attitudes across generations undertaken in 1981 and 1982. In answer to questions about whether they had the same attitudes as their parents, West Germans scored consistently lower than the European average. Whereas 63 per cent overall spoke of having the same ideas of morality as their parents, the figure for West Germans was only 49 per cent (and 38 per cent for those aged between 18 and 24), while the figures for similar political views were 36 per cent overall and 28 per cent in the Federal Republic (Greiffenhagen and Greiffenhagen 1993: 441).

What is the situation today now that the student movement generation has itself become middle-aged and its children represent youth? This is a difficult question to answer because in a fragmented post-modern society, where young people attach themselves to various subcultures, such as punk or techno (the leading musical craze in Germany), the picture is more amorphous than ever before. This was illustrated in the summer of 1995 when the Berlin 'love festival' (*Liebesfest*) of the techno fans was followed shortly afterwards by the punks' *Chaostage* in Hanover when policemen were attacked and property vandalised. What cannot be claimed is that young people have reverted to the model against which their parents rebelled. It is only necessary to look at the world of fashion to see that the age of sartorial conformity has not returned. What is beyond doubt is that the greater part of the younger generation is hedonistic, with the pursuit of enjoyment taking precedence over traditional political activities. This state of affairs has led the sociologist Gerhard Schulze to describe contemporary German society as an 'experience society' (*'Erlebnisgesellschaft'*), that is to say one in which young people primarily seek excitement and stimulation.

This does not necessarily mean that young people have no interest in politics or have reverted to traditional German attitudes. The large numbers of young males refusing military service and choosing the option of *Zivildienst* (a period of, at the time of writing, thirteen months, as opposed to the ten months of an army conscript, working, for example, with handicapped or old people), particularly among those who have attended *Gymnasium*, suggest that the Prussian military ethos holds little appeal. The average number of those refusing military service and having their refusal accepted has generally been around 20 per cent with the figure rising to 23 per cent at the time of the Gulf War. There was also a large increase in the first half of 1995 when the situation in former Yugoslavia doubtlessly had an influence. As for the all-important question of young people's attitudes to politics, polls taken in 1992 at the height of the *Politikverdrossenheit* debate and reproduced in a major study of youth published in 1995 entitled *Jugend und Demokratie in Deutschland* (*Young People and Democracy in Germany*) suggest that in both parts of Germany satisfaction with democracy was high (75.6 per cent in the west and 61.8 per cent in the east) (Hoffmann-Lange 1995: 172); it is just that Greenpeace appears a more sympathetic organisation than established political parties.

In conclusion, it is possible to claim that German youth increasingly resembles that in other comparable countries, certainly in its cultural preferences. What is more, differences between young people in both parts of Germany, although present, are less than might have been expected given forty years of separation and the attempts of GDR politicians to influence their citizens.

OTHER SOCIAL QUESTIONS

Every month the Federal Press and Information Office (Presse- und Informationsamt der Bundesregierung) publishes statistical material including polls showing which issues most concern the citizenry. Following unification, there was a marked difference between the perceptions in east and west. Whereas economic and labour market problems featured at the top of eastern concerns, questions relating to foreigners and asylum seekers headed the western lists. Following the amendment to the law relating to asylum seekers, both parts of the country began to share the same economic concerns. For a period in the 1980s, when prosperity was at its height, West Germans regarded the environment as their major concern. In the autumn of 1994, admittedly an election period when basic economic issues tend to come to the fore, only a fifth as many people in the west regarded the environment as equally important as unemployment. In the east, it did not show up as an issue. This gives the lie to any suggestion that the Federal Republic is a post-materialist society. In any case, other indicators, such as the government refusal to introduce speed limits on motorways, show that, despite what was said in the previous chapter, environmental issues, although arguably taken more seriously than in other comparable countries, do not dominate the agenda.

Besides the question of unemployment, the second issue exercising minds in the east was crime, a matter of concern in the west too. The strength of feelings in the east can be attributed to the change from GDR days when crime rates were low. All the other issues that showed up as a matters of concern have been dealt with in this or the preceding chapter. How far they make up a society undergoing some form of crisis will now be examined.

113

CONCLUSION

By 1990, the society of the Federal Republic, like that of other advanced countries, was no longer based on the traditional model of clearly differentiated strata consisting of homogeneous social classes. It was not the case that no barriers now existed, but rather that the increased individualisation that had accompanied prosperity had led to a fragmentation within what had once been more clearly distinguishable large social groupings. The working class was no longer dominated by those employed in the traditional heavy industries whose economic significance had declined rapidly in the previous decades, while within the middle classes various distinct lifestyles had developed, of which the most obvious is the alternative lifestyle associated with the Greens.[13] With unification, a very different kind of society was grafted on to the existing Federal Republic, one that had been organised according to very different principles and in which there were generally no extremes of wealth or poverty. In so far as the changes that have taken place reflect developments that apply in numerous other countries or, in the case of unification, are a consequence of a unique event, wholesale condemnation of national politicians is inappropriate. What can be demanded is that they address issues that have arisen as a result of the changes that have occurred. The majority of these issues, as described in this chapter, can be subsumed under the general heading of inequality, something that has appeared to increase over recent years.

The claim that little can be done to cushion inequality because global competition requires a massive reduction of welfare and other social programmes is dubious not just for moral, but also for economic reasons. It is not just that the Federal Republic, in order to stay competitive, needs to exploit the talents of as many citizens as possible; the exclusion of a large minority from the mainstream of society might lead to additional costs, in particular expenditure to contain crime. Nursery education, which research has shown to bring great social benefit in that its beneficiaries are less likely to become involved in crime, is a better investment than the construction of prisons. There is also the constitutional requirement that the Federal Republic should be a *sozialer Rechtsstaat*. The issue that has to be faced is how far since unification the Federal Republic has maintained that ideal within the financial and economic limits that undoubtedly exist.

The challenge exists in three main areas: education, employment and the welfare state. It has been seen in this chapter that not all benefit from the education system and some are denied equality of opportunity; whether a wholesale reform of the system, in particular the more widespread introduction of the comprehensive principle would help, is as controversial a topic in Germany as it has been in other countries with opponents fearing a drop in allegedly already declining educational standards. What cannot be denied is that the *Hauptschule* is in danger of being regarded as a repository for failures, with pupils of foreign origin all too often coming into this category. This raises another – in the widest sense – educational issue: the need to encourage a greater acceptance and tolerance of all groups in society. Women and those born into certain social groups have yet to achieve their potential and the same is true of the children of foreign citizens. Whether the answer to their various difficulties is the promotion of the ideal of a multicultural society is another controversial issue with the objection being raised, as it is in a number of countries, that this could lead to minorities being compartmentalised into their particular group and therefore still liable to discrimination.

In the case of social welfare, certain measures taken by the Federal government can be judged on their effectiveness. The apparent increase in poverty suggests that there is still much to be done in this area, although it must be pointed out that about half of those who claim *Sozialhilfe* only do so for a limited period. Consequently, it is wrong to see the nearly 4 million who received this benefit in 1993 as being permanently confined to the margins of society.

Social welfare and employment are linked in that the relationship between levels of benefit and rates of pay is always a contentious issue, which has led some experts to demand that the two questions be separated.[14] Once it has been assured and accepted that the needs of families would be met by social welfare, it might be easier to consider more rationally the questions of wages and employment in an environment of increasing international competition. Another possible improvement would be for all citizens to regard themselves as potential beneficiaries of the welfare system and not, as many do, solely as contributors. This would surely be good for social cohesion.

As in the last two chapters, it is as well to end with a note of caution. Despite all the problems, it would be false to conclude

115

that German society is disintegrating. Most people are not only prosperous but also less insular than previous generations. The widespread interest among Germans in foreign travel, languages and even non-native cuisine are signs of this, even if it would be naive to conclude that an interest in foreign cultures excludes the possibility of xenophobia, at least where people of non-European origin are concerned. Nevertheless, it is remarkable how many bestselling books and popular television programmes originate outside Germany, not to mention the domination of the cinema by American products. It should also be pointed out that some 80 per cent of children in the west and 65 per cent in the east continue to grow up in stable two-parent families, that is to say in what are normally regarded as ideal conditions. Moreover, levels of crime and corruption generally compare favourably with many other European countries, as does the provision of social welfare. In this area, too, the Federal Republic can claim to be something of a model for others.

6

THE NEW GERMANY, EUROPE AND THE WORLD

AN ECONOMIC GIANT BUT A POLITICAL DWARF?

When the German Reich surrendered unconditionally in May 1945, the fate of Germany was transferred into the hands of its former enemies, who occupied the whole country within pre-agreed zones and divided its capital Berlin into four sectors. Until 1990 its destiny reflected the patterns of agreement and disagreement between the former wartime allies. Whereas the three western allies were able to agree on the creation of the political entity that became the Federal Republic of Germany, disagreements with the fourth ally, the Soviet Union, meant that no single German state emerged from the defeat of 1945 and that a second German state was set up under its auspices. Thus the impetus for the creation of both German states came from outside. The German population could only gain a voice and influence to the extent that they were willing to act within the parameters set by the sponsoring powers, in the west the United States, Great Britain and France and in the east the Soviet Union. The difference between the two German states as they developed was that the western powers set wider parameters and that the state they created gained legitimacy through democratic elections, in which the electorate invariably gave power to forces that were keen to co-operate with what were initially occupying powers and later became allies and partners.

In the early years of the Federal Republic, the forces of co-operation were represented principally by the CDU/CSU and Chancellor Konrad Adenauer. During his period in office, the Federal Republic became, as pointed out in Chapter 2, a member of NATO in 1955 and of the European Economic Community from its inception on 1 January 1958. Membership of NATO remained the cornerstone of the Federal Republic's foreign policy, as it was regarded as the guarantor of the survival of the state. As early as 1949 Adenauer's policies earned him the (in)famous rebuke from his SPD opponent Kurt Schumacher in a parliamentary debate that he was the *'Kanzler der Alliierten'* (the Allies' Chancellor), a claim that reflected the priority the SPD gave at that time to the preservation of national unity above integration with the west. By contrast, Adenauer's CDU, despite lip-service to reunification, was unwilling to pursue the cause of unity by dealing with the Soviet Union.[1]

The success of Adenauer's policy for the Federal Republic, even if it achieved nothing for the Germans living in the GDR, can be seen in the way that the Federal Republic gained a voice within western organisations, in particular NATO and the European Community, and gradually took over responsibility for more aspects of its own affairs. The most significant steps included permission to set up its own foreign ministry in 1951, the end of the official occupation and the regaining of sovereignty in 1955 and with the controversial Emergency Laws (*Notstandsgesetze*) of 1968 the end of Allied rights of intervention at times of civil strife.[2]

Despite all these measures that in principle gave the Federal Republic greater freedom of action, there was a general feeling throughout much of the pre-unification period that the Federal Republic remained a 'political dwarf', that it did not take on a role in international affairs commensurate with its status as a leading economic power. This was felt on the right of the political spectrum where there were objections to the way that the Federal Republic rejected the option of nuclear weapons (and arguably major power status) by signing the Nuclear Non-Proliferation Treaty in 1969, and on the left by those who believed that by following the Cold War policies of the USA the possibility of dialogue and improved relations with the east was being ignored. This latter feeling disappeared with Brandt's *Ostpolitik*, although it must be remembered that, as stated in Chapter 2, this was launched at a time of *détente*.

The widespread disquiet that the Federal Republic did not take enough interest in the wider world surfaced at the time of the Grand Coalition, when it was only after a long campaign by intellectuals that the Vietnam War was debated in the *Bundestag*. This may have reflected the partial exclusion of the Federal Republic from world affairs, as illustrated by its non-membership of the United Nations until 1973. Now, with unification, the Federal Republic is free, in theory, to play a full and independent role in world affairs. The negotiations that took place in Moscow in 1990 under the heading Two plus Four (two being the two German states and four being the wartime Allies) provided the framework not only for unification but also for full sovereignty with the former Allies/occupying powers, who had until then retained a final say over the future of Germany, relinquishing their control. It could be argued that within these negotiations, by agreeing, on the insistence of the Soviet Union, that the size of its army should not exceed 370,000, the Federal Republic had made its last concession as a state that as a result of the German defeat in 1945 did not have full control of its own affairs.

This chapter will concern itself with the question of possible changes in the area of foreign policy now that the post-unification Federal Republic is, because of its size and economic strength, a potentially more powerful fully sovereign state. In particular, the question must be considered whether, far from being a political dwarf, it is in danger of becoming a powerful destabilising factor in European and world affairs, as is feared, for example, on the right of the political spectrum in Great Britain.[3] At the outset, however, it must be stated that the Federal Republic remains tied by international treaty obligations, not to mention the political will that exists to maintain a large measure of continuity after unification. Nowhere is this better illustrated than in the first area to be considered in greater detail: the relationship of the Federal Republic with the rest of Europe.

EUROPEAN POLICY

The Federal Republic's membership of the various European organisations that were founded after 1945, in particular what was first known as the European Economic Community, then became the European Community and in 1993 the European Union, reflected a genuine enthusiasm among the population for European integration. Given that German nationalism was totally discredited in the postwar era, the ideal of Europe offered an alternative whose distinguishing features were friendship and international co-operation rather than rivalry and war. This ideal was particularly expressed in the new found friendship between the Federal Republic and the France, the country that had once been charac-terised as the *Erbfeind* (traditional enemy). In 1963 the changed

119

relationship was sealed by the Franco-German Friendship Treaty, the conclusion of which was accompanied by a ceremony of reconciliation in Reims Cathedral in the presence of Adenauer and the French President Charles de Gaulle. This treaty, which underlines the central importance of Franco-German co-operation within the European Community/Union, has been enshrined not only by regular summit meetings of political leaders but also many opportunities for contact between the two peoples. Where it has been less successful is in persuading many Germans to learn the French language, which remains far less popular than English.

It goes without saying that German support for European unity has not solely been a matter of idealism. Membership of European bodies gave the new Federal Republic an acceptable role in international affairs; it was also in the country's economic interests. With exports to the other members of the EU making up 54.1 per cent of the total German exports in 1992 (and this figure has increased to 57 per cent with the expansion of the EU in 1995), it is small wonder that the Federal government has always sought to support measures that would make the organisation stronger. Accordingly, it has generally been a co-operative member of the organisation, using its power of veto much more sparingly than some of its partners. This enthusiasm has gone beyond the support for measures, such as the Single European Market, that primarily aim to make trade easier; it has also led to support for policies that would indeed make the union, as was always intended, more than just a trading bloc. The expressed aim of both major parties is something more akin to a Federal Europe or a 'United States of Europe'.

This conception lay behind German support of the Maastricht Treaty agreed by the member governments of the European Community in 1991. Its provisions included easier movement between countries for the community's citizens and common citizenship, the doctrine of 'subsidiarity' whereby decisions should be taken as far as possible at the level of the people affected, a greater role for the European Parliament and moves towards a common foreign and security policy. These items coincided with the German agenda to a large degree. Subsidiarity was a reflection of German federalism, which already had a link with Europe through the offices of the *Länder* in Brussels (viewed as a vital link in the promotion of regional development), while increased powers for the European Parliament fitted in with the democratic ideals of the Federal Republic. The free movement of people across boundaries as

120

agreed at Schengen came into force in 1995 with the Federal Republic one of the original seven participating EU states. Nevertheless, the Maastricht Treaty proved controversial in the Federal Republic (and not just in those countries, such as Great Britain and Denmark, where lack of enthusiasm for ever closer European union meant that they had to be allowed to opt out of certain of the treaty's provisions).

Opposition to Maastricht in Germany centred on one provision of the treaty: the proposal to work towards the achievement of economic and monetary union by the end of the decade. This was seen in certain quarters as endangering German prosperity, based as it is on the strength and stability of the D-Mark, as guaranteed by the independence of the Bundesbank. This enthusiasm for the national currency was disparagingly described as *'D-Mark-Nationalismus'* by the philosopher Jürgen Habermas. It expressed itself in worries about inflation, if a single European currency were to be in the hands not of prudent bankers but profligate politicians. These sentiments were expressed particularly strongly by the CSU and in parts of the media, not least the magazine *Der Spiegel* whose founder Rudolf Augstein was especially polemical in his columns. There is no doubt that such concerns about the national currency reflect widespread unease, which as yet has not generally been at the centre of political debate but may well emerge more strongly as the projected date of monetary union approaches. In his public pronouncements Chancellor Kohl continues to insist on the importance of the introduction of a Single European Currency as planned. Nevertheless, the decision of the *Bundesverfassungsgericht*, to which the Maastricht Treaty was referred, to require European Monetary Union to be agreed by the *Bundestag* indicates the importance of the issue.

There is also some concern about the Federal Republic's role as a net contributor to the EU's funds; in 1993 it contributed 29.8 per cent of the EU's budget (just over ECU19 billion), while only receiving 11.3 per cent. Nevertheless, despite occasional murmurings – Helmut Schmidt during his time as *Bundeskanzler* once stated that the Federal Republic was not Europe's 'paymaster' – the question of payments to the EU has never developed into a major political issue in the way it did in Great Britain in the early 1980s when Mrs Thatcher demanded 'our money back'. Whether, along with monetary union, it turns into one may depend on the overall success of European integration; it has again to be borne in mind that the idea of 'Europe' has been popular in the Federal Republic not just for idealistic reasons. The process of European integration has been accompanied by economic success. As long as the two are regarded as linked, anti-European sentiment is likely to remain somewhat muted, at least in the mainstream political parties.

Internal worries about Maastricht in the Federal Republic reflect a fear that by its acquiescence in the idea of a single currency, the government is making concessions to its partners who fear the power of the D-Mark. By contrast, doubts about Maastricht outside Germany are based on fears about German domination of the EU. There is no doubt that the economy of the Federal Republic is, with over a quarter of the EU's GNP in 1992, the most significant within the Community. The influence of the Bundesbank on the basis of its power to set interest rates can be seen by the way other countries have felt obliged to follow German rates.[4] It can also be argued that the German economic model is increasingly influential. Part of the agreement on possible monetary union reached at Maastricht demanded that to be eligible for incorporation into the single currency, individual currencies (and the economies of the relevant countries) had to meet certain conditions in the areas of inflation, budget deficit, interest rates and debt.[5] These have traditionally been areas in which, at least before unification had such an effect on public debt, the Federal Republic operated a stringent policy. This may well have been good for the German economy, but is arguably less so for other countries.[6] Where efforts have been made to follow the German model in other countries by shadowing the D-Mark within the Exchange Rate Mechanism of the European Monetary System, the first stage towards monetary union, this has resulted in deflation and unemployment, with France, where the *franc fort* policy has coincided with very high levels of unemployment (around 12 per cent at the time of the 1995 presidential election), providing a prime example. The influence of the Federal Republic on monetary policy appears to be further underlined by the decision to locate the European Central Bank in Frankfurt, the seat of the Bundesbank, even if the new bank's brief encompasses the whole of the EU.

The most extreme expression of the fear of German domination of the EU would be the view that any such domination would represent a continuation of the attempt made in the two world wars to impose German hegemony on Europe. A claim of this sort,

NEW GERMANY, EUROPE AND THE WORLD

however, is historically inaccurate in that it ignores the point that concepts of a united Europe within Germany were never based solely on the idea of domination through military and economic might. The ideal of a Europe united on the basis of co-operation goes back at least as far as the ideas for a United States of Europe to be found in the programme of the SPD at its Heidelberg Party Congress of 1925. For Helmut Schmidt, a member of the generation that remembers the Second World War, a united Europe in which Germany plays a full part is an antidote to any attempt at German domination. He also makes the point that Germany cannot maintain its present prosperity without partnership with other countries. For Chancellor Kohl, the vision is based more on postwar idealism, although he too appears aware that it would be wise to create a more united Europe while there is still a degree of enthusiasm for the project among the German people and the public memory of the dangers of a nationalistic course remains strong. What is common to both is the view that the aim should be a European Germany and not, as some fear, a German Europe. To this end, the Federal Republic appears prepared to give up some of its sovereignty, for example, to the European Parliament; where it favours the extension of its own model to a united Europe, it should be remembered that it is a highly decentralised and largely democratic model which should not cause undue fear among European partner states.

The other major fear expressed in connection with German policy towards Europe stands in complete contradiction to the one just expressed. It is that the post-unification Federal Republic might turn its back on its previous partners in the west and look to the east. This conjures up unhappy historical memories, specifically the Treaty of Rapallo of 1922 when the defeated Germany entered into co-operation agreements with the other pariah state of the time, the Soviet Union, and the Hitler–Stalin pact of 1939 that facilitated the attack on Poland by both countries that marked the start of the Second World War. Now that a kind of vacuum exists in eastern Europe following the collapse of the Soviet Union, it is claimed, Germany might be tempted to fill the gap, with such events as the takeover of Skoda by Volkswagen, in the face of competition from other European car-makers, already indicating the potential advance of German power.

Such a view must be dismissed as nonsense. Statistics show that trade with eastern Europe is minimal in comparison to that with

EU countries, with figures for 1993 revealing that exports to all (former) communist countries, including those in Asia, amounted to well under 10 per cent of total exports. Accordingly, it would be suicidal for the Federal Republic to turn its back on its western partners. Given the problems of the new democracies, any German engagement would also be extremely expensive. What is reasonable and legitimate is that the Federal Republic should be interested in their becoming relatively stable and prosperous, not least because of the possibilities of mass immigration and the temptation, already apparent, for criminal elements from the east to try to gain more from one crime in Germany than from months or even years of legitimate work at home. Accordingly, the Federal Republic accepts growing links and possible eventual membership of the eastern European states within the EU. Whether it will be possible to reconcile expansion of the community with the process of closer integration agreed at Maastricht, while keeping the potential costs of admitting less affluent members within limits that will be acceptable to the Federal Republic as the largest contributor to the EU budget, is a question that is difficult to answer. Nevertheless it remains within the interests of all European countries that it is not left to a single state, Germany, to control developments in eastern Europe.

Some attempt to resolve these problems was made in 1994 in a paper that appeared under the name of the CDU member of parliament Karl Lamers, but was also associated with Wolfgang Schäuble, the parliamentary leader of the party and heir apparent to Chancellor Kohl. He presented the idea of a multi-speed Europe with the Federal Republic at the centre of a core group pressing for greater integration. This idea has not found favour with some other countries, not least Britain despite its hostile attitude to further European integration. An alternative might be to accept that deepening and widening are irreconcilable aims and set one as a priority. The real danger is that by pursuing contradictory goals, the EU might become discredited, and this is a particular danger in the Federal Republic as the major country within the community. Again, it is as well to remember the importance of success within German political culture. This applies not just to economic matters, but also to areas where idealism plays a part. The failure of the EU, despite its protestations of moves towards a common foreign policy, to halt the conflicts in the former Yugoslavia is something that has caused concern in Germany, even if, as will be seen later

(p. 134), the Federal Republic can be partly blamed for those conflicts. At present, however, the European ideal retains its positive aura in the Federal Republic. This is underlined at symbolic level by the frequent flying of the European flag (a rare occurrence in some member states) and the incorporation of the EU stars into car number plates in 1995. Although such gestures cost little, they do suggest that commitment to Europe is a cornerstone of German policy.

GERMANY AND THE MAJOR POWERS

Despite the importance of its western European partners, the key relationship for the pre-unification Federal Republic was undoubtedly that with the United States, the leading member of NATO and the country with whose approval the process of European integration began. For most West Germans in the postwar years it was the United States, as the leading world power, that through its aid policies had made possible economic recovery and through its resolution in the face of Soviet communism, exemplified in the Berlin Airlift in 1948 9 when the blockaded western part of the city had been kept supplied by air, preserved freedom in one half of Europe. Although Great Britain flew a third of airlift flights, it was the USA that gained nearly all of the credit. Accordingly, once it became a member of NATO, the Federal Republic was almost invariably happy to follow the lead of the United States and prove itself the most loyal of allies. The partnership did come under some strain at the time of the Franco-German Treaty as the United States was suspicious of President de Gaulle's efforts to reduce American influence in Europe. However, when the Treaty was debated in the *Bundestag*, the importance of the American links was stressed by the adoption of a preamble to that effect, which led de Gaulle to say that treaties, like roses and young girls, flourished only for a limited period.[7]

There were also strains during the time of the *Ostpolitik* when there were some suspicions in the USA that *détente* was being taken too far; the relationship between President Nixon's security adviser and subsequent Secretary of State Henry Kissinger and the chief *Ostpolitik* negotiator Egon Bahr was strained. Otherwise there were only occasional minor problems, for instance, when co-operation between Chancellor Schmidt and President Jimmy Carter proved to be less than easy,[8] but in general terms West

German politicians recognised the importance of the USA as the perceived guardian of their liberties and specifically the guarantor of the status quo in West Berlin. In the eyes of certain groups of people, in particular the student protesters, the reputation of the USA suffered during the Vietnam War. Nevertheless, the sense of gratitude remained among the vast majority of the population with experience of the postwar years and the USA's role at that time.

At the time of unification the Federal Republic also had reason to be grateful to the USA. Given the terminal weakness of the USSR, it was only the USA who might have prevented the move to unity. President Bush, possibly after some hesitation, chose not to do so, preferring to have tangible evidence of victory in the Cold War in the form of German unification. Against his endorsement, the scepticism of other western partners revealed in the public pronouncements of the Thatcher government in Great Britain and the apparent support for the GDR shown by President Mitterrand by his decision to visit the country shortly after the fall of the Berlin Wall did not carry much weight. The Federal Republic had become the major European partner of the USA with little to cloud the relationship.

The same has largely remained true since unification. It is difficult to think of issues that might strain the relationship in the same way that the relationship between the USA and Japan is put under stress because of economic rivalry or that between the USA and France by, in part, cultural rivalry. That is not to say that the relationship is unchanged; the future of NATO following the end of the Cold War is a matter of concern for both countries, as is the whole question of the USA's future role in Europe. The Federal Republic favours continued American commitment; within such commitment it seems destined to play a major role as the USA's most important partner. The unstinting devotion of the German people to the American model can be seen in the pervasive role of American culture referred to in the previous chapter (p. 116).

By contrast, the pre-unification Federal Republic's relationship with the USSR was very strained, particularly in the years of CDU-led governments. The USSR embodied an ideology that stood in direct opposition to the values of private ownership that were categorised by the postwar CDU as the hallmarks of western Christian civilisation. Mutual recriminations focused on the German side on the denial of democratic rights to 17 million Germans in the GDR, a state of affairs that was underlined by the suppression of the 17 June 1953 uprising, while the USSR presented the Federal Republic as an aggressive state intent on changing post-1945 frontiers out of a desire for revenge. The visit by Chancellor Adenauer to Moscow in 1955 did bring about diplomatic relations and the release of the remaining small number of German prisoners of war (less than 10,000); it did not lead to progress on the future of Germany. The limits on diplomatic co-operation were also soon underlined by the adoption of the Hallstein Doctrine by the Federal Republic.[9] This stated that, with the exception of the USSR, the Federal Republic would not have diplomatic relations with states that recognised the GDR. The initial consequence was that the Federal Republic had no diplomatic relations with the allies of the Soviet Union that were part of the Warsaw Pact until the doctrine was relaxed in the case of Romania during the time of the *Große Koalition*. Relations with communist but non-aligned Yugoslavia were broken off when it recognised the GDR in 1957.

The death knell of the Hallstein Doctrine was sounded with the start of Willy Brandt's *Ostpolitik*. This led initially to an improved relationship with the Soviet Union. Indeed the 1970 Moscow Treaty was the precondition for the whole process, as relaxation of tension with the Soviet Union was needed before anything similar could be attempted with its client states. As part of this treaty the USSR relinquished the right it demanded under the United Nations charter to intervene in the affairs of the Federal Republic, something it had claimed might be necessary in the event of right-wing extremists coming to power, an eventuality it chose to portray as at least possible. Thereafter tensions relaxed until the return of the CDU government more or less coincided with a return to Cold War attitudes between the USA under Ronald Reagan and the USSR.[10] The continuing suspicions of the CDU were visible when Chancellor Kohl, responding to the changed tone of USSR policy following the accession to power of Mikhail Gorbachev, warned in 1986 against any such blandishments by comparing the new leader to the Nazi propaganda chief Joseph Goebbels. The effect of this infelicitous remark, over which the Chancellor had to eat humble pie, had been largely overcome by 1989 when the revolution took place in the GDR and the USSR refused to intervene to prop up the Honecker regime, the decision that put German unity on the agenda.

One reason why the USSR was willing to accept German unity was undoubtedly the hope for financial and economic support

127

given the fragility of its economy and the resulting danger of instability. Some semblance of order and stability was also in the German interest given the proximity of the area in question. It has remained the major concern since the break-up of the Soviet Union. The first priority was to ensure the withdrawal of the troops that had been stationed in the GDR. This was completed in 1994 with the help of financial support intended to aid the repatriation of the troops in question. The extent of German willingness to support the new Russian Federation, the major successor state of the USSR, can be seen by the debts to the Federal Republic to the tune of DM500 billion it had acquired by 1995. A wider willingness to support the status quo in the person of President Yeltsin (a concern shared with the USA) was seen in the same year when official reactions to the murderous events in Chechenia were very muted. It remains to be seen whether this is a wise policy.

THE WORLD ROLE

In so far as the pre-unification Federal Republic played a role outside Europe, its policies were to a large extent an extension of the Cold War priorities that dominated its whole political existence. The Hallstein Doctrine was also applied in the Third World until the advent of *Ostpolitik* and, within its own terms, largely success-fully in that few Third World countries chose to recognise the GDR. This was because the Federal Republic was able to keep waverers in line by the offer of development aid. The policy of linking aid to politics was restated by the CDU government in the 1980s with the pronouncement that aid would only go to those countries whose economic and political policies were in line with those of the west. Only for a brief time during the Brandt government, when Erhard Eppler, the SPD politician whose ideas have frequently been close to those of the Greens, was Minister for International Co-operation (*Bundesminister für Internationale Zusammenarbeit*), did development policy have a more idealistic element.[11] In absolute monetary terms, the Federal Republic was as generous, if not more so, than others, although aid never reached the level of 0.5 per cent of GNP. Recent years have seen a decline in real terms as well as as a percentage of GNP. This fell from 0.4 per cent in 1991 to 0.36 per cent in 1993. Besides money, personnel were provided by the Deutscher Entwicklungsdienst (German Development Service), which was based on the Peace Corps founded in the USA by President Kennedy. Whether all the projects that were supported either financially or by German personnel made sense in development terms is a controversial issue that goes beyond the scope of the current discussion. There was certainly the expectation that some of the money should return to the Federal Republic in the form of orders for German companies. Accordingly, in the mid-1980s, Mercedes vans for the police in Guatemala, at the time not the most democratic state, were provided from the overseas aid budget.[12]

The Cold War also affected the role of the Federal Republic in international organisations. Until the process of *détente* got under way, both German states were generally excluded from international organisations or confined to observer status, as the Soviet Union would not allow the sole admission of the Federal Republic and the western powers, in keeping with the policy of diplomatic isolation, would not recognise the GDR as a sovereign state. Accordingly, admission to the United Nations did not take place until 1973. In certain areas, a pretence of unity had to be maintained. A single German team took part in the Olympic Games in 1960 and 1964 after 'Germany' was readmitted to the Olympic movement. Rivalry even extended to the field of culture; the rival to the Goethe-Institut, mentioned in Chapter 4, in the area of promoting German language and culture was the Herder Institut which managed to establish itself in the neutral country of Finland and in several Third World countries. Competition in this area meant that the two German states vied with each other in seeking to attract students from the Third World, who in the future might become part of their country's elite and thus be in a position to exert influence in favour of the land of their former *alma mater*.

The other factor that influenced the Federal Republic's policy towards countries outside Europe and North America was the German past. This legacy affected the sale of German arms abroad, with official policy being that arms would not be delivered to what were termed 'areas of tension', although the exact definition of these inevitably proved difficult. One controversy in the 1970s centred on the possible sale of tanks to Saudi Arabia, not solely because of the overall problems in the Middle East but principally because of the complications that inevitably existed in the relations between the Federal Republic and Israel. As early as 1952, under the provisions of the Luxembourg Treaty of the 10 September of that year, the Adenauer government, acting it seems almost entirely on its own initiative, had agreed to pay DM3 billion to Israel to help with the integration of Jewish refugees from National Socialism. At the same time, money was clearly not the main issue. The Federal Republic could not be seen doing anything that might endanger Israel, not least in the eyes of that large number of their own citizens who wished to atone for the past. This feeling manifested itself in the widespread public support for the Israelis during the Six Day War in 1967, something that was encouraged by the Springer Press, one of whose guiding principles was support for Israel, and the sense of outrage felt when Chancellor Kohl appeared to behave less than diplomatically during his visit to Israel in 1984.[13]

The sensitivity of German–Israeli relations re-emerged after unification in 1991 when during the Gulf War there was the possibility of missile attacks on Israel by Iraqi rockets, the development of which owed much to German technology and the willingness of certain parts of the German business community to supply Iraq.[14] In this area, there has been no change since unification; elsewhere the Federal Republic is less constrained now that Cold War priorities no longer come into the equation. Indeed, a major question is whether the Federal Republic should emerge from the shadows and play a more significant role in world affairs, one that befits its status as a major economic power. One specific issue that has arisen is whether the Federal Republic, along with Japan, should become a permanent member of the United Nations Security Council. Such a step has the support of the United States, as Secretary of State Warren Christopher made clear at the UN General Assembly in September 1995, but would form part of a wider restructuring that is less easy to achieve. However, the major difficulty that has come to the fore in this whole area has to do with military policy. This can best be illustrated by considering recent debates about the future deployment of the army.

A NEW MILITARY ROLE?

When the *Bundeswehr* was founded, a conscious attempt was made to break with the Prusso-German military tradition. At the symbolic level, this meant totally new uniforms, whereas the GDR's National People's Army (*Nationale Volksarmee*) largely restored the traditional ones along with the infamous goosestep. More importantly, discipline was no longer to be based on blind obedience to orders but on a concept called 'innere Führung' (internal guidance) whereby the soldier was to consult his own

130

conscience at critical moments. Another break with the past was articulated in the idea of the 'Staatsbürger in Uniform' (the citizen in uniform), which expressed the ideal of an army that would in no sense be any kind of state within a state or 'Schule der Nation' (academy of the nation), the role it had been assigned by the Prussian state. Moreover, the supreme commander was a civilian, the Federal Minister of Defence. Finally, the army was to have a purely defensive role in the service of NATO on the occasion of any offensive action by the Warsaw Pact, the military alliance led by the Soviet Union. Article 87a of the *Grundgesetz* stressed that the army existed for the purpose of defence and that any other use must be explicitly named within the constitution.

Given the shadow of the German past, these parameters were largely uncontentious until the Gulf War of 1991. At that time voices were raised, not least among the Federal Republic's NATO partners, expressing disquiet that the Germans were not pulling their weight. All that seemed constitutionally possible (except for financial contributions) was that the air force should station units in Turkey, a NATO country bordering Iraq, in case that country should be attacked. What were described as 'out of area' operations were deemed impossible.[15] Nevertheless, it is not true to say that the Federal Republic's military forces had never been involved outside NATO; the air force had taken part, as had that of the GDR, in relief flights to Ethiopia during the 1980s famine. Following unification, there seemed no problems with the involvement of medical teams in the UN mission to Cambodia; this was followed by participation in the UN's Somalia operation. This was justified by the Federal government on the basis of Article 24 of the Basic Law, which refers to the Federal Republic's obligations as a member of organisations of collective security, that is to say the UN and NATO. By contrast, the opposition SPD made a distinction between peace-making and peace-keeping UN activities with the latter being acceptable. Whereas peace-making might involve fighting and therefore be inappropriate, there appeared to be no objection to merely keeping an established peace. The issue was ripe for adjudication by the Constitutional Court, which ruled in 1994 that the *Bundeswehr* could take part in UN operations of all kinds. This was welcomed by the CDU/CSU but less so by the SPD which stresses the requirement laid down by the Court that all operations need parliamentary approval. Nevertheless the way is open for the army to play a wider role than in the past.

In fact, it was not long before the decision of the Court had practical consequences. When NATO became more involved in the crisis in former Yugoslavia in 1995, the *Bundestag* was faced with the question of increased German involvement. Whereas the air force had already been used on AWACS reconnaissance patrols flown by NATO on behalf of the UN, the question now was whether air force units should be sent to take part in combat missions. The decision was made more problematical because of the memories evoked by German military activities in the Balkans in the Nazi era. Any potential engagement with Serb forces was bound to evoke memories of the support the German occupiers gave to the wartime fascist Croat regime that massacred large numbers of Serbs. When the issue was debated in June 1995, the government, which supported the deployment of the air force in a combat role, was assured of victory because of its parliamentary majority. It also attracted the support of forty-five SPD members, who broke with their party's oppositional stance, and, even more surprisingly given the party's history of pacifism, that of four Bündnis 90/Die Grünen parliamentarians. That public and sections of intellectual opinion was increasingly on the side of the government was suggested shortly afterwards when Jürgen Habermas declared that he had reluctantly accepted that the use of force against Serbian 'fascism' could be justified. What is more, the leading Green politician Joschka Fischer began in the summer of 1995 to disassociate himself from his party's previous pacifistic stance.

The momentous decision of June 1995 was followed six months later by the decision to commit ground troops to former Yugoslavia as part of the extended NATO mission. This time opposition was restricted to the PDS, just under half of the Bündnis 90/Die Grünen parliamentary group, fifty-five SPD members and one solitary CDU member. This suggests that there is a broad consensus among the political elite about the need for Germany to play a greater role in world affairs.

CONCLUSION

In its 30 January 1995 edition the news magazine *Der Spiegel* reported remarks made by Klaus Naumann, the *Generalinspekteur* of the *Bundeswehr* and as such the leading military adviser to the Federal Minister of Defence, about the future of German defence policy. The magazine referred to Naumann's view that it was necessary to keep any future conflicts away from German soil. This was to be achieved, should the need arise, by German military operations anywhere in the area between Morocco and the Indian Ocean. Specifically, *Der Spiegel* quoted Naumann as speaking of Germany's 'behaving no longer reactively but taking action up to and including preventive action' (*Der Spiegel* 5, 1995: 73). In a speech to the Deutsche Gesellschaft für Auswärtige Politik (German Institute for Foreign Affairs) in March 1995 President Herzog spoke of the need for the Federal Republic to abandon the habit of *Trittbrettfahren* in world affairs. This word, which originates from the immediate postwar period when passengers had to ride on the carriage steps of the few overcrowded trains, implies that the Federal Republic was some kind of parasitic political hitchhiker. Even if the idea that it was some kind of 'passenger' is accepted, a more appropriate metaphor would have referred to seats in the first-class carriage given its financial role. Nevertheless the implication is that, if the metaphor based on (steam!) railway terminology is continued, it is time for Germany to jump on to the footplate and help to drive. In concrete terms, Herzog meant that a military dimension within foreign policy had to be accepted. Although the speech did not restrict itself to contemplating possible military operations, he nevertheless spoke of the need on occasions to risk 'Leib und Leben' (life and limb).

Even if neither Naumann nor Herzog carry ultimate political responsibility, the views they expressed reflected a widespread mood before and after the June 1995 decision. In a *Bundestag* debate in December 1994 both Foreign Minister Klaus Kinkel and Defence Minister Volker Rühe had seemed to accept that an extended military role for the Federal Republic was inevitable, while the changing mood among intellectuals, as illustrated by the example of Habermas, was mentioned in the previous section. The growing assumption is that political responsibility inevitably involves a willingness to use force. Against this classical view it might be more idealistically argued that the Federal Republic, given the burden of history, could show global responsibility by setting an example in, for instance, ecological and humanitarian areas under the auspices of the United Nations. It is interesting to note that in his 1995 speech President Herzog praised the use of 'soft power' in foreign relations, by which he meant solving problems through the use of intelligence rather than brute force, citing scholarships for foreign students as a positive example. Those who dismiss such a view as unrealistic should remember Willy Brandt's claim that cultural policy was the third pillar of foreign policy along with security policy and external trade relations. In any case, the implication that the Federal Republic did not bear enough responsibility before unification is open to challenge. It can be maintained that its loyalty to NATO, which showed itself in the number of nuclear weapons it was prepared to accept on its soil, reflected a very responsible attitude that prevented any possible aggression.

What is less at issue is that unification inevitably means that the Federal Republic has to exercise a new kind of responsibility, seeing that the former preconditions of the Cold War no longer apply. Equally important is that, as was stated at the beginning of this chapter, given the increased significance it has bestowed, unification potentially allows the Federal Republic to exert greater influence. The question is: how will that influence be used? There is one example of misuse it would be hard to deny. When the Federal government, with the then Foreign Minister Hans-Dietrich Genscher in the forefront, decided to press its European partners to recognise Croatia and Slovenia in 1991, it can be said to have precipitated the catastrophe that has taken place in former Yugoslavia.

Despite its consequences, the significance of this diplomatic initiative should not be exaggerated. It would be a mistake to regard the decision to send troops to former Yugoslavia as the crossing of some kind of Rubicon on the road to the Federal Republic's becoming a world military power. This is underlined by the size of the contingent sent to former Yugoslavia – 4,000 as opposed to the 13,000 and 20,000 committed by Great Britain and the USA respectively – and its largely supportive role. If the last three chapters of this book have shown anything, it is surely that the German people, and their political leaders, remain extremely loath to indulge in grand projects. As has been seen, this has provoked claims that the Federal Republic is not facing up to today's challenges in either the political or the economic area. On the basis of the dangerously 'experimental' nature of previous German politics, it is possible to claim that some degree of caution, if not outright pragmatism, has much to recommend it. Moreover, the results seem to show that such caution is not wrong.

Given the present-day generation of politicians and the influence the war and its aftermath continue to have on them, it remains unlikely that they will indulge in too many adventures, in either foreign affairs or elsewhere. The limits imposed by the past were clearly visible in the international dispute over French nuclear tests in 1995. Despite its disapproval, the Federal government could not be seen to be condemning France too harshly not just because of its current alliance with that country, but also because of sensitivity in France to any idea that it was being browbeaten by its former enemy. Equally important to bear in mind in any speculation about possible irresponsible acts by the Federal Republic in the area of foreign policy are the constraints imposed by treaty obligations. Many young Germans, as the wave of pacifism that swept Germany at the time of the Gulf War showed, appear to be anything but bellicose. As was pointed out in the last chapter, the number of young men refusing military service rises at times of international crisis. In the history of the Federal Republic it has in fact tended to be intellectuals rather than politicians who have demanded grand schemes. This tendency can be traced over the years from the complaint made in Ralf (now Lord) Dahrendorf's influential book *Gesellschaft und Demokratie in Deutschland* (*Society and Democracy in Germany*) that nobody in the Federal Republic set goals and that the country was run by a *Kartell der Angst* (cartel of fear) (Dahrendorf 1965: 297), to the title of a 1994 collection of critical essays *Politik ohne Projekt?* (*Politics Without a Project?*) (Unseld 1993). It will be the projects and ideas of intellectuals that will form a major concern of the next part of this book.

Part III
THE SEARCH FOR IDENTITY

7

COMING TO TERMS WITH THE PAST

DER DEUTSCHE SONDERWEG

A word frequently used in connection with German history is 'particularity'. It implies that German history took a distinctive course (*Sonderweg*) that marks it off from the history of other European nations and that carried within it the seeds of the calamitous events of 1933 to 1945. It is not intended here to consider the merits of various historical theories. Nevertheless, the idea of 'particularity' contains at least two major factors that indisputably affected the course of German history: first, the fact that Germany did not achieve statehood until very late and was in the words of the title of a much acclaimed book by Helmuth Plessner *Die verspätete Nation* (*The Belated nation*) (Plessner 1974); and, second, that a tradition of democratic government based on popular acceptance of this form of rule was unable to establish itself in Germany.

When German unity was achieved in 1871, the governance of the new state, although it contained certain democratic elements such as a parliament (*Reichstag*) elected on the basis of universal male suffrage, was based on the authoritarian Prussian model. Parliament did not determine the composition of the government; nor had it any control over the armed forces. Moreover, it was Prussian force of arms that made the post-1871 state possible, first, by the defeat of Austria in 1866 which excluded that state from the unification process (this was referred to as the *kleindeutsche Lösung* (the lesser German solution) as opposed to the *großdeutsche Lösung*, which would have included Austria), and, second, by the defeat of France in 1870/1. That the foundation of the German state at this time did not conform to the model of a state created from below based on the clearly articulated wishes of a nation is underlined by the way it was proclaimed on foreign soil, in the Palace of Versailles.

Two decades previously an attempt to create a unified German state, that incidentally planned to include Austria, had failed. In that case the impetus had been more democratic. Popular agitation for greater unity and democracy in the decades following the defeat of Napoleon led to a series of revolutions in 1848 and the convening of a parliament in Frankfurt am Main in the same year to create the foundations of a unified state. When this attempt failed because of the weakness of the revolutionary movements in the face of the power of the established forces, the pathway to a united democratic Germany was blocked. When Germany unity did come in 1871, largely without democracy, the majority of the middle classes, who had been at the forefront of the 1848 movement, accepted the status quo. In this way the link between nationalism and democracy was severed. Democracy on the western model came to be seen by many as alien to the German people and therefore something to be shunned. It is only too clear where this rejection of democracy helped to lead Germany in the first half of the twentieth century.

The other factor that is linked with the 'belated' nature of the German state is its aggression. As German power based on its growing industrial might grew – incidentally the Industrial Revolution was also delayed in Germany, gathering its full strength only after unification – the desire for a greater voice in world affairs also increased. In the title of a book by the historian Fritz Fischer, it was this *Griff nach der Weltmacht* (*Grasping for World Power*) by Germany that led to the outbreak of war in 1914 (Fischer 1961). The Second World War can also be seen to some extent in the same light; Hitler and his followers spoke of creating a 'New European Order' of German domination, something that was to a degree achieved for a brief period in the early 1940s before the tide turned against the Nazis.

It goes without saying that the Second World War was more than just a repeat of 1914. It is the policy of genocide pursued in particular against Jews and gypsies, but also against other races such as the Poles and the Russians in so far as attempts were made to destroy their elites, that makes the Nazi regime the greatest historical burden on German identity. It is proposed in this chapter to consider how major questions of history affect contemporary Germany. In the space available, it will be impossible to consider every element of German history; at the same time the focus will be wider than merely the Nazi period, since, as this section has attempted to show, this cannot be viewed in isolation. Nor, it should again be pointed out, can every element of Germany's history be seen, on the basis of some kind of philosophy of historical fatalism, as the precursor of that one disastrous period.

THE ROLE OF PRUSSIA

To concentrate on Prussia is not to equate the whole of Germany with Prussia. It is again important to recall the importance of different traditions within Germany. Nevertheless, as was stated in the previous section, it was Prussia which guided the process of German unity and forged the post-1871 state with its king as Kaiser and its leading statesman Bismarck as Chancellor. The rise of Prussia to displace Austria as the leading German power is a remarkable story that developed from unpropitious beginnings. Although the name Prussia derives from territories close to the Baltic, the original Prussians being a Baltic tribe that was Christianised and Germanicised at the time of the Crusades, the heart of Prussia (and the original name for the state) was Brandenburg, the area around Berlin.[1] This is a sandy area with few natural resources. It was only at the end of the Napoleonic Wars when Prussia gained the Rhineland that it began to develop industrial might, something that undoubtedly contributed to its growing power in the nineteenth century.

Prior to that, Prussian power rested largely on its military strength. In the eighteenth century it built up an army of 89,000 men by 1740, the year that Frederick II ascended the throne. He immediately used that army for aggressive purposes by capturing the Austrian province of Silesia, now a part of Poland and one of the territories lost by Germany in 1945. What is more, he managed to keep it throughout a series of wars, thus establishing a tradition that military force was an acceptable option provided it was crowned with success. The acceptance of war is contained within the famous dictum of the Prussian strategist Clausewitz: 'War is nothing other than the continuation of politics by other means.' As already indicated, it was Prussian arms that forged German unity, the doctrine of 'blood and iron' associated with Bismarck, the 'Iron Chancellor'.

The continuity between the Prussian military tradition and Hitler's Third Reich was symbolised by the 'Day of Potsdam', 21 March 1933, a carefully chosen day as the date coincided with the opening of the first post-unity *Reichstag* by Bismarck in 1871.

Hitler had come to power on 30 January of that year when the last President of the Weimar Republic, Field Marshall Paul von Hindenburg, the 'hero' of the First World War and embodiment of the Prusso-German military tradition, had overcome his previous patrician distaste and appointed the Nazi leader Chancellor. There followed the *Reichstag* fire and elections on the 5 March, which gave the Nazis 43.9 per cent of the vote, a long way short of an absolute majority despite the holding of the elections under less than ideal conditions of fairness with the Nazis already in control of the state and the left-wing parties, especially the KPD, suffering persecution.

The Nazis clearly had obstacles to overcome, one being the army which in its upper echelons still largely yearned for the days of the Kaiser. The 'Day of Potsdam' was Hitler's attempt to ingratiate himself with the army and conservative forces generally. Potsdam, where Frederick II had built his palace of Sans-Souci, was the city associated with Prussian military glory and in his speech at the Garrison Church (*Garnisonkirche*) Hitler stressed the link between his régime and the imperial past. Although there was subsequently resistance to the Nazis within the army, its leaders were prepared to have it swear an oath of allegiance to Hitler personally on Hindenburg's death in 1934 and to fight his war in 1939. Hitler himself, although an Austrian by birth, continued to present himself as the heir to the Prussian tradition, particularly towards the end of the war, when he sought comfort from the precedent of Frederick II, who had retrieved an apparently hopeless military situation in 1762. In accordance with this perception of history, the victorious Allies in 1945 also saw a clear link between Prussian militarism and Nazi Germany and in a rare example of postwar agreement expunged the name Prussia from the map of Germany.

This entirely negative view of Prussia, although in many ways justifiable and certainly understandable in the context of 1945, does ignore certain other factors. In the 1994 federal election campaign, the Greens sought to counter the extreme right-wing slogan, 'Ich bin stolz, ein Deutscher zu sein' (I am proud to be a German), by a satirical poster in which caricature images of right-wing thugs, short-haired and suitably attired, expressed their pride in German achievements such as the philosopher Kant's 'categorical impera- tive' and the German Literature Archive in Marbach, Schiller's birthplace. Another achievement that was highlighted were the Stein–Hardenberg reforms. This was a reference to reforms of the

Prussian system of government following defeat by Napoleon. Although the context was partly frivolous, such a reference suggests that even for a party with pacifist traditions the legacy of Prussia was not entirely negative.

Alongside the military, the second pillar of the Prussian state was the civil service, whose members were the forerunners of today's *Beamte*. The reforms of Stein and Hardenberg were part of a process whereby Prussia developed an effective system of government and administration, not least at the municipal level. With the foundation of the Humboldt University in Berlin in the Napoleonic era, it created the system of higher education, based on its founder Wilhelm von Humboldt's principle of 'freedom of teaching and research' ('Freiheit von Forschung und Lehre'), that remains the basis of German higher education today. The qualities expected of the Prussian *Beamter*, among whose numbers were university professors, included orderliness, punctuality and a sense of service, an ideal encapsulated in Frederick II's axiom that the king was the 'first servant' of the state. These are the basis of the 'Prussian virtues' that continue to be alluded to today,

The question that has to be asked is whether they form the basis for a reappraisal of the state of Prussia today. That German politicians are willing to identify themselves with Prussia was seen following unity when Chancellor Kohl took part in a ceremony in 1991 in which the remains of Frederick II and his father, which had been exhumed in 1945 so that they should not fall into the hands of the advancing Soviet army, were reburied in Potsdam. The city of Potsdam too is keen to make play of its Prussian heritage; the rebuilding of the Garrison Church, blown up after the war by the communist authorities as a symbol of militarism, has also been discussed. In as far as any activities appear to glorify the Prussian military tradition, they are not to be welcomed. As for the Prussian virtues, although they are not negative in themselves, they cannot on their own form the basis of a modern democratic society. Not only has it to be remembered that Prussia itself was not a democratic society, it also has to be borne in mind that the Prussian ethic of efficiency and doing one's duty can be used for evil purposes, as it was in the Nazi era. Combined with the worst excesses of German nationalism, the Prussian tradition has much to answer for. It would be inappropriate to seek a positive historical identity in the state of Prussia despite that state's achievements in the areas of administration and education or even the remarkable degree of religious tolerance shown to minorities in keeping with another of the dictums of Frederick II that everybody 'should get to heaven in his own way'.

GERMAN NATIONALISM

Despite the clear link between the Prussian tradition and the aggressive nationalistic policies pursued by Germany in the first half of the twentieth century, it is important to make certain distinctions. The Prussian state was bent on establishing itself on the basis of military strength; it did not seek to do so on the basis of nationalist ideology. It was keen to attract new citizens, for example, French Huguenots and it was also relatively tolerant towards Jews. It is also possible to see Bismarck, despite his role as the creator of a unified German state, as someone who sought to control German nationalism. By the exclusion of Austria he created a German state in the interests of Prussia rather than the German nation as a whole; he also showed scant interest in creating an overseas empire, as well as maintaining a non-aggression pact with Russia. Once he had been removed from office, however, the state he had created was vulnerable to nationalistic excess that drew on earlier traditions.

German nationalism developed as a political force in the struggle against Napoleon. Although, as indicated in the first part of this chapter, it was linked with demands for democracy, it nevertheless contained unsavoury elements. Nowhere is this more visible than in the political writings of one of the great names of German literature Heinrich von Kleist. His poem 'Germania an ihre Kinder' ('Germania to her children') contains horrifically violent anti-French sentiments, not least in the line:

Dämmt den Rhein mit ihren Leichen
(Dam the Rhine with their corpses).
(Kleist 1971: 840)

Incidentally, this is only one of a number of poems and songs inspired by anti-French sentiments and the glorification of the Rhine as the great German river. In 1840 when certain forces in France sought to expand its frontiers to the Rhine, an amateur poet, the clerk Nikolas Becker, penned the poem 'Der deutsche Rhein' whose defiant anti-French tones inspired a whole popular movement. Among the composers who set it to music was Robert

144

Schumann, while its sentiments were echoed in other nationalistic outpourings.

If there was some legitimacy in these nationalistic demands, however crudely expressed, to fight French domination, it is difficult to find justifications for certain sentiments expressed in Kleist's 'Katechismus der Deutschen' of 1809. This consists of sixteen short chapters made up of dialogues in the manner of religious catechisms between a father and son, the former taking on the role of interrogator. In the second chapter, the son rejects such reasons as political and cultural achievements for loving his fatherland; his only reason is because it is his *Vaterland* (Kleist 1971: 898f.). In the final chapter, he is happy to contemplate fighting for the freedom of Germany even if this were to prove unsuccessful and it were to involve the death of everyone, including women and children. Such a statement is part of a tradition that glorifies fighting to the bitter end – a well-known painting by the naval artist Hans Bohrdt (1857–1945), *Der letzte Mann* inspired by the Battle of the Falklands in 1914, shows a lone sailor defiantly waving the flag as his ship sinks – a cult that became reality in 1945 when few were prepared to lay down their arms in spite of the approaching certain defeat and those that sought to avoid further misery were often executed by the SS shortly before the arrival of the Allies.[2]

Something else that besmirched the movement for German unity in the years leading up to the 1848 revolution was anti-Semitism. Among those demanding unity were groups of students who met at the Wartburg, where Luther had translated the Bible, in 1817. This celebration was marked by a mood of anti-Semitism that had developed during the Wars of Liberation. At the same gathering, various objects were burned, including a corporal's stick (a symbol of repression) and books by politically disliked authors, including the popular dramatist August von Kotzebue who was murdered by a student two years later. Also confined to the flames was a copy of the Code Napoleon (the system of statutes often seen as the major achievement of the revolutionary period in France), whose rejection can be regarded as a sign that the Wartburg students were not inspired by the wish to create a modern state. The events at the Wartburg illustrate the ambivalent nature of parts of the movement for unity at this time. Heinrich Heine correctly referred to the 'irrationality' and 'ignorance' of those who burned books (Heine 1978: vol. 5, 259) in a ceremony that prefigured what the Nazis did in Berlin on 10 May 1933 when

145

the works of among others Heinrich Mann and Sigmund Freud were incinerated.

The struggle for German unity prior to 1848 was in fact a mixture of liberalism and at times virulent nationalism. Not surprisingly, the struggle against France was glorified under the Nazis, while the authorities in the Soviet Zone in 1948 made great play of the revolutionary activities of a century earlier. By contrast this anniversary was largely ignored in the western zones, where greater emphasis was put on Bismarck's 1871 achievement, the state whose restoration, at least in geographical terms, was the aim of official policy. Two decades later, following the student movement, it became popular in progressive circles in the Federal Republic to play records of songs dating from the revolutionary period. As with the state of Prussia, the nationalist movement of the nineteenth century presents an ambivalent legacy to contemporary Germany.

THE NAZI ERA

In the case of the twelve years of Nazi rule, there can be no question of an ambiguous legacy. The only question is the nature of the attempts made to come to terms with the horrific events that occurred. The official line adopted in the GDR which saw fascism as something almost alien and therefore did not lead to a demand for individuals to consider their own behaviour was referred to in Chapter 1. The problems of what became known as the *unbewältigte Vergangenheit* (the past that has not been overcome) were much more complex in the Federal Republic where the possibility of free debate existed, at least in theory.

That there was a reluctance to face up to the events of the immediate past was suggested by the subtitle 'A play which no theatre wants to perform and no public wishes to see' which Wolfgang Borchert, a former soldier who died in 1947 at the age of 26, gave to his drama *Draußen vor der Tür* (*The Man Outside*) (Borchert 1990). This work was originally a radio play and was first performed on stage the day after his death. It tells of a man returning from the Eastern Front with the death of a number of comrades on his conscience, a burden from which nobody is prepared to release him, least of all his former commanding officer. Borchert's play has become a classic, so its subtitle is not literally correct; nevertheless it does reflect the unwillingness of many in the postwar period to be reminded of the Nazi past, a motif that recurs throughout postwar literature, for instance, when the hero of Heinrich Böll's novel, *Ansichten eines Clowns* (*The Clown*) (1963), angers his mother by telephoning her and announcing himself as a 'Jewish Yankee'. Although the efforts of German writers such as Böll, Günter Grass and Martin Walser to deal with the Nazi regime in literature are not to be belittled, it cannot be said that they provoked a mass concentration on the issues involved. This was only achieved on three occasions, the publication of the Anne Frank diary, the showing in the late 1970s of the American television series *Holocaust* and in 1994 by Steven Spielberg's film *Schindler's List*. The nearest 'conventional' literature came to evoking such an echo were two plays which raised the spectre of Auschwitz, Peter Weiss's *Die Ermittlung* (*The Investigation*) (1965), which is a documentary drama based on the trials of former Auschwitz guards, and Rolf Hochhuth's *Der Stellvertreter* (*The Representative*) (1963), which attracted attention less for its attempt to show Auschwitz on stage than for its claim that the Pope had turned a blind eye to Nazi genocide.

At other times silence led to ignorance, particularly on the part of the younger generation. An example of this ignorance came to light in 1977 when schoolchildren were asked to write essays on what they knew about Adolf Hitler and their answers appeared in book form (Bossmann 1977). This refusal to face the past has been described by the writer Ralph Giordano, himself of Jewish origin and a survivor of the Nazi era, as *Die zweite Schuld* (*The Second Guilt*), the title he gave to the book he published on the subject in 1987. He defines this second guilt as the 'suppression and denial' of the Nazi era, something that he sees as one of the decisive elements in the political culture of the Federal Republic (Giordano 1990: 11). The same phenomenon was analysed earlier by the psychologists Alexander and Margarete Mitscherlich, the title of whose major work spoke of *Die Unfähigkeit zu trauern* (*The Inability to Mourn*) characterised by defensive attitudes towards the facts of the Third Reich (Mitscherlich and Mitscherlich 1988).

What Giordano and the Mitscherlichs are referring to is the failure of most Germans to accept any responsibility, let alone any guilt for the events of the Nazi era, as was visible in Chancellor Kohl's reference during his 1984 visit to Israel to crimes committed 'in the German name' rather than to crimes committed by Germans. At the opposite extreme stands the doctrine of 'collective guilt', the idea that all Germans were guilty for Nazi crimes, favoured for a time by the Allies at the end of the war. This doctrine was problematical in that guilt is invariably something individual and in the way it fails to differentiate between varying degrees of responsibility. It may also have helped to provoke the reactions condemned by Giordano and the Mitscherlichs, or at least to have helped to encourage an attitude that put the blame solely on Hitler and a few acolytes rather than considering the whole range of issues involved.

This attitude can be seen in the language used in connection with the beginning and end of the Nazi era. In the pre-unification Federal Republic, it was common to talk of the Nazi seizure of power (*Machtergreifung*), as if Hitler had achieved his aims by some quasi-revolutionary act that violated the political order of the Weimar Republic. In fact, as was indicated at the beginning of this chapter, he was offered the position of Chancellor by the President acting – extremely misguidedly – within his constitutional role. The events of 1945 were invariably described as the collapse (*Zusammenbruch*), a term which continued the dramatic but obfuscatory language used in connection with 1933 and veiled any continuity between the Nazi era and the postwar period. The use of the term 'Year Zero' (*Jahr Null*) for 1945 only underlined this tendency which ignored elements of continuity, particularly in the economic field and in the occupancy of elite positions in society.

It was the numerous perceived elements of continuity between the Nazi era and the Federal Republic that infuriated those writers and intellectuals who longed for a new kind of German state and only saw a process of what they called 'restoration' in the first post-war decades. They pointed especially to the continuing presence of former Nazis in positions of prominence, the worst case being in their view that of the civil servant Hans Maria Globke who had written the commentary to the Nuremberg Race Laws of 1935 which, for instance, had forbidden intermarriage between Germans and Jews. After the war he became the Secretary of State in the Federal Chancellery under Adenauer, that is to say the leading civil servant in the Federal Republic. Intellectuals also perceived a reluctance to pursue war criminals, along with a fateful continuity in foreign affairs through which the Soviet Union continued to be cast in the role of arch-villain, as it had been for most of the Nazi era. In this way, it was felt, the suffering of the Soviet Union at German hands in the Second World War was being conveniently overlooked. The moral outrage felt can be seen in the following

statement made by the dramatist Rolf Hochhuth in a collection of
essays edited by the writer Hans Werner Richter that appeared in
1965 (in these prominent writers declared their support for the
SPD in the elections of that year):

> The state pays war criminals and judicial murderers, who
> punished the concealment of a Jewish child threatened with
> the gas chamber with the guillotine, 1400 marks per month,
> even more. Eight or nine times as much as the parents or
> widowed mother of two sons killed in the war.
>
> (Richter 1965: 83)

That Hochhuth and fellow intellectuals did have a case is suggested
by the failure of the Federal Republic's authorities to punish any
judge or lawyer involved in Nazi injustices. It was invariably
claimed that those involved were only carrying out the law as it
existed at the time, the standpoint adopted by the then *Ministerpräsident* of the *Land* of Baden-Württemberg Hans Filbinger in
1978 when his involvement in the Nazi judicial process came to
light, incidentally following research by Hochhuth. In this case
Filbinger had to resign, an unusual example of intellectual protest
achieving an immediate tangible result. By contrast, it was also only
after considerable debate that the normal statute of limitations on
murder proceedings, which means that a case cannot be brought
more than twenty years after a murder is committed, was waived in
the case of war crimes in 1965. In general, the example of the legal
system illustrates only too clearly the difficulties the Federal
Republic had in dealing with the legacy of the Nazi past.

This is not to say that there are no objective difficulties in facing
up to these problems, beyond those of political expediency,
specifically the need of the Federal Republic in its early years not
to alienate large numbers of its citizens. The events of the Nazi era
require a rethinking of many basic issues associated with history
and politics.[3] One example is that of resistance, in this particular
case the resistance to the Nazis shown by some Germans, many of
whom paid with their lives. In both German states, the legitimacy
of such resistance was accepted, with tribute being paid to those
who in Nazi eyes were 'traitors'. However, each was selective
when it came to particular manifestations of resistance. In the
Federal Republic, respect was shown to those involved in the
conspiracy which culminated in the unsuccessful bomb plot of 20
July 1944 when Hitler avoided major injury and lived to wreak

terrible vengeance on those involved or suspected of being involved in the assassination attempt. The majority of plotters were army officers; accordingly, they were presented in the Federal Republic as the embodiments of an honourable military tradition that could be distinguished from the barbarities of the Nazis. What such a conception ignores is that many of the plotters were anything but democrats and continued to envisage a peace settlement in which Germany might retain many of the territorial gains achieved by the Nazis. On the wider question of the role of the army, it is impossible to distinguish between the SS and other inherently Nazi forces who committed atrocities and a 'normal' army, the *Wehrmacht*, who fought within the accepted conventions of war and whose 'healthy' patriotism was somehow misused by the Nazis. This became fully clear in 1995 when an exhibition showed how far the regular army was involved in the racial policies of the Nazi regime.[4]

The other group viewed favourably in the pre-unification Federal Republic were the *Weiße Rose* (White Rose) conspirators of Munich whose foremost members were the student brother and sister Hans and Sophie Scholl. The esteem in which they were and are still held can be seen from the way streets or squares near universities and schools are frequently named Platz der weißen Rose or Geschwister-Scholl-Straße. Although it would be totally wrong to belittle their opposition to the Nazis which ended in martyrdom, it can still be pointed out that their religious inspiration fitted in with the Christian ideology of the early years of the Federal Republic. They provided a contrast to those Christian leaders who had compromised with or even supported the Nazis. The worst example of such support had been that part of the Lutheran Church known as *Deutsche Christen* (German Christians) whose *Reichsbischof* Müller was a convinced Nazi. Other Lutherans had resisted the Nazis, founding the *Bekennende Kirche* (Confessing Church) whose best-known leader, Pastor Martin Niemöller, was imprisoned from 1937 to 1945. That Niemöller became a critic of the policies being pursued in the Federal Republic meant that the new state was not entirely comfortable with the Christian tradition he represented.

The different attitudes in the GDR and the Federal Republic towards resistance to the Nazis can be seen by the way the conspirators of the 20 July 1944 were regarded with deep suspicion in the GDR. Although the idealism of certain individuals was accepted, the plot tended to be seen as an attempt by conservative, capitalist forces to maintain their leading status. For GDR historiography Hitler was a tool of the capitalists, who not only helped him to power but also continued to hold sway. If this had been the case, one wonders why these all-powerful forces had to resort to a risky assassination attempt to rid themselves of their servant. By contrast the GDR stressed, as might be expected, the communist opposition to the Nazis; Erich Honecker, for instance, had spent the years 1935 to 1945 in prison. The opposition of communists tended to be a taboo subject in the Federal Republic. Neither did another attempt to assassinate Hitler, the bomb planted by the carpenter Johann Georg Elser in 1939, that would have achieved its aim if Hitler had not left a gathering earlier than planned, attract much attention, although Elser was the eponymous hero of a 1982 play by the left-wing writer Peter-Paul Zahl.[5]

What these varied interpretations show is the difficulties of achieving a consensus view towards the most difficult period of German history. How far a rethinking of attitudes might be necessary becomes even clearer when the events of 1945 are considered. Should Germans be pleased that their country was defeated? If so, it would seem to follow that those who deserted their army during the war deserve some kind of recognition or rehabilitation, something that has never happened. This too was an issue that surfaced in 1995, the anniversary that once again concentrated attention on the Nazi past.

THE DIFFICULT ANNIVERSARIES

It has become a feature of recent years for historical anniversaries to be commemorated in a variety of ways, not least by some form of quasi-official ceremonial attended by politicians, who no doubt hope to gain something from the presence of television cameras. This was very much the case in May 1995 with commemorations taking place in London, Paris, Moscow and Berlin, all largely attended by the same political leaders. Although it would be totally wrong to restrict consideration of history to such events or only to the years in which anniversaries fall, they do provide a focus for the consideration of issues and, inevitably in the case of Germany, confrontation with difficult questions. As Federal President Gustav Heinemann put it in his broadcast speech in 1971 to mark the hundreth anniversary of the foundation of a unified German state, such anniversaries come 'ungerufen' (uncalled), that is to say inexorably without anyone having to summon them.

In this speech, Heinemann sought to identify positive forces in German history that might be seen as the precursors of the democracy of the Federal Republic. He highlighted Social Democracy (noting its opposition to the authoritarian post-1871 German state and its rejection of Nazism), Liberalism and political Catholicism, as represented by the Zentrum, which had resisted Bismarck's attempts to fight Catholicism and along with the Social Democrats and Liberals had formed the core of democratic parties within the Weimar Republic. Although this was a brave attempt to stress the common democratic bonds between the various political forces of the Federal Republic, Christian Democracy, Social Democracy and Liberalism, and pointed to more positive forces in German history, it did overlook certain uncomfortable facts, for instance, that it was only the Social Democrats who voted against the Enabling Law (*Ermächtigungsgesetz*) of 1933 through which Hitler was able to assume dictatorial powers within the framework of the Weimar Constitution.

If 1871 is a difficult year in German history in that it gave unity without true democracy, it pales into insignificance besides 1945. As the journalist Thomas Kielinger put it (1995), in a brochure published by *Inter Nationes*, an official organisation that seeks to encourage international interest in Germany: 'No other date in modern history has made such a deep impression on the German psyche as 8 May 1945.' Initially, it was generally regarded, as already mentioned, as a day when Germany collapsed in defeat. It was not until the fortieth anniversary of that date that a perceptible change to a more positive attitude occurred. This change was set in motion by the speech to mark the occasion by Federal President Richard von Weizsäcker, which, in printed form, achieved a remarkable circulation of 650,000. Weizsäcker, a member of the CDU, had been an officer in the Second World War and his father, a diplomat, had been arraigned at the postwar Nuremberg Trials, when those accused of war crimes were tried by an Allied court. In his speech Weizsäcker broke with convention by describing the German defeat as in fact liberation, the term also used, for obvious ideological reasons, in the GDR. He made the point quite simply: 'The 8. May was a day of liberation. It freed us all from the violent rule of National Socialism and its contempt for humanity' (Weizsäcker 1986: 280). This clear statement was in contrast to the previous terminology and was enough to cause tension within his own party, parts of which continued to regard the war, or at least the campaign against the Soviet Union, as in some way justified.

Ten years later, the term 'liberation' had largely established itself. Opinion polls showed that 80 per cent of Germans regarded 8 May 1945 as a day of liberation and the theme was taken up by politicians in their official comments. In his statement to mark the anniversary Chancellor Kohl made the point: 'There can be no doubt that the liberation from the Nazi barbarity was necessary to open the way for democracy in Germany and for peace and reconciliation in Europe.' Similarly, President Herzog, in his speech at the official gathering in Berlin on 8 May 1995 spoke of the end of the war opening 'a gateway to the future'. In this and earlier speeches, for example, at the ceremony to mark the liberation of the concentration camp at Bergen-Belsen, and by his deportment during the commemoration of the liberation of Auschwitz, which unfortunately was marked by tensions between Jewish and Polish representatives, Herzog set a high standard which, as the next section will show, was not emulated by all who expressed themselves on the subject of the end of the war.

Although President Weizsäcker had shown a different way of dealing with the difficult legacy of the past, the years immediately following his speech did provide one major scandal in connection with an anniversary. This was the speech made by the President (Speaker) of the *Bundestag*, Philipp Jenninger, in 1988 to commemorate the fiftieth anniversary of the *Reichskristallnacht*, the anti-Jewish pogrom of 9 November 1938 when synagogues were attacked and Jews arrested and tortured. Jenninger set out to explain the popularity of Hitler among the German people in the years following his coming to power, referring, for example, to his apparent economic success. To concentrate on such questions was bizarre enough given that the speech was meant to commemorate the victims of Nazism. What made matters worse was that Jenninger failed to convince his audience, in particular invited Jewish listeners whose body language betrayed their feelings of revulsion, that he was not giving his own opinions but trying to convey the mood of the time. It was said following his speech that he should have shown he was using indirect speech, which, as students of the German language learn, is expressed in the subjunctive and distances the speaker from what is being said. That Jenninger had to resign can be justified in terms of his lack of sensitivity.

Unfortunately there was no retribution against the many department stores who at roughly the same time 'celebrated' their fiftieth anniversary and ignored the fact that they had come into existence in their present form in the late 1930s because the previous Jewish owners had been expropriated.

REWRITING THE PAST

If the Jenninger episode was, at least in part, a case of clumsiness rather than malice, it is less easy to play down other attempts to reinterpret German history so that the German past appears in a better light. Two approaches have been prevalent – one that casts Germany or at least Germans as victims rather than aggressors or perpetrators and the other that seeks to relativise Nazi crimes by comparing them with other examples of inhumanity. In as far as such views are widespread and found in the political mainstream, they are to be taken at least as seriously as the untenable claims of right-wing extremists that the horrific events of Auschwitz never occurred.

The casting of Germans as victims has a long history. It goes back at least as far as the pre-1914 cry, 'We too want our place in the sun', used to justify imperial ambitions and to suggest that the other powers had disadvantaged the Germans. Nazi propaganda made use of the same sense of frustration when it pointed to what it saw as the iniquities of the 1919 Versailles Treaty. After 1945 these perceived injustices could be regarded as the catalyst that had enabled the Nazis to come to power. Even if the Versailles Treaty was far from perfect, it cannot be right to use it to absolve those who supported Hitler from all responsibility or to cast them as victims of the Allies. That former Nazis were somehow victims of the Allies was also implied by such terms as *Siegerjustiz* (victors' justice), used in connection with the Nuremberg trials, which exploited the failure of the Allies to include representatives of neutral states in the judicial process, and by negative reactions to the process of 'denazification' pursued in all zones of occupation after the war, which did in fact in the western zones often seem to involve minor party members rather than those in positions of real power.[6]

One episode that is particularly relevant in this context is the postwar expulsion of the German inhabitants of those territories that had previously been part of Germany or incorporated by the

Nazis but that were now to be given to other states (the territories to the east of the Oder–Neisse line to Poland and the Soviet Union, or, in the case of the lands gained as a result of the Munich Agreement of 1938 returned to the former governing power Czechoslovakia). Although the Potsdam Agreement of the summer of 1945 laid down that such expulsions had to be conducted in a humane manner, it is estimated that in the process about 2 million people died, many from starvation and illness but many also as a result of acts of brutality. How sensitive this subject is was shown by the way a generally respected publishing company, Piper Verlag, withdrew in early 1995 their planned publication in German of a book by the American John Sack, *An Eye for an Eye* (1993), purporting to document atrocities committed by Jews who had escaped the Holocaust on Germans in the immediate aftermath of the war.

It is in part the events surrounding the expulsion of Germans from their former homes that has led many to reject any idea that 1945 was a year of liberation. In *Die zweite Schuld*, Ralph Giordano quotes an example of such thinking, which was originally a letter to the *Frankfurter Allgemeine Zeitung* in 1985 from a retired pastor and goes far beyond the specific issue of deportation:

> Those of us who experienced and suffered the 8 May 1945 know that on this day the German became an outlaw. It was then that arbitrary acts and thefts of all kinds began, expulsion from house and home, the hunting down of people, hunger in the camps – not only in the east – the dismantling of our industry, the theft of our patents etc.
>
> (Giordano 1990: 267)

Ten years later a similar spirit informed a statement which appeared in the *Frankfurter Allgemeine Zeitung* on 7 April 1995 under a large number of names, many of whom were known for their right of centre views. Among the most prominent were the Minister for Overseas Aid Carl-Dieter Spranger (CSU) and more surprisingly the former SPD cabinet minister Hans Apel. It acknowledged that 1945 saw the end of Nazi terror but also spoke of 'expulsion terror, new oppression in the east and the beginning of the division of our country'. What such statements ignore is the sequence of events. By using the phrase 'at the same time' the signatories to the manifesto omit the absolutely essential point that any crimes perpetrated against Germans came after *and* as a

155

direct result of crimes perpetrated by Germans. It is also sad to note that when in 1994 President Havel of the Czech Republic bravely conceded in defiance of the general view held by his own citizens that the expulsion of the German minority in Czechoslovakia was wrong, he was not met with an equal generosity of spirit in many quarters but rather confronted with legalistic demands for restitution of former property rights. One example of this kind of attitude was the comment made by Foreign Minister Kinkel that any compensation the Germans paid to Czech victims of Nazism should be matched by equal compensation for 'German victims of similar violent and unjust deeds committed on the Czech side' (*Die Spiegel*, 22, 1995: 29).

On the wider issue of deportation, it is also sad that the April 1995 manifesto only refers to those Germans who were forced to leave their homes after May 1945, not those that were removed by the Nazis. It is morally reprehensible that the signatories do not mention the German Jews who suffered this fate – unless, basing their views on an abhorrent racial philosophy, they do not consider them to have been real Germans. One also wonders how a Social Democrat like Apel, who, it must be pointed out, did subsequently withdraw his support from this initiative, could at any time overlook those of his own party who were driven into exile or put into concentration camps, or how CDU/CSU signatories can forget those Christians who suffered a similar fate. The really tragic date in German history was not the 8 May 1945 but 30 January 1933 when Hitler came to power and deportations and worse began.

The statement published in the *Frankfurter Allgemeine Zeitung* was part of a campaign, '*Gegen das Vergessen*' ('Against Forgetting'), that was to have culminated in a rally in Munich. When the main speaker, the veteran right-wing CDU politician Alfred Dregger withdrew following pressure from his party, the event collapsed. Nevertheless, it would be wrong to say that the campaign had no influence on the general debate. Chancellor Kohl, in particular, for all his references to liberation, seemed keen to placate those with different views, thus creating a large degree of anger, not least among the Board of Deputies of British Jews. In his comments to mark the end of the war he said: 'There is no common denominator for all these memories and feelings. We should therefore respect each other's experience of that era and not trivialise it through excessive discussion.' Similarly, the politician seen as his possible successor, Wolfgang Schäuble, the leader of the CDU/

CSU parliamentary group in the *Bundestag*, descibed 8 May as a date 'that does not allow unambiguous and uncontroversial evaluation' (cited by Roderich Reifenrath, in *Frankfurter Rundschau*, 106, 8, 1995: 3). Whilst it is true that different people will hold different attitudes about this kind of historical event, it does not follow that all subjective views and experiences are equally valid. If this were the case, all mass murderers (and other criminals) could exonerate themselves by saying they thought they were justified in their deeds. There are clearly Germans who experienced distress at the end of the war, through rape or the revenge killing of relatives for instance, but the unprecedented barbarity of Nazism means that its defeat must be regarded as by far the greater good.

The general casting of Germans in the role of victims amounts to the weighing of one set of suffering against another and thereby to an attempt to relativise the crimes of the Nazis. How dubious such comparisons of suffering are was pointed out by Federal President Herzog in his speech in Dresden in February 1995 to commemorate the fiftieth anniversary of the bombing raid, and, much to its credit, by the CSU, the most right-wing of the mainstream parties, in its statement to mark the fiftieth anniversary of the end of the war. Such statements provide a counterbalance to attempts by certain academic historians to put the crimes of the Nazis into a context that denies their unique nature and thus relativises their horror.

The major example of this was what became known as the *Historikerstreit* (historians' dispute) that broke out in 1986. In a newspaper article the well-known Berlin professor Ernst Nolte claimed that the system of concentration camps operated by the Nazis had been preceded by the Soviet Gulag (other apologists have pointed to the British rounding-up of Boers into camps during the Boer War), and with the exception of the use of gas (a somewhat major exception, one might think) the Nazis had merely copied the communists. Moreover, the war against the Soviet Union was seen by Nolte as a preventive war to forestall a coming attack from that quarter on Germany. If this had been the case, the plan must have been in the very long term, as Soviet forces were totally unprepared for the 1941 invasion, not least because Stalin had earlier purged the Red Army of many of its leading generals, hardly the action of someone who was preparing for war, even in the medium term.

Nolte was answered by the philosopher Jürgen Habermas, who

stressed that it was impossible to compare the systematic genocide of the Nazis with any other political crime. Many other academics took part in the debate, with the Hitler biographer, Joachim Fest, supporting the idea of a link between Stalin's crimes and those of the Nazis by postulating that Hitler's paranoia was fed by reports of events in the Soviet Union. Against this Professor Ernst Jäckel pointed out that any possible link did not diminish the horror of the crimes committed particularly against Jews, while the Berlin historian Hagen Schulze made the seminal point in the 26 September 1986 edition of *Die Zeit*: 'The rationality and technical nature of the murder of the Jews have no equivalent either in Stalin's Russia or in Pol Pot's Cambodia – the industrialisation of mass murder is a German invention' (cited in Giordano 1990: 347).[7] There is nothing to add.

CONCLUSION

The *Historikerstreit* provides a clear example of how far the shadow of history, in particular the Nazi era, affects contemporary Germany. Demands that it should somehow be forgotten are clearly impossible. The demand of the right-wing Bavarian politician Franz Josef Strauß made in 1969 that Germans had a right to forget Auschwitz because of their economic success was not only reprehensible but impractical.[8] Much closer to the truth is William Faulkner's statement, 'The past is never dead. It is not even past', that provides the opening of works by two distinguished postwar novelists. Alfred Andersch places it before the text of his novel *Winterspelt* as a kind of motto (Andersch 1977: 7), and it is similarly used, with a slight variation, by the GDR writer Christa Wolf. She writes as the opening sentence of her novel *Kindheitsmuster* (*Patterns of Childhood*), 'The past is not dead' and does not acknowledge the quotation (Wolf 1983: 9). Günter Grass takes the argument a little further with his statement at the beginning of another fictional work, *Das Treffen in Telgte* (*The Meeting at Telgte*), 'Yesterday will be what tomorrow was' (Grass 1979: 7). What this initially baffling statement means is that views of history change according to who writes the history. This is the issue in contemporary Germany, the interpretation of the past and how this affects current behaviour.

The ideal would be for history or what can be learned from it to contribute to a German identity characterised by democratic values. How far this has been achieved will be a concern of the concluding part of this book. This is the issue rather than any requirement that the collective of society should feel guilty. The latter is a ridiculous proposition in the case of Germans too young to have been actively involved in the Nazi era, unless the view is taken that Germans are by nature evil, which would be a case of applying racist ideology to the Germans themselves, by claiming unchanging biological characteristics and thus using similar arguments to those employed by the Nazis about the Jews. Non-Germans should hope that the process of forging a democratic identity begun in the pre-unification Federal Republic will be a success. What is not required is arrogance or a sense of superiority. It has to be remembered that, in addition to the Nazis, there were fascist movements in nearly all European countries (as well as neo-fascist groupings today) and that in many of the countries occupied by the Nazis there were those who were willing not only to collaborate at home but also to take up arms and fight alongside the Germans in the SS.

How difficult it remains to create a common democratic identity can be illustrated by the example of street names, which should not be regarded as trivial or frivolous. In both the pre-unification Federal Republic and, particularly, in the former GDR the names of streets remain a political issue to do with who (or what) should be remembered. In an interview with me in 1984, the leading literary critic, writer and Professor of Rhetoric Walter Jens complained that nearly every town in the Federal Republic had its Hindenburgstraße or Hindenburgplatz, although Hindenburg had been opposed to democracy and had helped Hitler to come to power, whereas a Kurt-Tucholsky-Straße was exceedingly rare. Tucholsky was a left-wing intellectual of Jewish origin who, during the years of the Weimar Republic, was an inveterate opponent of the German military tradition and of the Nazis.

In the GDR, street names often reflected communist ideology. The question now is whether these should be changed. In the case of Karl Maron, who gave his name to a suburban station in (east) Berlin and was a Minister of the Interior in the GDR, or in the case of Lenin the decision to change names can be understood, although there were protests against the removal of the massive statue of Lenin in Berlin at the centre of what was the Leninplatz and is now the Platz der Nationen. The question becomes more acute when it is a case of communist victims of Nazism. One example of someone who was a hero in the GDR but not well-known in the Federal Republic is Ernst Thälmann, the leader of the KPD who died in Buchenwald. He gave his name to endless streets in the GDR, but now seems to be a person less worthy of memory. In the town of Jena, for instance, what was the Ernst-Thälmann-Ring has reverted to its original name of Löbdergraben.

The issue of names has led to massive controversy in Berlin. Under threat have been, among others, Rosa Luxemburg, the communist leader murdered in 1918 and an opponent of Lenin in that she championed free speech, and Clara Zetkin, one of the first women in the Weimar parliament but also a communist. The idea that there should be a Clara-Zetkin-Straße in the centre of the political district of Germany's restored capital city was anathema to those wanting change. By contrast, left-wingers protested successfully against the name Baltenplatz (literally Square of the Baltic People), which was said to commemorate the independence of the Baltic states but to many invoked the medieval Teutonic knights who conquered the region and German expansionism generally. How complicated a name can be is shown by the example of Scharnhorststraße, which continues to exist in (east) Berlin. Scharnhorst was responsible for the reform of the Prussian army following defeat by Napoleon and was in fact praised for this in the official historiography of the GDR. Nevertheless, his name was given to a warship in the Nazi era. Such an example only underlines the problems for German identity that continue to be presented by German history.

8

CONCEPTIONS OF GERMANY AND THE GERMANS

NATION OR *VOLK*

Zur Nation Euch zu bilden, Ihr hoffet es, Deutsche,
vergebens;
Bildet, ihr könnt es, dafür freier zu Menschen euch aus.
(Germans, you hope in vain to make yourselves into a
nation;
Make yourselves instead, you can do it, more freely into
human beings.)

(Schiller 1966: vol. 2, 737)

These well-known lines by Friedrich Schiller were written shortly after the French Revolution when the idea of a French nation based on liberty, equality and fraternity was born. Although (as was seen in the Introduction to this book) the word 'Nation' has been part of political discourse in Germany – the emphasis on the existence of a single German nation despite division into two states was part of Willy's Brandt's *Ostpolitik* and was encapsulated in the phrase '*Zwei Staaten einer Nation*' – traditionally the Germans preferred to characterise themselves as a people rather than a nation. This is because the idea of nationhood in Germany has frequently been built around the sense of belonging to a single people (*Volk*) rather than on the basis of shared political ideas, which make up a common sense of citizenship. This is the ideal not only of France but also especially of the United States, which built a nation by accepting immigrants from many countries and backgrounds. Reviewing the German conception of nationhood in an essay entitled 'Nation und Nationalismus in Deutschland', the sociologist Rainer Lepsius has described the concept of the *Volk* as 'a pre-political essence ... which subsumes individuals' (cited in

161

Jeismann and Henning 1993: 200). Hence the dedication 'dem deutschen Volke' on the *Reichstag* building in Berlin, which was constructed following the achievement of German unity in 1871, reflects both a specific German linguistic tradition and underlines that the post-1871 state was not based on democratic principles of nationhood. This is still the case, even if the Kaiser objected to the inscription at the time. The same tradition can be seen in the way that philosophers and writers have devoted their attention to the German *Volk* and its claimed characteristics.

One of the first to do so was the philosopher Johann Gottfried Herder (1744–1803), a close collaborator of the young Goethe. His major work, *Ideen zur Philosophie der Geschichte* (*Ideas on the Philosophy of History*), examines the characteristics of various peoples including the Germans and the Slavs. Within his comments on the Germanic peoples there are statements that, from a crude present-day perspective, can cause a shudder. They are characterised by 'enterprising, bold and persevering courage in war', have a 'big, strong and handsome body structure, fearsome blue eyes' and with their 'spirit of faithfulness and abstinence' (Herder 1978: vol. 4, 387f.) were the right people to conquer Rome: 'We can be very pleased that peoples of such strong, beautiful and noble form, of such chaste morals, upright understanding and honest spirit as the Germans were – and not, for instance, Huns and Bulgars – occupied the Roman world' (ibid.: 399).

Although such comments are clearly capable of misuse by nationalists, Herder's interest in differences between peoples are to be seen as part of the relativism that characterised eighteenth-century thought and emphasised the influence of such factors as climate on different groups of people, an idea initially developed by the French philosopher Montesquieu. Herder specifically rejects the idea of there being four or five races throughout the world, that is to say ideas that are reminiscent of Nazi speculations about the superior Aryan race and other inferior races, preferring to stress the common humanity of all people. His warning about how negroes should be treated, 'You should therefore not oppress him, not murder him, not abduct him, for he is a human like you are' (ibid.: 111), is clearly totally at odds with Nazi racial ideology.

By contrast, the eulogies of the Germans contained in the philosopher Johann Gottlieb Fichte's *Reden an die deutsche Nation* (*Orations to the German Nation*) (cited Ripper 1974: 186–7) contain a much clearer political dimension in that they appeared shortly before the Wars of Liberation against Napoleon and have to be understood against the background of that particular historical context (see pp. 144f). Unlike Herder, he made a clear differentiation between the Germans and other Germanic nations; moreover, he emphasised the Germans' superiority, which was based on their having retained their original language (*Ursprache*) and their being the only people capable of true love of their nation. Most ominously, Fichte saw an inextricable link between the individual and the people to which that individual belongs:

> The belief of the noble being in the eternal continuation of his effectiveness on this earth too is accordingly based on the hope of the eternal continuation of the people from which he has himself developed and of its particular characteristics according to that particular law: without interference and corruption from anything alien.
>
> (Fichte in Ripper 1974: vol. 2, 186)

It is not difficult to see this kind of thinking as a precursor to the most extreme forms of German nationalism. In its own historical context, it stands in contrast to the reality of division and sub-jugation, something that was to continue even after Napoleon had been defeated, hence the use of the phrase 'die deutsche Misere' to characterise the condition of Germany in the first half of the nineteenth century. The contrast between historical reality and the ideal of Germany undoubtedly helped to create an almost mystical quality in some expressions of German national feelings at this time. A good example is the second stanza of Hoffmann von Fallersleben's 'Deutschlandlied' in which the adjective 'deutsch', used in connection with women, loyalty, wine and song ('Deutsche Frauen, deutsche Treue/Deutscher Wein und deutscher Sang'), attains the status of a totem through which uniquely positive qualities are expressed. It is small wonder that such intense feelings had dire consequences once they entered the realm of political reality. In the years prior to the failed 1848 Revolution German nationalism had found its expression in the creation of national singing competitions and the formation of clubs and associations, the 'Vereine' that still play a part in leisure activities today; even the academic discipline of German Studies (*Germanistik*) has its origins in this period. When the Romantic ideas that lay behind these compensatory expressions of national feeling subsequently became allied with the might of the Prussian state after 1871, the way was open for the aggressive nationalism that was to lead to two world wars.

Although, as the third stanza of his anthem proves, Hoffmann von Fallersleben held liberal views about justice and liberty, he was also an anti-Semite. The same is true of the philosopher Ernst Moritz Arndt, who, along with Fichte, was one of the inspirations of early nineteenth-century nationalism, a movement, as seen in the last chapter, that was not free of anti-Semitism. Arndt spoke of his desire to keep Jews out of Germany because they are 'a thoroughly alien people and because I wish to keep the Germanic stem as far as possible free from foreign elements' (cited in Ripper 1974: vol. 2, 191). That one of these foreign elements was democracy became a core belief for many German nationalists, for whom it was, in the words of Richard Wagner, a 'triumph of the modern Jewish world' (cited in Bergmann 1987: 126). German nationalism was based, therefore, arguably more than other nationalisms, on the sense of belonging to some special group with special characteristics that had to be defended at all costs. These, rather than political achievements or institutions, were what counted, especially once the forces of liberalism had been largely crushed in 1848.

GERMAN SELF-HATRED AND ADMIRATION OF OTHERS

At the opposite extreme to this glorification of the German *Volk* stands a tradition of extremely negative statements about Germany and the Germans. In an interview in the 15 September 1989 edition of *Die Zeit*, the doyen of postwar (west) German literary criticism, Marcel Reich-Ranicki, himself of Jewish origin and a survivor of the Warsaw ghetto, responded to a question about Jewish self-hatred by saying that it was the Germans who, of all people, showed most self-loathing (*Die Zeit* 38, 1989: 61). It is in fact easy to cite examples of criticism of Germans by leading writers of the past that contrast sharply with the ideas of Fichte or those of Kleist. One of the most celebrated examples is the diatribe generally referred to as the '*Deutschland-Schelte*' (stricture) by a contemporary of Fichte, the writer Friedrich Hölderlin. His prose work *Hyperion* contains the following diatribe about the Germans:

> Barbarians from ancient times, made more barbarian by diligence and knowledge and even by religion, deeply

164

incapable of any divine feeling . . . crude and devoid of harmony, like the pieces of a thrown-away pot. . . . I can think of
no people more fragmented than the Germans. You see
craftsmen, but not humans, thinkers, but not humans.
(Hölderlin 1970: vol. 1, 737f.)

Hölderlin continues in this vein for several paragraphs. Nor was he
an exception in his own day. Goethe, too, in his old age was moved
in his conversations with the diligent chronicler Johann Peter
Eckermann to comment on aspects of life in Germany that
displeased him, specifically the role of the police who invariably
intervened if children were enjoying themselves noisily on the
street. The results of this atmosphere Goethe saw in young
German academics who were 'young without youth' (cited in Buch
1978: 143) and lacked any interest in the world of the senses,
preferring instead the realms of abstract speculation. This kind of
negative comment by Germany's greatest writer stands in contrast
to the invocations of England by Shakespeare, for example, at the
end of *King John*. Nor did the tradition of deprecating things
German die out with Goethe and Hölderlin. Negative comments
about the Germans can be found in the writings of other major
nineteenth-century figures.

The work of Heinrich Heine, who spent many years in political
exile in France during the first half of that century, contains many
criticisms of Germany and the Germans. He describes the German
people collectively as a 'very big fool' (Heine 1978: vol. 4, 26),
and speaks of Germany as a land that, unlike the countries to the
south, may be short of lemons and laurels but has an abundance of
'rotten apples' (ibid.: vol. 2, 7).[1] His mock-epic poem, *Deutschland,
ein Wintermärchen* (*Germany, a Winter's Tale*), also contains a celebrated passage in which the poet, Heine himself, is given a vision of
Germany's future, which consists of a foul, stinking substance
(ibid.: 155). However, it would be wrong to see Heine's criticisms
in the same terms as Hölderlin's diatribe. Heine's concerns are
essentially political. His criticism of the German people results
from his frustration at their acceptance of repression, his true
enemy being the Prussian state, which he describes as 'rigid' and
'hypocritical' (ibid.: vol. 4, 17). It is in keeping with these views,
and, one fears, his Jewish background, that Heine long remained
a controversial figure, at least until the 1960s. It required, for
example, a long struggle before the new university in his home
town of Düsseldorf could be named after him.

165

Much more in keeping with Hölderlin's remarks are comments made later in the century by Friedrich Nietzsche, the philosopher whose ideas are often seen as forerunners of Nazi ideology, in particular on the basis of his apparent cult of the 'super-man' (*Übermensch*), who is not constrained by conventional morality. Whatever justification there may be in such claims, there are clear statements in his writing that show him to be anything other than a conventional German nationalist. He describes the Germans as the 'race of misfortune' (Unglücksrasse) and speaks of 'German philosophy, the Wars of Liberation, the foundation of the German Reich at the end of the nineteenth century' as events that have held up the progress of 'culture' (Nietzsche 1980: vol. 13, 587). In fact, even some avowed nationalists were unhappy with the post-1871 state. The relatively restrained policies of Bismarck, in particular the exclusion of Austria from the new German Reich, did not find favour with those, including many university professors, who dreamed of a return to the days when the Emperor Friedrich Barbarossa ruled most of Europe or, at the other extreme, with those who found Bismarck's policies too militaristic. A poem entitled 'Germania' by the admittedly not very eminent Ferdinand von Saar complains that respect is only felt for German power and not 'deutsche Liebe und deutsches Herz' ('German love and German heart') (Lamprecht 1969: 221).

That sentiments of dislike or even loathing towards Germany did not die with the nineteenth century is only to be expected, given recent German history. One typical, relatively recent example of a diatribe against Germany is an essay 'Die dauernde Ausbürgerung' ('The lasting expatriation') written by the poet Peter-Paul Zahl in the 1970s while he was in prison for involvement with terrorism, his sentence having been raised from four to fifteen years after appeal by the prosecution. He speaks of 'lick-spittles, arse-creepers, crawlers, informers, creeps' as admittedly existing in other countries but not in such a 'sly' way *'so typically German'* (Zahl 1978: 98f.). Although Zahl's use of italics may suggest a certain irony, his use of the phrase *'typisch deutsch'* in such a negative way is reminiscent of a comment by Martin Walser in his 1960 novel *Halbzeit* (*Half-Time*). Walser's narrator Anselm Kristlein comments on the way that anything that is to be criticised in German society is invariably labelled in this way; it is irrelevant that the phenomena described as typically German might be totally contradictory (Walser 1960: 605ff.).

The fictional context in which Walser's Kristlein makes his comments has to do with the pronunciation in German of foreign names. It points therefore to another dimension of German self-criticism, the way it is frequently characterised by enthusiasm for all things non-German. The propensity of the language itself to adopt foreign words, since 1945 in particular English words, might be an example of this. It has certainly provoked criticism, for example, the author Reinhard Lettau's assertion: 'Now that this people has betrayed almost everything about it that was beautiful, loveable and delicate, it is now losing its language as well' (Lettau 1978: 121). Similar sentiments were expressed more recently in the 23 June 1995 edition of *Die Zeit* by one of its long-standing writers on cultural affairs, Dieter E. Zimmer. Interestingly, he connects the tendency of the German language to incorporate foreign words unthinkingly with problems of identity. Whilst accepting the inevitability of foreign words, he asks that they be adapted to the patterns of German so that the language might remain intact. Although it would be wrong to accuse Zimmer of this, it should still be remembered that demands for total linguistic purity are just as dubious as demands for any other sort of national purity. By contrast, the desire to exhibit erudition or cosmopolitanism by a surfeit of English or French words is merely silly or pretentious. What is most important in the present context is how the use of foreign words relates to the tradition of lauding other countries and their cultures by juxtaposing them with the situation in Germany.

This tendency can be shown from the example of France, although it should be pointed out that the eulogies have not been only in one direction, many Germans having frequently felt flattered by Madame de Staël's characterisation of their country at the beginning of the nineteenth century as the 'land of poets and thinkers' ('Land der Dichter und Denker'). Nevertheless, it remains remarkable, particularly given the course of history, how many Germans have seen France as a paragon compared with their own country. Despite his reputation as a great German leader, Frederick II of Prussia had no time for the German language or for German culture, preferring the company of Voltaire to that of any German philosophers and showing no interest in the German literature that was burgeoning in his lifetime. At the beginning of the twentieth century, the novelist Heinrich Mann championed France against Germany, whereas his brother Thomas favourably contrasted German 'culture' with French 'civilisation'. Specifically, Heinrich embraces the ideal of the French writer who involves himself with social and political questions rather than indulging in the abstract speculation that had attracted Madame de Staël. He also praises the French people for their openness to the social concerns of writers with the result that, unlike in Germany, there is a link between the world of intellect and that of action. These two terms provide the title for the 1910 essay entitled simply 'Geist und Tat' ('Intellect and action') in which Mann extols the close relationship between writers and the people in France:

> They have found it easy, the writers of France, who, from Rousseau to Zola, have confronted established power. They had a people. A people with literary instincts, which questions power, and of such warm blood that power becomes unbearable to it when it is refuted by reason.
>
> (H. Mann 1960: 9)

What is relevant here is less the exact truth of Mann's claims than the clearly implied contrast with Germany, where the worlds of intellect (*Geist*) and power (*Macht*) have traditionally been seen as being in total opposition to one another. This appreciation of the French intellectual tradition was revived in the years after 1945 when many German writers sought both to assimilate the recent French thought from which they had been cut off by Nazism and to emulate the social role of their French counterparts such as Jean-Paul Sartre. In 1968 this development reached its apotheosis when the poet and essayist Hans Magnus Enzensberger, looking to the alliance between students and intellectuals in Paris during the events of May of that year, demanded the creation of 'French conditions' in Germany (Enzensberger 1969: 20).

That admiration for France has not necessarily been based on left-wing ideas is shown by the example of Martin Walser's essay 'Deutsche Gedanken über französisches Glück' ('German thoughts on French fortune'), which originally appeared in France in 1980. Walser speaks openly of his envy for France, but bases this envy less on any specific French achievements and traditions than on the uncomplicated patriotism of the French, a feeling that is denied Germans because of their history. Walser concludes his essay by recounting incidents from a family holiday in France, finishing with the comment: 'A touch of nationalism is nice' (in Walser 1982: 114). Although the tone of this final statement is reminiscent of the world of advertising (or perhaps because of it), Walser's essay underlines the problematical nature of the championing of others when this is used only for an ideological purpose, in this instance to advance the case for a greater degree of nationalism in Germany. As with some of the eulogies and criticisms of Germany already cited, which equally belong to the world of wishful thinking and escapism, it shows an unwillingness to engage dispassionately with the concrete issues relating to Germany and its history.

A much better example of a balanced attitude to France is found in the writings of Heinrich Heine. He was in fact often accused of being pro-French, and therefore anti-German, in his political ideas. His answer was that his vision of democracy was based not on the example of France, even if greater political progress had been made in that country, but on the ideal of human rights that came from 'heaven, the fatherland of reason' (Heine 1978: vol. 4, 8). This is written in the introduction to his *Französische Zustände* (*Conditions in France*), the collection of his writings that seeks to mediate between France and Germany, the two European countries he valued most highly.

THOMAS MANN: *GERMANY AND THE GERMANS*

Another person to attempt a wider-reaching explanation of Germany and its people was Thomas Mann, who had turned his back on German nationalism during the Weimar Republic, in a speech he made in the Library of Congress in Washington shortly after the end of the war in 1945. Mann does not attempt to disassociate himself from Germany and its fate, despite his having spent the Nazi years in exile, saying that attempts to reach the truth can only be 'the product of self-examination' (T. Mann 1945: 3). He regards himself as steeped in the German tradition of 'inwardness' (*Innerlichkeit*). This is a frequently used term in connection with German culture, which denotes the tendency for writers to search for personal utopias rather than for social progress, something that can be explained by the course of German history in the nineteenth century. Mann relates inwardness to both positive and negative aspects of German development, seeing the wickednesses of the recent history of Germany as manifestations of 'good Germany gone astray' (ibid.: 18). By inwardness Mann means, on the one hand, a penchant for music and speculation and, on the other, a rejection of politics, something he finds exemplified in the person of Martin Luther, who incorporated the 'German dualism of boldest speculation on the one hand and political immaturity on the other' (ibid.: 9).

It is this political immaturity, which in the case of Luther manifested itself in his willingness to be subservient to the German princes of his day, that is Mann's greatest concern. He points to the way that liberty in Germany only ever related to freedom from foreign interference, not to the internal political order: 'it meant the right to be German, only German and nothing else and nothing beyond that' (ibid.: 10). This is of course the attitude encountered in Kleist's 'Katechismus der Deutschen' (see p. 145) and in the statements by Fichte and Arndt quoted above. What it leads to, according to Mann, is the total rejection of politics, if politics is regarded as the art of the possible and as being based on the necessity of compromise. That this claim has some validity can be seen at a linguistic level in the way that the word *Kompromiß* is often accompanied by the adjective *faul* which in this context means rotten rather than lazy. Mann goes on to say that since Germans believe that politics is something essentially negative, they invariably behave abominably when indulging in political activity. Despite these comments, Mann stresses in conclusion the positive sides of the German tradition, hoping that they can contribute in some way to a less nationalistic world.

Given the historical circumstances following 1945, it is small wonder that Mann's concerns about Germany and the Germans should have been felt by other writers and intellectuals. He himself entitled a volume of essays on Germany published in 1946 as *Leiden an Deutschland* (*Suffering through Germany*) (Mann 1946), a condition in which he was far from alone. The remainder of this chapter will examine attitudes to Germany over the past fifty years, concentrating on what they reveal about continuing problems of German identity.

THE POSTWAR YEARS:
HOPES OF A NEW GERMANY

The years following 1945 were ones in which the Germans had little influence over their own destiny with the result that differences between the occupying powers led to the division of their country. This did not prevent a widespread discussion among

German intellectuals about the future of their land; in fact, the situation demanded it with all the Allies intent on creating a new Germany which should break with its tragic past. This discussion encompassed proposals for a new political order in Germany and Europe and, inevitably given the history of such debate, speculation about Germany and the Germans.

Some continued the debate in a manner reminiscent of Thomas Mann. In the first edition of *Frankfurter Hefte*, one of the many periodicals that sprang up in the years immediately after the war, the co-founder Eugen Kogon, who had been imprisoned in Buchenwald, considered the character of the Germans in an essay 'Gericht und Gewissen' ('Tribunal and conscience'). Kogon's starting-point is very close to that of Mann in its view of the German people:

> Roaming in the realm of the imagination, a prey to inexhaustible plans, to many feelings and dreams, it sees in every concretisation a limitation of the lofty and the ideal. Just as it succumbs to a false creed from an excess of credulity, it also easily succumbs to a real bond that does not even arise in its midst.

(Kogon 1946: 33)

The bond that is specifically implied here is that of National Socialism, whose success in Kogon's view was made possible by the Germans' propensity to submit to authority. The conclusion he reaches, which is again similar to Mann, is that Germans should learn to know themselves better, both their good and bad characteristics.

By contrast, others espoused the hope of a totally new beginning based on positive German traditions. The strength of belief in such traditions is encapsulated in the phrase 'the other Germany' ('das andere Deutschland') to express all that is good in Germany and all that was largely suppressed in the course of history. One example of this feeling is the 1945 essay 'Deutsches Bekenntnis' ('German confession') by the poet Johannes R. Becher, who, having spent the Nazi years in Moscow, was to become the Minister of Culture in the GDR (however, in the title of this essay he was still willing to use not only the religious term *'Bekenntnis'* but also *'deutsch'* in the quasi-mystical manner referred to above). In fact, the same tone prevails throughout the essay, as the following passage shows: 'We believe in the capability of our people to live and in its strength to

171

change, this we confess. Germany's resurrection is our certainty' (*Vaterland* 1979: 39). Similar tones are to be found in the declarations of the group of writers from all the zones of occupation who met at the *Erster Deutscher Schriftstellerkongreß* (First Congress of German Writers) in Berlin in 1947. In fact, it was to prove to be the only such gathering, as the realities of Cold War division and confrontation soon began to spread into the realm of culture too. The danger of such division led the assembled writers to stress the eternal existence of Germany and the 'permanent community of those who speak the German language' (ibid.: 74).

Expressions of worry about Germany were increasingly heard as the process of division continued. A volume published in 1951 under the title *Wir heißen Euch hoffen. Schriftsteller zur deutschen Verständigung* (*We Bid You Hope. Writers on German Understanding*) with the aim of preserving the idea of German unity is particularly revealing in the way that reference to Germany is frequently made in largely metaphorical terms (Schwarz and Weber 1951). Both Walter von Molo, a writer who had remained in Germany throughout the Nazi period, and Johannes R. Becher refer to Germany as a 'heart'. Von Molo, in his essay entitled 'Ja, wir wollen uns retten' ('Yes, we wish to rescue ourselves'), provides a basic lesson on anatomy, before making use of the idea of the heart as the seat of emotions to underline his plea for unity: 'We have two legs, two arms, two eyes, two ears, two lungs but only one heart, on which our life depends; and it is really a requirement of our heart to preserve ... unity' (Schwarz and Weber 1951: 33), while Becher in his verse contribution sententiously states at the end of his poem 'Deutschland, dich suchend!' ('Germany, seeking you'):

Man kann ein Herz nicht in zwei Teile spalten.
(A heart cannot be split in two.)

(ibid.: 26)

By the time these outpourings appeared, the political division of Germany was a *fait accompli*.

Whereas postwar statements about Germany expressed in metaphorical or declamatory language are reminiscent of the nineteenth-century tradition in which German reality was compensated by flights of fancy, others did use what appeared to be the chances for a new start after 1945 to make more political statements about Germany and its possible future. This was the

172

case with the short-lived magazine *Der Ruf* (*The Call*) whose leading associates were subsequently to be at the forefront of the Gruppe 47, the literary grouping that had a major influence on cultural life during the first twenty years of the Federal Republic's existence. Looking back in 1962 in the introduction to a collection of pieces from the magazine, one of the editors, Hans Werner Richter, summed up the hopes of his generation in the following terms: 'Their hope was a united socialist Europe. They were passionately opposed to the division of Germany, not out of chauvinism but because they were aware that a new Europe could never be built on the basis of divided nations' (1962: 8). What Richter and his colleagues hoped for was a merger within Germany of elements of both east and west, in other words of socialism and democracy. Similarly they hoped that Germany might act as a bridge between east and west and thus prove a focus for a united Europe.

Richter and the authors of *Der Ruf* were not the only ones to conceive of a role for Germany between the blocs of the western and eastern powers. Some hoped to make Germany into a neutral zone between the two blocs, while others aspired to Germany being a third force, armed and neutral, rather than neutralised. One particular group, the 'Nauheimer Kreis' envisaged a neutral zone encompassing the centre of Europe and including Finland, a united Germany, Austria and Switzerland. Although these projects were not feasible, they should not necessarily be condemned in the context of their time when attempts to preserve unity that went beyond mere incantations did have a place as long as it was possible to believe that the future of postwar Germany was still open. This does not mean that they should be resurrected today. Today's united Germany does not have to reconcile the interests of two superpowers, as the plans of the 1940s were designed to do. As was seen in Chapter 6, its interests are now tied primarily to those of its western neighbours, while the westernisation of German politics and society has proved largely successful and should not, given the lessons of history, be abandoned.

The realities of the postwar situation meant that a new Germany could not be built on the moral and political aspirations of those who sought a total break with the past. In fact, the voices of those who appeared to represent a different Germany, namely the émigrés from National Socialism, were soon stifled. Tensions between those who had left and those who had stayed were soon apparent when Thomas Mann, in reply to an open letter from Walter von Molo asking him to return to Germany, stated that in his view all books published in Germany during the Nazi period carried 'the stench of blood and shame' (*Vaterland* 1979: 48). This provoked the response that Mann hated Germany. Some of those who did return were soon disillusioned, for example, Alfred Döblin, the author of the celebrated novel of city life set during the Weimar Republic, *Berlin Alexanderplatz* (1975), who returned to France in 1953 feeling that there was no place for him in the new Federal Republic. The situation was different in the GDR where émigrés were welcome as representatives of a different German tradition, although they too had to accept the political priorities of that state, something not all were prepared to do. In all events, the visions of a new united Germany soon faded and a period of disillusionment followed. Hopes that the experiences of émigrés might contribute to a new sense of identity were largely thwarted.

DENIAL OF NATIONALITY: THE CASE OF HANS MAGNUS ENZENSBERGER

Following the failure of the various projects to create a united and different Germany after 1945, many writers and intellectuals in the west of Germany, as was seen in Chapter 2, adopted the unenthusiastic attitude encapsulated in the phrase '*ohne mich*'. It was only in the 1960s that this changed with their increased interest in the political life of the Federal Republic, a development that culminated in the widespread identification with the figure of Willy Brandt, the embodiment of the 'other Germany'. What took place was a kind of recognition of the Federal Republic. The changing atmosphere was indicated by the publication in 1961 of a volume entitled *Ich lebe in der Bundesrepublik* (*I Live in the Federal Republic*) in which various authors expressed their feelings about the country. Although many of the essays are critical, a desire for identification is visible in the sentiments expressed by the editor Wolfgang Weyrauch in the Introduction: 'I love my home. Because I love it, I worry about it. Because I worry about it, I have put together and edited this . . . volume' (Weyrauch 1961: 7).

As this interest in the Federal Republic grew, there was less concern with Germany as a whole. Intellectuals were in part deterred from this area by the official policy of reunification propounded by the Adenauer government. This was based on a 'policy of strength' whereby concessions would be extracted from the Soviet Union on the basis of western strength. In that it was backed by an anti-communist rhetoric that reminded many of the ideology of the Nazis, this policy was anathema to intellectuals. It also appeared to have been proved wrong by the building of the Berlin Wall which indisputably deepened division.

One author to show particular exasperation with what at the time was called the German Question was the poet and essayist Hans Magnus Enzensberger. His exasperation with Germany was visible in his contribution to *Ich lebe in der Bundesrepublik*, the title of which, 'Schimpfend unter Palmen' ('Cursing under palm-trees'), expresses in itself the distance felt towards Germany. Enzensberger expresses his abhorrence of German coffee-houses – they are enough to 'teach us fear of the eternity of hell' (Enzensberger 1961: 25) – while the essay concludes, apart from a postscript, in which a more mellow tone is adopted, with the brilliant but slightly opaque aphorism: 'On the two disputing piles known as Germany there live in part people partially' (ibid.: 30).

Enzensberger's exasperation with Germany is again visible in a collection of essays published in 1967. The title of this collection, *Deutschland, Deutschland unter anderem* (*Germany, Germany among Other Things*), is a deliberate contrast to the idea of Germany being '*über alles*'. The first essay in the collection originally appeared in English in the magazine *Encounter* under the title 'Am I a German?' (Enzensberger 1964). It begins with the seemingly naive statement, 'I have never really understood why nations exist' (ibid.: 16), goes on to suggest that the division of Germany proves that nationality is a dubious principle on which to base judgements and then adds that it is a mystification to speak of a German character. He also claims that the great problems facing the world as a whole, in particular the threat of nuclear obliteration, make the division of Germany only a matter of secondary importance. Another article in the same collection with the title 'Versuch, von der deutschen Frage Urlaub zu nehmen' ('Attempt to take leave of the German Question') underlines the point:

Today Germany is an anomaly, a special case that is no longer part of the future. 'We are someone again in the world', somebody in Bonn is supposed to have said. It will

have been some Federal Chancellor or other. We are someone again, we count again, about as much as the two-headed
calf at the fair.

(Enzensberger 1967: 47)

These dismissive comments are comparable to Hölderlin's tirade
against the Germans. At least Enzensberger never went so far as
to change his name to show his disenchantment with Germany.
This was the course taken by the artist Hans Herzfelde, better
known as John Heartfield, at the time of the First World War to
show his lack of identification with the German cause. There are
many cases when individuals have changed (or have been forced
to change) their name; in most cases it has to do with assimilation
(at the most basic level it might be that the original name cannot
be pronounced in the new country of residence); a change of name
as an act of political protest against one's nation seems a peculiarly
German phenomenon.

THE RETURN OF AN ISSUE

Given the apparent permanence of division at the time, it is at
first sight surprising that the theme of Germany again became
an issue of intellectual debate in the late 1970s. What is even more
surprising is that the debate took place largely on the left of
the political spectrum, that is among people whose patriotism had
been called into question ever since Kaiser Wilhelm II had called
the Social Democrats 'vaterlandslose Gesellen' ('fellows without a
fatherland'). In 1981 Herbert Ammon and Peter Brandt, the son
of Willy, edited a volume entitled *Die Linke und die nationale
Frage* (*The Left and the National Question*) which sought to show
that post-1945 interest in the German Question had never been
confined solely to the right of the political spectrum (Brandt
and Ammon 1981). A little earlier the author Hermann Peter
Piwitt had demanded that the Left should show more patriotism,
asking why the national colours were never displayed at gather-
ings of the New Left. Piwitt went on to attack the citizens of
the Federal Republic for what he perceived as their insipid
cosmopolitanism:

They cannot even be proud any longer of their home, they
have made a single dirty production factory out of it, into
which they drag home, from their journeys and forays, the

176

cultures of the whole world. The cuisine Greek, the dress Indian, wall-hangings and Weltanschauung from the Far East.

(Piwitt 1978: 20)

Piwitt's criticisms suggest one reason for the reawakened interest in Germany as a whole at this time, the birth of the ecological movement and, along with it, the peace movement. With the increase of superpower tension in the early 1980s and the subsequent stationing of more nuclear weapons in both the Federal Republic and the GDR, there was a growing fear that both German states might be united in nuclear obliteration. This led to the first quasi-official meetings of writers from both parts of Germany since the 1947 gathering mentioned above, this time to discuss the nuclear threat. The link between the peace movement and the national question was underlined in a memorandum 'Denkschrift Friedensvertrag – Deutsche Konföderation – Europäisches Sicherheitssystem' ('Memorandum for Peace Treaty – German Confederation – European Security System') that appeared in the 27 April 1985 edition of the *Frankfurter Rundschau* and with which, among others, the artist Joseph Beuys – a doyen of the peace and ecology movements – was involved.

How controversial this kind of link between peace and nation was at this time is shown by an essay that appeared in the 31 October 1981 edition of *Die Zeit* under the title 'Ein Volk, ein Reich, ein Frieden' ('One people, one reich, one peace'). Its author, Wolfgang Pohrt, suggests that the sense of national identity developing in the peace movement might one day turn against the Turks (*Die Zeit* 45, 1981: 41f.). Pohrt's point is that any expression of national feeling in Germany is likely to turn into excessive nationalism. The counter-argument, frequently presented by Günter Grass, is that by abandoning questions of nation to the Right, the Left is encouraging extremism rather than directing it into more acceptable channels.

Despite the national concerns of sections of the peace movement, it should not be concluded that the renewed interest in Germany at this time expressed itself in positive tones. Other events of the late 1970s, in particular what had been felt in certain quarters to be the excessive government reaction to the terrorism of the Baader–Meinhof Group/Red Army Faction in the form of new draconian laws, provoked memories of undemocratic German traditions and practices. A volume simply entitled *Deutschland, Deutschland* that was published in Austria in 1979 contains among its forty-seven contributions from writers living in both German states comments that are fully reminiscent of previous expressions of uncertainty and disenchantment with Germany. Commenting on terrorism and reactions to it, Klaus Stiller in his essay, which is simply entitled 'Deutschland', says that, unlike colleagues who are concerned about a lack of German identity, he is only too aware of it. In a comment that alludes to Goethe's difficulties in locating Germany he says: 'I do not claim there is no such thing as Germany. Let others claim it does not exist. I know exactly where it is' (Stiller 1979: 267). Other contributions show a lack of identification that is similar to Enzensberger's. Angelika Mechtel speaks of herself in her essay, 'Deutschland drinnen und draußen' ('Germany within and without'), 'as a coincidence allocated by coincidence to this country' (Mechtel 1979: 203), while Ludwig Fels simply states in his contribution 'Und hier ist das Märchen zu Ende' ('And this is the end of the fairy tale'): 'my presence is a mistake' (Fels 1979: 58).

By keeping the question of Germany on the agenda, writers and intellectuals did arguably contribute to the survival of national feeling at a time of division. That does not mean that they were concerned directly with the re-creation of a single German state. It is true that this did have some attraction to those of an older generation with memories going back beyond the time of division. In a 1979 publication edited by Jürgen Habermas, *Stichworte zur 'Geistigen Situation der Zeit'* (*Key Points on the 'Intellectual Situation of the Present'*) – the title refers to a similar volume produced during the Weimar Republic – which sought to survey the intellectual climate of the Federal Republic, two authors of this generation sought to explain their feelings towards Germany as a whole. Dieter Wellershoff in his essay 'Deutschland – ein Schwebezustand' ('Germany – a state of suspended animation'), despite his praise for the democracy of the Federal Republic, could only compare it with a club whose rules he respected but to which he could not feel an emotional bond; this was reserved for Germany. He speaks of a 'love that has lost its target but is untransferable' (Wellershoff 1979: vol. 1, 78). By contrast, in his contribution, 'Händedruck mit Gespenstern' ('Shaking hands with ghosts'), Martin Walser is much more conventionally nationalistic. He proclaims defiantly: 'I am incapable, just because I live in the

FRG, to think and feel only as an inhabitant of the FRG. And even less can I adopt the GDR' (Walser 1979: vol. 1, 18).

Over the course of the next decade Walser was to become a ceaseless campaigner for German unity, often promoting strong criticism for his apparent espousal of nationalistic stances and making the subject of division the theme of a 1987 fictional work, the novella *Dorle und Wolf*.[2] Other commentators in the 1970s who were from a younger generation did not show the same emotional attitude towards German nationalism. For the critic Heinz Ludwig Arnold, introducing a collection of writings on Germany, German nationalism is 'the frustration complex which grew out of the Germans' lack of national self-awareness' (Arnold 1972: xi), while for Hans Christoph Buch writing in 1978 Germany remains a 'literary fiction' (Buch 1978: 4). He goes on to castigate Germany in the time-honoured way, claiming that civic courage (*Zivilcourage*), the quality Germans are seen as having lacked during the Nazi era, fairness and tolerance continue to be alien to the country.

DEBATES AT THE TIME OF UNITY

It was inevitable that the theme of Germany and the Germans should come even more to the centre of public debate in the years 1989–90 as the unification process gathered momentum. Whereas certain writers, in particular Günter Grass and Martin Walser, who took opposite standpoints, concentrated principally on the political events taking place at the time, as will be seen in the next chapter, others continued to agonise on a more abstract level. The early months of 1990 saw a series of lectures by prominent intellectuals in the German State Opera building in (east) Berlin, in which writers such as Rolf Hochhuth and Günter Grass as well as the scientist Carl Friedrich von Weizsäcker discussed the subject of Germany.[3]

Another volume from 1990, *Mein Deutschland findet sich in keinem Atlas* (*My Germany is Not to be Found in any Atlas*), shows already by its title that the tradition of seeing Germany as some kind of abstract ideal was continuing. The title comes from a comment in the book by the western novelist Elisabeth Plessen and is reinforced by the GDR author Brigitte Burmeister's statement that for her Germany is more than the (at the time) two German states, the word evoking rather landscapes and images of towns. The other contributions include some of the attitudes that have been noted throughout this chapter. The GDR poet Uwe Kolbe, who had been a leading dissident in that country, speaks of his confusion over his nationality in a manner that is superficially reminiscent of Enzensberger, making the title of his contribution the claim 'Ich war nicht darauf vorbereitet, ein Deutscher zu sein' ('I was not prepared for being a German') (Kolbe 1990: 68). In fact, his situation is exactly the opposite to that of Enzensberger. Whereas Enzensberger was trying to escape being labelled and stereotyped, Kolbe is complaining that his upbringing in the GDR denied him any sense of German nationality and identity so that it was only when he was able to travel abroad that he understood the concerns of Heine and Hölderlin.

This collection also contains the obligatory tirade against the Germans, this time by the GDR writer Winfried Völlger under the title 'Von der Schwierigkeit, ein Deutscher zu sein' ('On the difficulty of being a German'). He claims:

What has traditionally characterised the Germans is their overpowering thoroughness, their quality of pursuing every single thing to the bitter end; it is known that the Germans did not invent fascism, but they became, as Fellini put it its classical exponents.

(Völlger 1990: 86)

Finally, there are at least two contributors, one from each of the German states, who associate themselves with France. The westerner Christoph Meckel speaks of his desire to be buried in France, while the GDR dissident Frank-Wolf Matthies claims that he feels much closer to French than to German literature and culture. These examples suggest that some writers' attitudes to Germany have not changed much in over a century.

CONCLUSION

In an essay published in 1985, 'Der Traum vom "anderen" Deutschland. Schriftsteller leiden am deutschen Weg' ('The dream of the "other" Germany. Writers suffer through the way of Germany'), the political scientist Karl-Rudolf Korte advances six theses to describe the interest of writers in the phenomenon of Germany (Korte 1985: 122–9). They include several of the themes that have been visible in this chapter: writers' self-images as the true patriots along with their visions of the 'other' Germany, the belief that Germany should play a mediating role in Europe because of its central position and the continuing factor of '*Leiden an Deutschland*'. Korte concludes that the concerns of writers are to be understood as part of the search for national identity.

The reasons for this state of affairs lie primarily in German history. It is not just a question of the negative course of German history, specifically the factors of division and authoritarian and totalitarian rule, but also of the brevity of any sense of German identity. In 1962 Martin Walser began a series of observations entitled 'Ein deutsches Mosaik' with the remark, 'My grandfather still did not know that he was a German' (Walser 1965: 7). He is not in the manner of Enzensberger denying the significance of nationality, only pointing to how recently it was that any sense of nationality developed among members of his family. If one adds to this some of the uncertainties about Germany that were mentioned in the Introduction to this book, in particular the uncertainties about its geographical limits, it is small wonder that the establishment of an identity based on a sense of what constitutes Germany and being German has proved extremely difficult. A further complicating factor has been the divisions within Germany, the differences between regions and traditions. One example already referred to is the difference between the westward-looking Catholic milieu of a city such as Cologne – its famous son Heinrich Böll was always proud of the fact that, because of this, the Nazis received a relatively low share of the votes in that city – and the military and aristocratic ethos of Prussia. Referring to the division of Germany, Böll stated in 1976 that he was not worried about the disappearance of Bismarck's 1871 Reich, a creation with which he could not identify and which he described as a 'swindle', although he did worry about the lot of the people in the GDR (Böll 1978: 582).

The only possible conclusion is that the extent of writers' concern with Germany and the way this expresses itself in such abstract and at times almost mystical forms is the result of the lack of any firm ties based on clear historical, political and cultural foundations. This is a phenomenon that goes beyond writers and intellectuals. It has been argued that the division of Germany after 1945 would have been impossible if the Germans themselves had felt strongly enough about unity. This viewpoint probably underestimates the importance of power politics; after all other countries such as Vietnam and Korea have also experienced division as a result of great power rivalry, but there are hints that ties to Germany as a whole were never as strong as they appeared on the surface. Reporters in 1945 noted that as soon as areas of Germany were occupied by the advancing Allies, the inhabitants abandoned any sense of identification with the Nazis.[4] This is not to equate Nazism with Germany; nevertheless it must be remembered that the Nazi movement was based on the stimulation and mobilisation of national feeling. To claim that identification with Germany was always shallow may seem to contradict what was said in the previous chapter about many Germans fighting to the bitter end or about the wave of suicides that accompanied the defeat of 1945. This need not necessarily be the case, as it is psychologically credible that people try to cover up what is only a shallow identification with a cause or set of ideas by outward displays of fanatical loyalty. The same could be said of Germans in the GDR. Whereas in other communist states, such as Hungary and Poland, most citizens did not hide their hostility to the prevailing ideology, even when acting in a quasi-official capacity, those in positions of any authority in the GDR rarely showed signs of doubting official policy. It is a tragedy of German history that, because of its un-certainties, there was a lack of powerful countervailing forces to combat harmful ideologies, which many were therefore willing to embrace.

It is small wonder that, in the face of historical reality, German intellectuals often took refuge in mystifications, be they idealisa-tions of some imagined idea of Germany or a total condemnation of all things German. Even in the case of Thomas Mann, who did seek to balance positive and negative aspects in 'Germany and the Germans', it is possible to point to his lack of attention to concrete political and economic developments. This may be partly excusable among those who work in the realm of ideas. What is inexcusable is politicians upholding the idea that being German is something that has an almost mystical dimension, which is surely the implication of the *jus sanguinis* with its disregard of where people are born and brought up. A glance at a German telephone directory in which Polish or French names abound shows how tenuous and hypo-critical any idea of nationality based on a myth of heredity is.

What this chapter has sought to show is how uncertain any con-cept of German identity is. It is not arguing that a single exclusive identity should be the ideal; it should be possible – and is probably desirable – that people have a variety of loyalties: to a district or region and to ideals that go beyond national boundaries. In short, why should someone not feel, let us say, Bavarian, German and European at the same time? Nevertheless, even if some kind of exclusive identity is not desirable, with the establishment in 1990 of what has the potential to be a stable German state there is the opportunity for a new kind of German identity to establish itself, one that might be less based on projections and abstractions. It is also likely that intellectuals will play a significant part in this. Accordingly, the next chapter will examine the intellectual debates that have already taken place since unification.

9

THE INTELLECTUAL
CLIMATE SINCE
UNIFICATION

CHALLENGING THE PAST: THE GDR

Since the fall of the Berlin Wall many aspects of life in the GDR
have come under critical scrutiny as more and more has been
revealed about the unwholesome consequences of the SED's dictatorial rule. Literary and cultural life have been no exception to
this development. As early as 1990, what was quickly dubbed the
deutsch–deutsche Literaturstreit (the German–German literature
dispute) broke out. The immediate cause was the publication of
Christa Wolf's text *Was bleibt* (*Something Remains*) (1990).[1] This
recounted in the first person a day in the life of a writer, recognis-
able as Wolf herself, who is under surveillance by the Stasi. What
was considered especially objectionable was that Wolf had waited
until the end of the GDR to publish a work whose origins were
much earlier and which had largely been completed a decade
before. This was taken as an act of cowardice that was typical of
many GDR writers in general and Wolf in particular.

The situation was compounded when the extent of Stasi involvement in literature became apparent. It was not difficult to take
sides in the cases of those writers, such as Reiner Kunze and Erich
Loest,[2] who, until their departure to the Federal Republic, had
been subject to surveillance and harassment. However, the real
shock came when it became clear that other writers, in particular
the GDR's leading dramatist Heiner Müller and Wolf herself,
along with certain younger authors, who were associated with an
alternative culture that had developed in the 1980s centred on the
Berlin district of Prenzlauer Berg, had been involved in some
degree of co-operation with the Stasi. Again, it was the case of Wolf
that received special attention, particularly as she responded to the

attacks made on her by comparing in a television interview her fate
following unification to that of German writers who suffered persecution and exile under the Nazis. Although this was an extremely
misguided comparison, the extent of her co-operation with the
Stasi did not merit the opprobrium that was heaped on her. Her
involvement dated back to a brief period in the late 1950s and early
1960s and did not involve any covert operations. Moreover, the
explanation she gave for her involvement, the guilt she felt as a
young German in the face of those communists who had opposed
the Nazis, is understandable.[3]

One of Wolf's critics, Ulrich Greiner, denounced her as the
'Staatsdichterin [state poet] der DDR' in an essay entitled 'Mangel
an Feingefühl' ('Lack of sensitivity') that originally appeared in
Die Zeit (Anz 1991: 66). The nub of the attacks was that writers
in the GDR had identified themselves far too closely with the
political system, an identification that was only underlined by the
involvement of some of their number with the Stasi. There clearly
were writers who fully identified with the GDR system and were
rewarded by large editions, an important factor in a system of
book production in which print runs were not determined by
the market forces of supply and demand but by political considerations and the limited allocations of paper within the planned
economy. At the other extreme, there were writers who were
totally at odds with the system or at least appeared to be so, as had
been the case with the Prenzlauer Berg poets who were regarded
as representing apolitical alienation from the state in which they
had grown up and as expressing their position through radical
formal and aesthetic experimentation that was entirely at odds
with the official tenets of 'socialist realism'. Between these two
extremes were the group that remained loyal to the socialist ideals
of the GDR but wanted extensive reform. It included Wolf and
many of the other names most readily associated with GDR
literature, for example, Volker Braun, Stefan Heym and, even if
he has subsequently claimed that his disillusionment with socialism
predated unification by two decades, Christoph Hein. In the eyes
of those responsible for official GDR literary politics, they were
unwelcome critics whose work might endanger the survival of the
socialist state; for their post-unification western critics their opposition was only token. These western critics could only see merit in
those writers who had left the GDR or consistently been refused
permission to publish. That those writers who criticised the GDR

from a reformist socialist standpoint were misguided in their views was confirmed for their critics in the way they continued to support efforts to retain the GDR as a separate state as late as the autumn of 1989, not least, in the case of the four individuals mentioned above, by signing the petition '*Für unser Land*' ('For our country'), which can be seen as a last ditch effort to prevent unification.

Although useful, such distinctions are not clear-cut. Critics of Wolf and comparable GDR writers would wish to consign them to the unreservedly pro-GDR group. What is true is that she and many others, despite their record of criticism of aspects of the GDR, differed from dissidents in other comparable countries, Vaclav Havel in Czechoslovakia being the most obvious example, by retaining their belief in socialism. Nevertheless, this does not mean that Wolf and others were unquestioning apologists of the GDR system. She herself frequently ran into difficulties with the authorities. When the SED indulged in one of its periodic clamp-downs on cultural activity in 1965, she protested vociferously enough for her name to be removed from the list of candidates for the party's central committee. She also attached her name to the open letter of protest signed by, among others, Volker Braun and Stefan Heym against the expulsion of Wolf Biermann. Heym himself suffered the penalty of expulsion from the writers' union in 1979, a fate that destroyed any chances of his work being published in the GDR and hardly fits in with any kind of status as 'state poet', even if he remained left-wing enough to stand and be elected for the PDS in the 1994 federal election.[4]

The strained nature of the relationship this group of writers had with the GDR authorities becomes even more obvious if some of their literary works are considered. Whereas, despite certain criticisms of dogmatic mentalities, Wolf's first major work, *Der geteilte Himmel*, 1963, clearly comes down in favour of the GDR (the decision of the heroine Rita not to follow her lover Manfred to the Federal Republic in the summer of 1961 is fully endorsed and the project of a mature GDR in which the guiding principle will be truth is embraced), her next novel, *Nachdenken über Christa T*. (*Reflections on Christa T*.), 1968, is much less positive in tone. The heroine who dies at an early age is disenchanted with a society in which lip-service often takes precedence over true political idealism. After its initial print run of 15,000 it was not reprinted for four years, suggesting that it is anything but a ringing endorsement of the GDR. An even more radical critique of the mentality of those in positions of authority in the GDR is found in Volker Braun's 1975 story *Unvollendete Geschichte* (*Unfinished Story*) (Braun 1989). Here two young people have their lives almost ruined by the authorities' unwillingness to trust their loyalty, preferring suspicion and control to open dialogue. The story, which is based on a real case, is unfinished because it is not resolved whether the situation can be patched up; the title, which exploits the two meanings of the word '*Geschichte*', history and story, underlines the challenge the book makes to those in power in the GDR, namely change or be confined to the dustbin of history. What happened in 1989 shows that Braun's demands had fallen on deaf ears. The question for Braun and other writers of his type is whether they should have still hoped for an alternative within the parameters of a separate GDR state.

Just as it is difficult for some to separate the writers who were outright apologists for the GDR from those seeking a reformed socialist society, it is even harder to distinguish the reformists from those generally seen as total opponents. A distinction based on whether writers were victims of censorship is impossible, as nobody could escape its vagaries. Whereas it remains true, as stated in Chapter 1, that nothing could be published officially in the GDR without its being subject to censorship, it does not follow that the system worked consistently. Even if changes in party attitudes – the periods of relative liberality followed by restriction already alluded to – and the possibility of the censors making, from the SED's point of view, 'mistakes' are allowed for, there are other factors to consider. On occasions a conscious decision was made to publish a critical work, albeit perhaps in a small edition, to combat the danger that a totally disaffected writer might do more harm by offering his or her work to western publishers, work that might then be even more critical because awareness of censorship did generally influence what was submitted to GDR publishers.[5] This danger of self-censorship could lead to the conclusion that even the submission of a manuscript was a form of collaboration with the cultural policies of the GDR. Such a fundamentalist view ignores the natural desire of writers to have works published in the society to which they relate; few of those GDR writers generally accepted at the time of unification as out and out opponents of the regime on the basis of extreme difficulties with the censor, such as Monika Maron and Wolfgang Hilbig, would pass the test, if the rigorous criterion of never having had a word published or never having submitted a manuscript were applied. In the case of Maron, her status as a model dissident disappeared in 1995 when it came to light that she too had been involved with the Stasi, something she had been as unwilling to admit as any of her fellow writers.

Similar difficulties arise if emigration is taken as a reliable criterion of dissidence. This can be illustrated by the example of Wolf Biermann. His emigration was enforced rather than wished, in that he was not allowed to return from a visit to the Federal Republic. In other cases, too, emigration was enforced in the sense that the only alternative was a period of imprisonment. That emigration was in certain cases involuntary does not reduce the hardship it may have caused; nor does it mean that the dislike felt by those who left the GDR towards those who remained, and appeared to enjoy privileges, is less understandable. Emigrés have been among the most vociferous critics of those who remained, with their stance contributing to the difficulties of 'uniting' German literature at an official level. After unification separate branches of the International PEN Club remained in existence and the prospect of their merging caused, for example, Reiner Kunze to resign temporarily from the organisation in 1995. In the event, however, although steps towards a rapprochement occurred – certain western writers declared their intention of being members of both groups – no merger was agreed, which left the two separate PEN clubs as a continuing monument to division.

Deciding on the merits of GDR literature is rendered even more complicated by the role culture played in that society as part of the search for legitimacy and status. This meant that writers and other artists attracted official attention that was not just based on the desire to suppress undesired political statements. That the authorities needed writers for reasons of national prestige led to writers being offered privileges if they were prepared to conform. This was a trap some were accused of falling into, with pictures of a smiling Honecker in the company of writers appearing relatively frequently. On the other hand, this situation enhanced the position of writers, who were taken seriously throughout society. More-over, the criticisms they made of GDR society, even if toned down by the censor, enhanced their popularity and status, especially as other media, which in different kinds of society have the function of voicing criticism, were even more rigorously controlled. The rapport more critical GDR writers, such as Christa Wolf, had with their readers makes it difficult to condemn them out of hand as willing tools of the regime. It is more appropriate to argue that their criticisms contributed to a weakening of the system and therefore to the events of 1989.

If it is impossible to subdivide GDR writers into neat groups who can then be praised or condemned according to the degree of identification with the state they displayed, there remains the question of what criteria can be applied if a resolution to the issues raised by the *Literaturstreit* is sought. What cannot be doubted is that certain individual GDR writers behaved in a shameful way towards certain colleagues. The name that springs to mind is that of the then President of the Writers' Union, Hermann Kant, who not only collaborated with the Stasi but was also willing to let himself be used in the process whereby Heym and others were expelled from this organisation. All such cases are, however, by their nature individual and it is just as difficult to speak of collective guilt in this area as in any other. Moreover, if judgements on works of literature were based on the morality of their authors, many celebrated works would have to be cast aside. Other criteria have to apply.

One question that immediately arises is whether a work of art that reflects distasteful ideas can have any aesthetic merit. If unquestioning support for the GDR system comes into this category, then this question becomes acute. Fortunately, although it is difficult to lay down a hard and fast rule, there does seem to be some correlation between content and aesthetic considerations; where a work of art conceals or simplifies the truth, this is likely to be reflected in the use of forms, and in the case of literature language, that are in some way equally dishonest and simplistic. Judging GDR literature – or art – on purely aesthetic terms is, however, a daunting task. Each work would have to be judged individually and some degree of speculation would be required about which works might stand the test of time. Both activities contain a strong subjective dimension.

What can be stated with some certainty is that GDR literature at least did appeal to many readers and fulfilled a need in their lives. Moreover, many writers, even if they supported the existence of a socialist state, were willing to voice criticisms of the Ulbricht and Honecker regimes. Accordingly, their writing attracted great attention in the west, not least among those who now decry it. It may be that its exotic nature, the insights it gave into a partially unknown society, led to a greater interest than it merited on aesthetic grounds, particularly in non-German speaking countries. On the other hand, rejection on the grounds that it largely used realistic techniques may rest on a view, prevalent in some German cultural circles, that realism has somehow been superseded by other developments in twentieth-century art, a view that transposes the concept of technological progress on to works of culture. The most obvious reason for its rejection remains nevertheless political, based on the belief that nothing good can have come out of the GDR. It is true that Thomas Mann's 1945 assertion (see p. 174) that all works of literature published under the Nazis carried the stench of blood has not been applied exactly and cannot be, since the GDR did not indulge in war and genocide. Nevertheless, there is still the implication that any work of art conceived in the GDR, unless it reveals total opposition, must bear some of the opprobrium due to that state. The essentially political nature of the attack on GDR culture is further confirmed by the parallel questioning of the cultural and intellectual life of the Federal Republic that took place at the time of unification.

CHALLENGING THE PAST: THE FEDERAL REPUBLIC

The role of writers and intellectuals in the development of increased political awareness in the pre-unification Federal Republic was discussed in Chapter 2, with particular emphasis placed on their contribution to the change of mood that took place in the 1960s and led to the change of government in 1969. Günter Grass especially believed that it was the duty of a writer not to live in some kind of 'ivory tower', a German tradition of which he totally disapproved, but to take part in social and political debate. In this way he and other colleagues hoped to play their part in the creation of a more democratic society. At the same time, given their experience of National Socialism, writers of Grass's generation remained suspicious of political power, in this sense perpetuating the dichotomy between *Geist* and *Macht* that had characterised the difficult relationship between politicians and intellectuals in Germany. Indeed, when CDU politicians described their intellectual opponents as pinschers rather than poets, as Ludwig Erhard did in 1965, or compared, as Josef-Hermann Dufhues did in 1963, Bertolt Brecht to the pimp Horst Wessel (who became a 'martyr' to be immortalised in song for the Nazis), little seemed to have changed.

Although Grass stressed that his involvement in politics was undertaken as a citizen – he distinguished between the world of poetry that knew no compromise and that of politics that depended on compromise – and, together with Heinrich Böll, disliked the idea that writers should be given the accolade of 'conscience of the nation', it would be ridiculous to suggest that his literary work, and that of many of his colleagues, can be divorced from his political concerns. For Böll in particular there was no distinction between aesthetic concerns and the moral concern for society. It was this tradition of socio-critical literature, together with active participation in political debate, that came under scrutiny at the time of German unification, when, just as with GDR literature and culture, it was felt that an era had come to an end.

The critics of the literary life of the Federal Republic detected a dominance of political ideology to the detriment of true aesthetic and literary concerns. How this had debilitated literature was the subject of an essay by Frank Schirrmacher, the literary critic of the *Frankfurter Allgemeine Zeitung*, entitled 'Abschied von der Literatur der Bundesrepublik' ('Farewell to the literature of the Federal Republic') that appeared in the 2 October 1990 edition, one day before unification. He equated this literature with the work of those authors associated with the Gruppe 47. This loose association of writers was established in 1947 but enjoyed most prominence in the early 1960s when authors associated with it, who included Grass and Böll, were coming to the height of their fame. Schirrmacher denied that this generation of authors had, as was generally held, adequately dealt with the questions that arose from the recent past. Rather than confront their readers, they had offered superficial and comforting explanations; a sign of this was the way that the past had frequently been narrated from the perspective of a child. One example of this is of course the figure of Oskar Matzerath in Grass's *Die Blechtrommel* (*The Tin Drum*) (1959), who retains the physical stature of a 3-year-old throughout much of the novel. As far as Schirrmacher was concerned, the choice of such a perspective, which offered the readers the simple answers they craved, amounted to the fulfilment of a set task. For this the readers were duly grateful and they rewarded writers with a special status. It has to be admitted that Schirrmacher's explanation is very neat; in reality it ignores the tensions between writers and parts of society and also simplifies the complex relationship between writers and their public.

Another critic who complained that German literature had been too dominated by social and political concerns was Ulrich Greiner. He popularised the term *Gesinnungsästhetik* (conviction aesthetics) to characterise works in which the political views of the author, invariably left-wing, took precedence over artistic concerns. When Günter Grass ended his membership of the SPD after unification because of his disagreement with the party's policy on asylum seekers, Greiner rejoiced that an era of political commitment among writers was over. He spoke scornfully of Cassandra – a reference to the Trojan priestess who had prophesied doom – now being unemployed (*Kassandra arbeitslos*); indeed this was the title he gave to his piece that appeared in the 8 January 1992 edition of *Die Zeit* (2, 1992: 41).

Because Greiner and Schirrmacher were both involved in the *Literaturstreit* – in fact the arguments about the literature of the Federal Republic can be seen as an extension of this dispute – it is necessary to consider how far the attacks on western intellectuals made at the time of unification were motivated by political considerations. One collection of essays edited by Cora Stephan, entitled *Wir Kollaborateure* (*We Collaborators*), clearly makes the connection between east and west (Stephan 1992). The thesis of the volume is that western intellectuals, a category in which she cleverly includes herself to show the requisite degree of contrition, had turned a blind eye to the failings of the GDR and thus collaborated in that repulsive system. To sum up: the essence of the case was that western writers and intellectuals had espoused misguided political ideas and, in the case of writers of literature, by their concentration on politics had not fulfilled their true literary role.

Inasmuch as these strictures involve aesthetic judgements, response to them is as difficult as in the case of GDR literature, if not more so, because a greater number of works is involved. Indeed, Schirrmacher's attack is based on the reduction of the literature of the Federal Republic to a single set of writers and a particular era. The fact that these writers have to be criticised because they proved popular to readers is reminiscent of Brecht's comment after the 1953 uprising that the SED needed to elect a new people, with on this occasion Schirrmacher and his supporters being in the role of the Communist Party. Incidentally, the same strictures would have to be addressed to foreign readers of German literature. Whereas Böll was awarded the Nobel Prize for Literature in 1972 and Grass enjoys a wide international following, other authors receive virtually no attention abroad, particularly those of the younger generation, with the occasional exception such as Patrick Süskind only proving the rule. What can be considered more easily than in the case of GDR writers is the political dimension, because intellectuals in the Federal Republic had outlets other than literary fiction through which to express their political ideas more directly. On this basis it might be possible to answer Greiner's charge that their political concerns had negatively affected their literary work and Stephan's claim that their views amounted to collaboration with the GDR. Given the pre-eminence afforded to it by Schirrmacher it is as well to begin with the Gruppe 47.

As a literary grouping whose origins were political (it grew out of the magazine *Der Ruf* referred to on p. 173), the Gruppe 47 (or some of the writers associated with it) had taken part in the sporadic protests that characterised the 1950s and early 1960s in the Federal Republic. The limits to such activities became manifest, however, when Hans Werner Richter, the co-ordinator of the Gruppe 47, limited his involvement in the fight against the *Bundeswehr* being equipped with nuclear weapons because he did not wish to become involved in the organisation of a co-ordinated campaign. In fact, this was typical of the group, which had no clear structure or membership, its existence being confined to its twice yearly meetings that writers attended on Richter's personal invitation. In so far as it had an ethos, it was primarily literary; meetings consisted of discussion of literary texts, with the emphasis, in the 1950s at least, being much more on modernist works than on simple realism with a clear political message.

Against this background it was a new departure when in 1965 Günter Grass undertook election tours to speak in favour of the SPD, frequently choosing as his venues the Catholic diaspora where the party's message invariably fell on stony ground. In the same year a group of young writers in Berlin were involved in writing speeches and inventing slogans for the SPD. However, when the party joined the Grand Coalition a year later many of the writers became disillusioned and turned to more revolutionary politics. Some felt so attracted by their political mission that they saw no further role for literature, a position proclaimed by the poet Hans Magnus Enzensberger in 1968, although not followed by him in practice. The mood at this time does support the claim that politics dominated aesthetics in the pre-unification Federal

Republic, although at this point it was less a case of 'conviction aesthetics' than of no aesthetics. When Grass sought to convey his political ideas in book form in *Aus dem Tagebuch einer Schnecke* (*From the Diary of a Snail*) (1972), there clearly was an aesthetic dimension as he wove together fictional and non-fictional elements and expressed his belief in gradual progress through the symbol of the snail.

If it could be claimed that politics dominated literary life in the 1960s, this soon ceased to be the case in the 1970s, when a spate of works, usually subsumed under the label 'New Subjectivity' (*Neue Subjektivität*), written in the first person and purporting to explore their authors' inmost feelings, began to dominate the literary market. At the same time, a number of writers and intellectuals turned away from politics, ending the era of enthusiasm for political commitment. In the 1970s, the word *Tendenzwende* (change of prevailing mood) entered political vocabulary to refer to a loss of enthusiasm for left-wing ideas and reform, a mood that made itself felt not least in the universities where traditional structures largely returned. By contrast, disillusionment with the SPD-led government led other writers and intellectuals to become attracted to the DKP (Deutsche Kommunistische Partei), which from its foundation in 1968 as the successor to the proscribed KPD invariably followed a pro-GDR line, not surprisingly since most of its funds originated from that state. In particular, Martin Walser, an erstwhile supporter of the SPD, created a stir in the 1972 election campaign by appearing to support the DKP, although he criticised its close links with the GDR. Others rallied to the party, whose members included the dramatist Franz Xaver Kroetz and the novelist Günter Herburger. It was at this point that Stephan's claim that writers were too close to the GDR might have had some validity. Subsequent events showed, however, that suspicion of communism, which was such a characteristic of the pre-unification Federal Republic, was equally widespread among intellectuals. Kroetz and most other intellectuals left the DKP and when, in the early 1980s, the writers' organisation, Verband deutscher Schriftsteller (which had been founded in the euphoric days of the late 1960s when there had been widespread belief in the effectiveness of collective action based on the trade union model), came under the control of individuals associated with the DKP, there followed mass resignations, including that of Günter Grass.

It has been argued that the other occasion on which intellectuals showed collective misjudgement was in the period 1989–90 when they allegedly failed to show sufficient enthusiasm for German unity. Whereas some, like Patrick Süskind, as was seen in Chapter 2 (p. 46), felt sorrow at the passing of the old Federal Republic, others, in particular Grass, were concerned that unification would inevitably lead to a new nationalism, a belief he expressed in two volumes of essays published in 1990 (Grass 1990a, 1990b). Grass argued that the moral opprobrium of Auschwitz had destroyed the justification for a single German state. Although this argument failed to take account of the changing political reality, it could not be claimed that it was based on sympathy for the GDR's political system, given Grass's long history of opposition which dated back to his comparison of the GDR to a concentration camp after the building of the Berlin Wall in 1961. Moreover, Grass had always been interested in the German question. His 1980 work, *Kopfgeburten oder Die Deutschen sterben aus* (*Headbirths or the Germans are Dying Out*), is a plea for the maintenance of German cultural unity, made in an era when political division seemed permanent. In fact, as the previous chapter showed, the 1980s were a time when many writers' interest in Germany as a whole was re-awakened. Peter Schneider's 1982 semi-documentary work, *Der Mauerspringer* (*The Wall-Leaper*) is devoted primarily to the division of Berlin, while in 1985 Thorsten Becker made his literary debut with *Die Bürgschaft* (*The Pledge*), an amusing tale in which a West and an East German exchange places for a limited period. On the basis of such works, it can be argued that writers were the only group interested in Germany as a whole at that time.

Attacks on certain writers and intellectuals for their lack of enthusiasm over unification were not based on the feeling that they were uninterested in politics, but rather that they did not share the same agenda as those in favour of the new developments. This is not to say that the sceptical writers were right. Nevertheless Greiner's complaint that writers had been too concerned with politics was largely the claim that they had been identified with the wrong issues. When, following unification, other questions arose, the same topos was visible: not so much objections to political stances as such, but rather to certain specific stances.

THE GULF WAR

When the Gulf War broke out in 1991, German society split between those who, in keeping with the policy of the Federal government, supported the action against Iraq and the pacifistic groupings who rejected violence in general and in this case doubted the motives of the USA and its allies, showing their suspicions in the widespread slogan, 'kein Blut für Öl' ('no blood for oil'). Opposition to the war was particularly widespread in universities with the normal lecture programme frequently giving way to seminars and demonstrations on the issue of the day. Despite the history of common causes between demonstrating students and intellectuals, intellectual opinion split more on the lines of society in general. Whereas it had long been impossible to talk of intellectuals in the Federal Republic speaking with a single voice (as pp. 184–192 showed), what was surprising at the time of the Gulf War was the vehemence of the reactions (which apparently led to the end of certain personal friendships among intellectuals) and the positioning of certain individuals on one particular side of the argument. Specifically the support for the war expressed by Hans Magnus Enzensberger, who at the time of the student rebellion had appeared to espouse the cause of revolution in the Federal Republic, and by Wolf Biermann, whose position as dissident in the GDR was based on his desire for a truly Marxist alternative, caused a degree of consternation.

Opponents of the war expressed their fears in a volume entitled *Ich will reden von der Angst meines Herzens* (*I will Speak of the Fear in My Heart*) (1991), the emotionality of which is compounded by the original German's unorthodox word-order. The subtitle *Autorinnen und Autoren zum Weltkrieg* (*Authors on the world war*) reflected the extent of concern, which clearly proved to be exaggerated. Some of the arguments contained in the book also lack the ability to differentiate, with the Swiss writer Peter Bichsel in his contribution 'Die Weltordnung der Weltmeister' ('The world order of the world champions') comparing the concept of the New World Order that became current after the end of the Cold War with Nazi terminology such as The Thousand-Year Reich (*Ich will reden* 1991: 13–16). Other contributions are not free of sentimentality, for example, a poem by Lutz van Dick which compares the suffering children in the Gulf with the demonstrating children in Germany. The poem 'zum golfkrieg' ('on the gulf war') by Gabi

196

Kachold, a former GDR writer who suffered imprisonment, is open to the charge of nationalism in that it states her hope 'as a German' that the Americans leave Germany. That she chooses the colloquial form 'rausgehen' (*Ich will reden* 1991: 62) puts the language almost on the level of crude chants and graffiti, whose English equivalent is approximately 'Yanks (or some other group) out'. By contrast Günter Grass examines German culpability that resulted from the supply of materials that helped Iraq to develop chemical weapons, seeing in such behaviour the same mentality that predominated in the western takeover of the GDR economy, while the novelist Gabriele Wohmann contributes a fictional satire, in which opponents of the Gulf War are so engrossed in their activities that the elderly mother of one of their number has to be transferred to an Old People's Home.

Wohmann's contribution clearly takes a different viewpoint from that of most of the rest of the collection. Accordingly, it provides a variety that is lacking in the volume that universally takes up an anti-pacifist stance, *Liebesgrüße aus Bagdad* (*From Baghdad with Love*) (Bittermann 1991). The subtitle, *Die 'edlen Seelen' der Friedensbewegung und der Krieg am Golf* (*The Noble Souls' of the Peace Movement and the War in the Gulf*), by referring in inverted commas to the paragons of the peace movement in terms taken from idealist philosophy, implies that opponents of the Gulf War were part of the German tradition of inwardness and other-worldliness that so concerned Thomas Mann. Accordingly Cora Stephan finds the 'decent German' someone to be feared in this context, while the Berlin author Eike Geisel speaks of moral anti-Semitism. It was the prospect of Israel becoming a target that partly motivated Wolf Biermann's stance, while the link with the past was particularly stressed in Enzensberger's essay 'Hitlers Wiedergänger' ('Hitler's repeat'), also contained in the *Liebesgrüße* volume. This essay was particularly controversial precisely because of the comparison made between Hitler and Saddam Hussein. The issue was not so much the question whether the Iraqi dictator had any redeeming qualities, but rather that by making the comparison Enzensberger was relativising the crimes committed by the Nazis in the manner of the historians who initiated the *Historikerstreit*. Although events quickly overtook the debate over the merits of the Gulf War and German reactions to it, the stage was set for further controversies, which broke out again in 1993, particularly over the question of nationalism.

A RETURN TO NATIONALISM?

In the course of 1993, the news magazine *Der Spiegel* published three controversial polemics by Botho Strauß, Martin Walser and Hans Magnus Enzensberger (see p. 202), the first two of which especially were seen as marking a re-emergence of traditional German nationalism. Botho Strauß, born in 1944 and therefore very much a member of a postwar generation, acquired his reputation in the 1970s and 1980s as both a dramatist and a novelist largely on the basis of non-realistic works that nevertheless betray acute powers of observation and an interest in questions relating to Germany. Where a more direct political statement could be discerned, for example, in the more accessible work *Paare Passanten* (1981), which is in part a portrait of the society of the Federal Republic, it appeared to be conservative in that the progressive ideas and mores of the time were treated with satirical disdain. The 1993 essay 'Anschwellender Bocksgesang' ('The swelling song of the sacrificial goat'), which first appeared in the 8 February 1993 edition of *Der Spiegel*, confirmed this impression (Strauß 1994).

The title of the essay is based on a literal translation of the Greek word for tragedy and it discusses the tragedy Strauß saw besetting the German nation. Accordingly, his essay is based on the tragic view of history beloved of German conservatives in the earlier part of the century, for example, Moeller van den Brück and Oswald Spengler, the title of whose most famous work, *Der Untergang des Abendlandes* (*The Decline of the West*) (Spengler 1993), in itself speaks volumes. Strauß's tragic conception is partly based on ecological concern, but more generally on a sense of the moral decay he perceives in the affluent society of the Federal Republic. That this decay is linked to a loss of nationalistic values is clear from his list of what is scorned in today's society: church, tradition, authority and the soldier. Moreover, he links what he calls 'das Unsere' (ours), which is under threat and which is something to be fought for, with the presence of refugees (Strauß 1994: 257). Otherwise, the enemies are the media (he perceives a connection between the talkshow and the show trial) and what he calls Mainstream, the cultural hegemony of the progressive intellectuals who have supposedly dominated the intellectual climate of the Federal Republic. It is the clash between the traditional values that are ultimately not to be denied and the superficialities of the present that, he predicts, will bring about some kind of tragic conflict.

Strauß's polemic led to a major debate in which both positive and negative views were expressed. One of the most damning reactions came from the SPD politician and thinker Peter Glotz, who dramatically announced that the situation was serious and that Strauß's ideas represented a danger to society.[6] He also makes the point that the right-wing violence that Strauß condemns, at least when it occurs in the former GDR, is not the result of an over-liberal society but is committed by people who were brought up on a diet of order and discipline. In as far as Strauß specifically attacks the activities of neo-Nazis, he cannot be described as a crude right-wing extremist. Indeed, there seems little prospect of his essay being read, let alone understood, by those who perpetrate acts of violence. The problem is rather that, at an intellectual level, he sees positive elements behind that which thugs put into practice. One example is his statement: 'Racism and xenophobia are "fallen" cultic passions, which originally had a sacred meaning to create order' (Strauß 1994: 263). He then goes on to say that traditionally the scapegoat, the outsider who was sacrificed, fulfilled the function of uniting and cleansing the city by being the focus of feelings that might explode in a more destructive manner. Even at this semi abstract level it can be objected that the scapegoat is being made an object whose views count for nothing. Equally, Strauß's more popular analogy with football has its limitations. He describes the true conservative as the supporter and the neo-Nazi as the hooligan. Yet, in terms of the analogy, they have something in common, football, which might therefore not just be the entirely positive pastime Strauß assumes it to be. The same is surely true of nationalism.

Walser's polemic 'Deutsche Sorgen' ('German worries') that appeared in the 28 June 1993 edition of *Der Spiegel* marked another step along a path its author had been treading for at least fifteen years. In the 1961 federal election Walser had supported the SPD, but by 1965 had becomed disillusioned, a state of affairs confirmed by his sympathies with the student movement and his support for the DKP, which was referred to earlier in this chapter (p. 194), where it was also pointed out that he had misgivings because the party appeared to lack a West German identity. In the following years, as his enthusiasm for the DKP waned, the interest in the national dimension grew with a number of essays (see also pp. 178f) stating his unhappiness with the division of Germany. Thus it was no suprise that, unlike Grass, he reacted with feelings of joy to the coming of German unification in 1989–90.

Why then was there reason for worry three years later? Again, it was the outbreak of right-wing violence. Walser saw this less as an ideological problem than as a manifestation of the natural tendency of young people to kick over the traces. Accordingly, he compared the skinheads of the 1990s with the terrorists of twenty years earlier despite the different social and educational backgounds (most members of the Baader–Meinhof Group and Red Army Faction were from the middle classes and were well educated) and the different political standpoints.[7] The blame for the violence that had accompanied unification he laid at the door of an intellectual climate that had scorned all manifestations of national feelings. Consequently, nobody was willing to enter into dialogue with those he called 'Skinhead-Buben' (skinhead lads) (Walser 1994a: 141). Others singled out for criticism include, as with Strauß, the media, along with captains of industry, who, driven by the demands of profit, brought so many foreigners into the Federal Republic. This argument is reminiscent of the populist anti-capitalism of the extreme Right, even if at the end of the essay Walser lends his support to initiatives seeking to encourage greater racial integration. Indeed, Walser is willing to blame almost everybody but the perpetrators of violence themselves. Clearly there will be arguments about how to deal with such offenders; what is puzzling about Walser's argument is that, on the one hand, he sees nationalism as a kind of costume donned by young people for show and at the same time nations as the driving force in history and the source of unchanging emotional attachment, something he accuses intellectuals of overlooking in their search for a European identity.

The sense of the primacy of national feelings has not only been expressed by Walser. Around the time of unification the journalist and critic Karl Heinz Bohrer launched a blistering attack on provincialism, by which he meant not simply an unwillingness to see beyond the parish pump but also the pseudo-internationalism of large sections of German society. Thus, for Bohrer, the Germans who frequently travel abroad are not indulging in any mind-expanding activity but 'abandoning the specifically political sphere in favour of an undifferentiated iridescent world bounded by the baguette and bathing in the Mediterranean' (Bohrer 1990: 1101). What Bohrer means by the political sphere includes, as it does with Walser, a sense of nationhood and history, something he claims most contemporary German politicians seek to ignore, preferring to reduce politics to less momentous issues such as the environment. In fact, Bohrer, as editor of the magazine *Merkur*, devoted a whole series of articles to the topic of provincialism in 1990 and 1991. What his strictures amount to, once the point is disregarded that 'provincialism' is an easy insult in the context of the Federal Republic that has lacked a single centre like London or Paris, is a demand for a new kind of political culture, one that has been repeated elsewhere. Before these other manifestations are discussed, it could be pointed out that what might seem the apotheosis of provincialism, Chancellor Kohl inviting prominent guests, as he did with President Clinton in July 1994, to eat in his family home in the Oggersheim district of Ludwigshafen, has something comforting about it that might dispel any idea that the Federal Republic is somehow getting too big for its boots.

KITSCH, CONCERN AND CORRECTNESS

In 1993 Cora Stephan published a volume entitled *Der Betroffenheitskult* (*The Cult of Concern*). This followed the volume about alleged 'collaboration' between western intellectuals and the GDR which she edited in 1992. Her target in *Der Betroffenheitskult* was what she saw as the typical reaction of many Germans to political developments, namely expressions of emotional concern but few signs of an acceptance of the necessity for hard political decisions. According to Stephan, it is impossible in many areas for matters to be left to the 'personal attempts at understanding by individuals' (Stephan 1993: 72) because the only body able to tackle them is the state. She cites as examples the issues of unification, immigration and the role of the Federal Republic in the world. In essence, she is demanding a return to 'hard politics' in which politicians take responsibility, in keeping with Max Weber's concept of the politician's *Verantwortungsethik* (ethic of responsibility), as opposed to the intellectual's *Gesinnungsethik* (ethic of conviction). It is this latter ethic Stephan sees as having been dominant in the Federal Republic, manifested in a combination for the citizen of 'prosperity and high morality' and for politicians an existence 'between provinciality and Europe – that is to say no man's land' (ibid.: 15). The question that immediately arises is where the new Germany is to be located. Stephan's references to responsibility and also to duty invoke visions of a return to Prussian virtues. Although she speaks of the importance of western political ideals,

201

there is still the danger that she might be throwing out the baby with the bathwater in her demand that a radical break be made with the world of the pre-unification Federal Republic.

Another intellectual to demand decisive action based on clearly delineated policies is Hans Magnus Enzensberger. The ideas he expressed in an article entitled 'Ausblicke auf den Bürgerkrieg' ('Views of civil war'), the third controversial essay published in *Der Spiegel* in 1993 (in the 21 June edition), are expanded in book form in a volume with a slightly amended, but in terms of meaning hardly different, title *Aussichten auf den Bürgerkrieg* (1993). Enzensberger's call for action comes after a survey of the various conflicts in the world lead him to the conclusion that it is impossible to intervene in all cases. He perceives a universal propensity to mindless violence that manifests itself both in civil wars and in urban vandalism, and makes the claim that any tramcar 'can become a Bosnia *en miniature*' (Enzensberger 1993: 30). The appropriate response according to Enzensberger is to intervene where there is a clear breach of international law, as was the case with Saddam Hussein's invasion of Kuwait, or where this is required by geographical proximity, as in the case of former Yugoslavia. Otherwise those whose irresponsible actions are self-destructive, especially in economic terms, are to be left to their own devices. Enzensberger's stance is a move away from the idealistic internationalism that he sees as characterising certain intellectual circles. He claims that those who preach the doctrine of sympathy with every victim of conflict in all parts of the world are likely to provoke the opposite response to the one they seek, because they are unable to offer any solutions. Enzensberger may be more pragmatic than Stephan but both clearly reject policies based on emotionalism.

Another attack on the traditional moralistic approach to political questions in the Federal Republic is found in Bodo Morshäuser's book, *Hauptsache Deutsch* (*German is the Main Point*) (1992). What began as an investigation into manifestations of right-wing extremism develops into a critique of German attitudes to politics in this whole area. Morshäuser's thesis is that no subject in German politics is dealt with 'so ideologically and moralistically self-righteously, so impersonally and abstractly' (Morshäuser 1992: 12) as the legacy of the past, with all shades of opinion seeking to instrumentalise Auschwitz for their own purposes. In particular, he claims that the moralistic approach based on conviction is likely to prove counter-productive in trying to fight a right-wing party such as the Republikaner, since it ignores the concrete concerns of those tempted to vote for such a party. Like Stephan and Enzensberger, Morshäuser is demanding more pragmatism, in this case in an area in which moral considerations have understandably prevailed.

The moralistic stances that have allegedly dominated the approach of intellectuals to politics in the Federal Republic are the target for scorn in a volume that appeared in 1994 entitled *Das Blöken der Lämmer. Die Linke und der Kitsch (The Bleating of the Lambs. The Left and Kitsch)* (Henschel 1994). In this book Gerhard Henschel has compiled examples of what he perceives to be kitsch and subjects them to ridicule. The objects of Henschel's satirical treatment include most of the leading figures of postwar German culture, including Grass, Böll and the leading film-makers Rainer Werner Fassbinder and Wim Wenders. In this context what matters more than the fairness of the examples chosen and the quality of Henschel's humour is the fact that a certain approach to politics is being labelled in this way (although to be fair to Henschel he does differentiate between the pragmatic left-wing policies of trade unions and the symbolic actions of intellectuals). A similar label is that of 'political correctness' which has been levelled at those who criticise the kind of political thinking that has been discussed in this chapter.

The term had already entered political discourse in the Federal Republic when Martin Walser launched his attack on 'rituals of permissibility and political correctness tests' in the 7 November 1994 edition of *Der Spiegel* (Walser 1994b: 138). He refers to attacks on his own political writing and the campaign that led to the withdrawal of Steffen Heitmann, Chancellor Kohl's original choice, from his candidacy for the post of Federal presidency after he was criticised for his views on the German past and the role of women. As in his essay 'Deutsche Sorgen' (ibid. 1994b: 130–50), Walser is critical of the media for their unwillingness to accept a variety of views, a stance that is comparable to Botho Strauß's attacks on 'Mainstream' referred to on p. 198. What is remarkable is that these criticisms do not distinguish between different sections of the media. They also overlook the point that they invariably appear in the organs they condemn. In fact, generalisations that condemn all sections of the media and label opponents 'politically correct' or, from the other end of the political spectrum, 'fascist' if they are not left-wing, do not serve much purpose. In the case of Walser, his strictures on his opponents reveal a desire to cast himself as the victim of powerful forces, when his prominence grants him a platform not available to many other citizens.

CONCLUSION

The first question that has to be asked is whether the tone of the debates discussed above means that a new right-wing hegemony in the intellectual world has been established in the Federal Republic in place of the proclaimed dominance of left-wing ideas established in the 1960s. Inasmuch as this chapter has considered debates, then this is clearly not the case, as a debate such as that over the morality of the Gulf War by definition has two sides. Moreover, those intellectuals associated with the pre-unification Federal Republic have not fallen silent, as the example of Günter Grass shows. His *Rede vom Verlust* (*Speech about Loss*) which was originally a lecture held in Munich in November 1992 and was reprinted three times in book form by the end of the year shows that his willingness to enter the political fray has not decreased, and that there was not a lack of public interest in his point of view (Grass 1992). Moreover, the speech is vintage Grass, in the positive sense that it does not mince words and in the negative sense that rhetoric often takes over from political substance. Nevertheless, the title suggests that Grass and his like are on the defensive; the losses he feels include the atmosphere of democratic debate that existed in the Brandt era and the opportunities for reform offered by unification. Another regret expressed by Grass is that large parts of the press have swung to the right, a view at odds with that of Walser.

Grass was again the centre of controversy in 1995 when he published his novel *Ein weites Feld* (*A Wide Field*). The title is a reference to the nineteenth-century novelist Theodor Fontane and the main character is a GDR Fontane devotee born exactly a century after his idol and nicknamed Fonty. Through his character Grass repeats the criticisms of the process of German unification previously expressed in essay form and referred to on p. 195. Such was the negative reaction of the reviewer chosen by *Der Spiegel*, Marcel Reich-Ranicki, that the magazine elected to make his comments the cover story of the 21 August 1995 edition and portray the critic on the cover ripping apart a copy of the book (something which led Grass to forbid the publication of an interview, as he objected to the visual presentation of such a barbaric act as the destruction of a book). Reich-Ranicki's objections to the novel were twofold: on the aesthetic level, he castigated Grass for submerging his own style by imitating Fontane, while in terms of content he severely criticised Grass for painting too positive a picture of the GDR. Similar criticisms were found in *Die Zeit* which devoted three articles to the novel. All found the novel a failure. Nevertheless, Gunter Hofmann, in a front-page article in the 25 August edition, praised Grass's contribution as an intellectual to the development of the Federal Republic. By contrast, in the 1 September edition Helga Hirsch, in an article entitled 'Das Boot ist leer', dismissed Grass and those who think like him as 'conservative left-wingers' who have not realised that the new Germany is far from being aggressively nationalist (*Die Zeit* 36, 1995: 55).

In the light of the kinds of disputes discussed in this chapter, which might be said to reflect nothing more than the prejudices of the people making their various claims, the important question is whether the opinions expressed should be taken seriously. There are good reasons for doing so, in addition to the general points made in the Introduction. The issues that have been raised in this chapter relate closely to those that dominated Part Two of this book, specifically the need for a new kind of politics, both domestically and in foreign affairs, after unification. In general terms, it is reasonable to speak of two groups of intellectuals: those who wish to preserve the ethos of the pre-unification Federal Republic and those who see change as necessary. Although it would be wrong to see the second group as invariably nationalistic, it is as well to remember that the democratic development of the old Federal Republic was in many respects exemplary. Furthermore, despite claims that German intellectuals forfeited their status through their failure to predict and appreciate unification, their voice still counts in political debate. How else is it possible to explain that the leading article in the 7 October 1994 edition of the prestigious weekly newspaper *Die Zeit*, that is to say immediately before the federal election, was concerned with this area of political debate, with the editor Robert Leicht championing the values of liberal democracy against those of Botho Strauß, whose ideas he saw as a continuation of an undemocratic German tradition of political romanticism? Finally, if intellectual debate is seen as a kind of seismograph of the condition of a country and its struggle for identity, the heated disputes of recent years suggest that much remains in flux in the Federal Republic.

CONCLUSION

A snapshot picture of the Federal Republic taken five years after unification would have confirmed most of the positive findings contained in this book. Indeed, some of these findings might have appeared slightly over-cautious. In October 1995, the governing coalition of CDU/CSU and FDP looked much stronger than might have been expected on the basis of the election results a year earlier, and consequently fears about the continuing governability of the country seemed less pressing. Although the continuing weakness of the FDP was undeniable, Chancellor Kohl remained largely unchallenged both at home and abroad. At home, his position was strengthened by the weakness of the major opposition party, the SPD, whose internecine strife appeared to have destroyed any hope of a rapid change of government. This was confirmed on 22 October 1995 by the results of the *Land* election in Berlin. Although the CDU lost votes, its share falling from 40.4 to 37.4 per cent, this was to be expected as the previous 1990 election had coincided with unification euphoria. It paled into insignificance alongside the disastrous showing of the SPD. Its share of the vote dropped from 30.4 to 23.6 per cent in the city in whose western part it had once attained around 60 per cent in the days of Willy Brandt and his predecessor Ernst Reuter. Such a result suggested there was little to fear from the domestic opposition. Abroad, Chancellor Kohl was undeniably the leading European politician, not least given the uncertain start of the Chirac presidency in France.

Whereas little happened in the following months to change the Federal Republic's status abroad – it could even be said to have been enhanced by the decision of December 1995 to shoulder more responsibility in former Yugoslavia and by the willingness of the Israeli president Ezer Weizman to undertake a state visit

207

in January 1996 – the domestic scene seemed less secure. In November 1995, the SPD chose to discard its increasingly hapless leader Rudolf Scharping in favour of Oskar Lafontaine who promised more vigorous opposition. Around the same time the FDP began to look even more vulnerable. The resignation of the Justice Minister Sabine Leutheusser-Schnarrenberger, a member of the party's more liberal wing, following the result of an internal party ballot, which endorsed the CDU/CSU's plans to introduce surveillance methods, in particular electronic listening devices, in the fight against organised crime, confirmed the impression of disarray. The spectre of further failure at the polls in the three *Land* elections of March 1996 brought speculation about an end to the ruling coalition in Bonn and talk of new elections. In the event, the FDP reversed its series of poor results, clearing the 5 per cent hurdle in all three states, while the SPD, despite its change of leadership, continued to lose votes. Nevertheless, as the continuing success of the *Republikaner* in Baden-Württemberg showed, a sense of malaise persisted.

An underlying reason for this political malaise was a change in the economic outlook. The early part of 1995 had brought renewed economic growth: 2.6 per cent overall during the first six months. However, this began to fade in the second part of the year with exports hit by the rise in value of the D-Mark. Growth estimates for the whole year were reduced to under 2 per cent with forecasts for 1996 speaking of only 1 per cent growth. What must be emphasised despite all the despondent comment of early 1996 is that nobody is speaking about economic collapse or a threat to democratic stability. Despite the worries about costs and taxation, it is as well to retain a sense of proportion. OECD figures comparing the percentage of economic performance that goes to taxes and social expenditure in various countries disprove any notion that the German economy is uniquely beset by such burdens, if that is the correct way to describe such costs. The organisation's figures for 1994 suggest that the amount in Germany is 39.2 per cent, higher than in Great Britain (34.1 per cent), but well below France's 44.2 per cent, the Netherlands' 47 per cent and Sweden's 53.3 per cent. Although cuts announced in 1996 have provoked anger and strikes, the situation is not comparable to France in late 1995.

Equally importantly, the situation in the former GDR has improved. The rate of growth in the eastern states reached 9.2 per cent in 1994, before it began to plummet in 1995. Moreover, because these states now export more to other countries than they import, it can no longer be claimed that all the progress is due to western subsidies. In the area of society, although it would be premature to speak of an end to the tensions between east and west, the '*Mauer im Kopf*' (the wall in the head) so frequently referred to, there is nevertheless evidence that the developments of the last five or six years have been generally welcomed. Material published by the Federal Press Office in August 1995 in connection with the approaching fifth anniversary of unity contained the following information. Gross wages in the east had risen from 35 per cent of western levels in 1990 to 74 per cent in 1995, pensions from 40 to 79 per cent. Moreover, polls taken in 1994 showed that 71 per cent of former GDR citizens felt that they enjoyed more freedom than before, 78.8 per cent were in favour of a market economy, while a later poll in March 1995 found that 57 per cent felt they were better off. What is more, a poll taken in June 1995 found that 51 per cent believed that their expectations of unity had been fulfilled, in contrast to the March 1991 figure of 36 per cent. Clearly, some dissatisfaction remains, but the development is in the right direction as far as the internal cohesion of the Federal Republic is concerned. Equally significant and unreservedly gratifying is an August 1995 poll of 16 to 29 year olds in the former GDR that showed that 89 per cent approved of democracy.

The fifth anniversary of unity also brought a statement from Foreign Minister Klaus Kinkel. This concluded with the promise that the Federal Republic would continue to be a reliable and responsible partner. Although it is possible to reply that any other kind of claim would be inconceivable, there remains little, if anything, in current foreign policy to arouse contrary suspicions. In his statement Kinkel spoke of the 'harmonious embedding' ('*harmonische Einbettung*') of Germany within Europe. It would be sad if potential European partners were not to take the opportunities this situation offers, especially if the consequences of a 'non-embedded' Germany earlier in the century are remembered.

The Introduction to this book spoke of a positive framework existing for the development of post-unification Germany. Given all the points mentioned above, it would be extremely difficult not to admit that what has been achieved so far bodes well for the future. This was the view reached by Professor Peter Pulzer in a 1994 survey of contemporary Germany in the magazine *German Politics*. He concluded the synopsis of his article by stating that 'the factors making for stability remain strong, as the experience of managing a democratic market economy continues to provide grounds for loyalty to, and confidence in, the first true nation state in German history' (Pulzer 1994: 1). Pulzer's article is entitled 'Unified Germany: a normal state?' Whilst such a title begs the question of what normality might consist of, it shows an awareness of the difficulties that have beset the development of Germany. Indeed, the article refers to the problem of identity that is the subject of the third part of this volume. The difficulty in coming to any assessment of contemporary Germany lies in weighing these less tangible factors against the concrete achievements referred to so far in these concluding comments.

What cannot be denied is that the shadow of history will remain. The various anniversaries of 1995 were, even if any of the participants might wish it, not the end of an historical episode. The impossibility of sending German combat troops to former Yugoslavia is just one proof of this. How the past continues to play a role at a different level was illustrated again in the summer of 1995 by the dispute over the planned Holocaust memorial in Berlin. Whereas the campaign led by the journalist Lea Rosh brought a widespread acceptance of the necessity for such a memorial, controversy surrounded its nature and its location. The original plan for a massive stone bearing the names of victims seems unlikely to be realised, while the less than entirely central location displeases those who wish the Holocaust to remain in the forefront of public consciousness. Generally, there is no shortage of individuals or institutions willing to draw attention to the significance of the past. One typical example is the statement issued by the central Lutheran Church organisation, the Evangelische Kirche in Deutschland (EKD), to mark the fifth anniversary of unification. It spoke of the need to secure liberty and justice after the experience of two dictatorships in Germany.

Another factor that implies that the post-1990 Federal Republic remains unsettled is the kind of debate that was discussed in Chapter 9. Here concern must centre primarily on the demands for a new kind of politics, specifically the nationalistic demands that manifest themselves most markedly in the cries for a 'self-confident nation' ('die selbstbewußte Nation'). This was the title given to a collection of essays published in 1994 that included and built on Strauß's 'Anschwellender Bocksgesang' (Schwilk and Schacht 1994). Happily, it would appear that at present few would wish to follow these cries if they mean a return to nationalistic attitudes. In fact, a different, and more welcome, display of self-confidence occurred in Berlin in the summer of 1995 with the reaction to the covering of the *Reichstag* building by the husband and wife team of artists known as Christo, who specialise in such activities. Whereas Chancellor Kohl fumed against the misuse of a national symbol, the public flocked to see something that was aesthetically pleasing and afforded the chance of communal enjoyment. The city of Berlin was happy to be the centre of a positive world attention for a while. Credit is also due to the majority in the *Bundestag* who agreed to the project.

Despite such rebuttals, demands for more nationalistic stances remain potentially dangerous. If certain attitudes become respectable, this only helps extremists. Even if violent thugs do not read the writings of rightist intellectuals, the general climate of opinion does influence them. It is no coincidence that the worst incidents of anti-foreigner violence coincided with the debate over asylum seekers. Accordingly, both politicians and intellectuals carry a responsibility not to encourage the growth of extremism. Specifically, politicians must cool to end the uncertainties surrounding the issue of German nationality. It is to be hoped that recent suggestions that the CDU/CSU will soon be prepared to face this question are true. At least, its coalition partner, the FDP, is being true to its liberal principles by demanding a relaxation of present legislation.

A second concern in this area is the way that, as some of the examples in Chapters 8 and 9 show, intellectual debate in Germany often seems to lapse into the adoption of extreme uncompromising stances. In certain cases, debate does not even take place, with many former dissidents from the GDR still frequently refusing to share platforms with those they blame for their experiences. This tendency was criticised by Ulrich Greiner in the 13 October 1995 edition of *Die Zeit*. He referred specifically to the reaction to Grass's novel *Ein weites Feld*, and to criticisms of the award of a major literary prize, the *Friedenspreis des Deutschen Buchhandels* (the peace prize of the German book industry), in 1995 to Annemarie Schimmel, an orientalist who in the eyes of her many critics has shown too much sympathy to those who pronounced the death sentence on Salman Rushdie. Whereas Greiner accepted the necessity of democratic debate – the article was entitled 'Streit muß sein' ('Conflict is necessary') – he criticised the continuing

211

CONCLUSION

tendency, highlighted by Bodo Morshäuser in *Hauptsache Deutsch* (1992), for those criticised to see themselves as victims of some kind of quasi-totalitarian conspiracy (Greiner 1995: 1).

That the attitudes of certain intellectuals are reflected in other areas of society was illustrated in the behaviour of CDU/CSU members of parliament during the first meeting of the *Bundestag* following the 1994 election. In accordance with tradition, it fell to the oldest member, in this case Stefan Heym, to open the parliamentary session. As Heym had been elected as a PDS candidate (he was not in fact a member of the party), this was anathema to the CDU/CSU. After an attempt to prevent his opening speech on the grounds of alleged Stasi links, CDU/CSU parliamentarians sat poker-faced during his largely uncontroversial speech, thus making no allowances for his having been persecuted by the Nazis for both racial and political reasons and for his treatment at the hands of the SED. Such reprehensible conduct shows an unwillingness both to face the past and adopt democratic standards in the present.

A key concept in this connection is that of reconciliation, both within Germany, not least across the divide between the two former states, and between Germany and other states. In Heinrich Böll's 1959 novel, *Billard um halbzehn* (*Billiards at Half-Past Nine*), both Heinrich Fähmel, its builder, and his son Robert, who organised its destruction in the last days of the Second World War, refused to take part in the ceremony, attended by leading figures from politics and society, to rededicate an abbey. This is because they are not reconciled with the forces that were responsible for German nationalism and still appear to hold sway in the Federal Republic. The same forces have also had a devastating effect on their own lives. There seems little doubt that these two fictional characters reflect Böll's own view at the time. It would also be hard to claim that Böll himself was ever fully reconciled with many aspects of the society of the Federal Republic before his death in 1985, although he was increasingly committed as a citizen to changing it. To some extent his individual development mirrored that of other intellectuals, who, as described in Chapter 2, increasingly identified with the West German state. Today, there are clearly those who are wary of unified Germany, not least Günter Grass. However, as suggested in Chapter 9, concern today centres on the preservation of the ethos of the pre-unification Federal Republic; it is not a case of total rejection of a whole state. As for

212

the relationship with other countries, the question of reconciliation was naturally to the fore in all the commemorations that took place in 1995. On his visit to the former concentration camp of Bergen–Belsen, President Weizmann of Israel openly stated that he could not offer any kind of blanket forgiveness for the past. Clearly the relationship with Israel remains the most difficult one for the Federal Republic and Israeli reservations remain understandable. In the case of Germany's western partners, any similar reservations are more problematical. The Federal Republic has generally proved to be a reliable and trustworthy ally, while the westernisation of Germany and the accompanying abandonment of traditional anti-democratic attitudes is something to be welcomed as a major historical change.

Nevertheless developments in Germany frequently continue to be viewed both within the country and outside with an intense suspicion that goes beyond the eternal vigilance that the proverb sees as the price of liberty. Even if it cannot be credibly claimed that unification has brought an upsurge of nationalism, critics still find pretexts for concern. The Germans are still frequently characterised as a nation driven by impractical concerns or beset by what is perceived as the most German of all emotions, *Angst*. In the 25 September 1995 edition of *Der Spiegel*, for example, Henryk M. Broder, a commentator renowned for his trenchant observations, spoke of the anxieties of the Germans expressing themselves in a 'tendency to moralistic megalomania', as reflected in environmental concerns and pacifistic campaigns (Broder 1995: 35). Broder attributes this to continuing amazement that the nation was not punished more severely in 1945. Despite the importance of the past, one should beware of such generalisations. How is, for example, the virulence of the 1995 protests in Scandinavian countries against French nuclear testing, which at least matches the strength of feeling in Germany, to be explained given the lack of a common past? It could be that the Federal Republic, admittedly partly influenced by the past, is moving towards the Scandinavian model of democracy and is set to enjoy a prolonged period of similar peaceful prosperity.

Such speculation is, however, ultimately pointless, for the banal reason that the future cannot be predicted. Equally dubious is speculation about 'the Germans'. In considering Germany and the Germans, the watchword should be the biblical commandment used by the Swiss writer Max Frisch in connection with his play

213

Andorra: 'Du sollst Dir kein Bildnis machen' ('Thou shalt not make unto thee any graven image') (1961). What the observer of German affairs can do, rather than make pretentious pronouncements, is to try to bring critical understanding and open-mindedness to bear on the subject. On this basis the conclusion has to be that the Federal Republic of Germany some five years after unity remains a success, not just because of its economic prowess and political stability but because of the commitment of so many to ideals and values that are the opposite of those frequently promulgated to such devastating effect in the past.

GLOSSARY

Aktiengesellschaft (AG) Share company. This is one of the commonest forms of company organisation in Germany.

Allianz für Deutschland Alliance for Germany. The three-party coalition led by the CDU (see p. 216) that successfully contested the GDR election on 18 March 1990. It was of no significance thereafter. Of the other parties, the Demokratischer Aufbruch (Democratic Renewal) merged with the CDU and the Deutsche Soziale Union (German Social Union) faded from prominence.

Arbeitsbeschaffungsmaßnahme (ADM) Job creation measure. Such measures have become more frequent with increasing unemployment, particularly in the ex-GDR.

Asylant Asylum seeker. A pejorative term for people seeking political asylum in the Federal Republic on the basis of Article 16 of the *Grundgesetz* (see p. 217).

Ausländerbeauftragter Commissioner for foreigners. A person appointed by the authorities in the Federal Republic to look after the interests of non-Germans, particularly foreign workers.

Aussiedler Immigrant of ethnic German origin. This group of people, previously resident mainly in Poland, Romania and the former Soviet Union, has an automatic right of entry to the Federal Republic.

Bayernpartei Bavaria Party. A Bavarian nationalist party that had some success in the early postwar years but is of no significance today.

Beamter Public servant. A person employed by a public body and enjoying privileges because of this status, for instance, job security. This group is much larger than in comparable countries and includes most teachers and, traditionally, post and rail workers.

Bund der Heimatvertriebenen und Entrechteten (BHE) Federation of expellees and victims of injustice. This political party was

215

formed in 1950 to represent Germans who lost their homes due to postwar frontier changes. It enjoyed some parliamentary success in the early 1950s.

Bundeskanzler Federal Chancellor. As head of government, he must be endorsed by a parliamentary majority.

Bundespräsident Federal President. The head of state whose duties are largely ceremonial.

Bundesrat Federal Council. As the upper house of parliament, it consists of representatives of the state (*Land*) governments, which, as part of the federal system, have the right to influence legislation, particularly that affecting their interests.

Bundesrepublik Deutschland Federal Republic of Germany. The official name of the west German state after 1949, which has been retained in post-unification Germany.

Bundestag Federal Assembly. The lower house of parliament, which is elected by universal adult suffrage and is the major legislative assembly. Its nominal membership is 656, but may be supplemented by *Überhangmandate* (see p. 220).

Bundesverfassungsgericht Federal Constitutional Court. This body acts to safeguard the constitution. Among other powers, it can proscribe a political party by declaring it unconstitutional. An individual may complain to the court if he/she feels that his/her basic rights are being infringed.

Bundeswehr Federal Defence Forces. The term embraces all branches of the armed forces.

Bündnis 90/Die Grünen Alliance 90/The Greens. The post-unification party formed from a merger of the ex-GDR party founded by active members of the 1980s civil rights groups and the western environmentalist Greens.

Bürgerinitiative (BI) Citizens' Action Group. The term is used for pressure groups made up of ordinary citizens who seek to influence official decision-making. They were particularly prominent in the environmental area in the 1970s.

Christlich-Demokratische Union (CDU) Christian Democratic Union. The major centre right party in the Federal Republic. It was founded in all states (except Bavaria) in the postwar period. Whereas the GDR CDU came under the control of the communist state, the western CDU provided the Federal Chancellor for twenty-eight of the forty-one years the pre-unification Federal Republic existed.

Christlich-Soziale Union (CSU) Christian Social Union. Although this party is often described as the Bavarian wing of the CDU and co-operates with it at federal level, it is a distinct party which is more rightist and populist than its counterpart.

Deutsche Bundesbank German Federal Bank. The powerful German central bank that has its headquarters in Frankfurt.

Deutsche Demokratische Republik (DDR) German Democratic Republic (GDR). The Soviet-sponsored east German state that existed from 1949 to 1990.

Deutsche Kommunistische Partei (DKP) German Communist Party. The western communist party that was allowed to re-form in 1968 following the banning of the KPD (see p. 218). In electoral terms it remained largely insignificant.

Deutsche Mark (DM) Currency introduced in 1948 following postwar inflation and lack of confidence.

Deutsche Partei (DP) German Party. A small right-wing party that provided two ministers as part of a coalition with the CDU/CSU following the 1957 election.

Deutsche Volksunion (DVU) German People's Union. Extreme right-wing party founded by newspaper proprietor Gerhard Frey. It has had some success in state elections in the last decade.

Evangelische Kirche in Deutschland (EKD) The umbrella organisation of the Lutheran churches in Germany. It was formed after the Second World War to cover all of Germany but in 1969 the GDR churches were forced to leave the organisation.

Freie Demokratische Partei (FDP) Free Democratic Party. The postwar (west) German liberal party that has almost invariably been the junior coalition party in both pre- and post-unification governments.

Freie Deutsche Jugend (FDJ) Free German Youth. Communist youth group founded in 1946 that became the only such organisation in the GDR. It was proscribed in the western zones in the 1950s.

Gastarbeiter Guest worker. The euphemistic term used to describe the foreign workers who increasingly settled in the Federal Republic from the late 1950s/early 1960s.

Große Koalition Grand Coalition. Any coalition between the Christian and Social Democrats. Such a coalition existed at federal level between 1966–9.

Grundgesetz Basic Law. The constitution of the Federal Republic.

Grundlagenvertrag Basic Treaty. The treaty agreed between the two German states in 1972.

Gymnasium Grammar school. The most academic of the three major kinds of secondary school.

Hauptschule Secondary school for the least academic pupils.

Industriegewerkschaft (IG) Industrial trade union. The term denotes a union that represents all workers in a specific industry.

Inoffizieller Mitarbeiter (IM) Unofficial associate. The name given to those GDR citizens who were willing to provide information to the Stasi (see p. 220).

Kommunistische Partei Deutschlands (KPD) Communist Party of Germany. The traditional communist party founded in 1918, whose name disappeared in the Soviet Zone after the foundation of the SED (see p. 220). The party was proscribed in the Federal Republic in 1956.

Krankenkasse Health insurance company. These bodies finance health care from the payments of contributors. Higher earners may be members of private *Krankenkassen*, whereas most citizens have to be insured with a public-sector *Kasse*.

Kulturkampf 'Cultural struggle'. The name given to Bismarck's largely unsuccessful anti-Catholic campaign beginning in the 1870s, whose lasting legacy is the compulsory civil marriage ceremony.

Ladenschlußgesetz Shop-closing law. Statute that restricts the opening hours of shops.

Land/Länder Federal state/states. There are currently sixteen: Baden-Württemberg, Bavaria, Berlin, Brandenburg, Bremen, Hamburg, Hessen, Mecklenburg-Vorpommern (Mecklenburg-West Pomerania), Niedersachsen (Lower Saxony), Nordrhein-Westfalen (North Rhine-Westphalia), Rheinland-Pfalz (Rhineland-Palatinate), Saarland, Sachsen, Sachsen-Anhalt, Schleswig-Holstein, Thüringen (Thuringia).

Landtag State parliament. The term is not used in city states.

Liberal-Demokratische Partei Deutschlands (LDPD) Liberal Democratic Party of Germany. Founded in the Soviet Zone in 1945 and one of the GDR 'satellite' parties. At the time of unification it merged with the FDP.

Ministerpräsident Prime minister. The head of a *Land* government. The title does not exist in city states.

Ministerrat Council of Ministers. The government of the GDR, which invariably carried out the policy of the SED (see p. 220).

Mitbestimmung Co-determination. A system whereby employees have a voice in the running of their company.

218

National-Demokratische Partei Deutschlands (NDPD) National Democratic Party of Germany. Political party subservient to the SED founded in the Soviet Zone in 1948 to integrate ex-members of the German military and low-level members of the Nazi Party. At the time of unification it merged with the FDP.

Nationaldemokratische Partei Deutschlands (NPD) National Democratic Party of Germany. Extreme right-wing party that enjoyed some electoral success in the 1960s in the Federal Republic.

Nationale Volksarmee (NVA) National People's Army. The armed forces of the GDR officially founded in 1956.

Ostpolitik Eastern policy. The term can apply to Germany's policy to its eastern neighbours at any time but in this volume is used in connection with the policy of *détente* towards the communist countries adopted by the Federal Republic after 1969.

Partei des Demokratischen Sozialismus (PDS) Party of Democratic Socialism. Successor to the SED (see p. 220), which adopted the new name in December 1989.

Pflegeversicherung Care insurance. A compulsory insurance introduced in 1995 against the risk of needing care in old age.

Politikverdrossenheit Disenchantment with politics. A concept that entered political debate in the 1990s.

Realschule Secondary technical school. The second level of the tripartite system of secondary education, the other parts of which are the *Gymnasium* and the *Hauptschule* (see p. 218).

Rechtsstaat Constitutional state. The term implies a state based on the rule of law.

Reichskristallnacht Night of crystal. Ironic term coined at the time to denote the anti-Jewish pogrom of 9 November 1938 that followed an assassination attempt against a German diplomat in Paris by a young Jew.

Reichstag Parliamentary building in Berlin built following the creation of the 1871 German state. It was also the name of the lower house of parliament post 1871. Historically it had the meaning of 'diet', as in the Diet of Worms (*Reichstag zu Worms*).

Republikaner Republicans. Right-wing party established in the 1980s, whose electoral success in West Berlin in 1989 and in the European elections of the same year caused widespread concern.

Rote Armee Fraktion Red Army Faction. The major terrorist group of the 1970s that emerged from the Baader–Meinhof group. It remained active until the 1990s.

GLOSSARY

Sozialdemokratische Partei Deutschlands (SPD) Social Democratic Party of Germany. Europe's oldest socialist/social democratic party that can trace its roots back to 1863. It remains the major centre left party in the Federal Republic.

Soziale Marktwirtschaft Social market economy. The economic order adopted by the new Federal Republic based on market forces and state intervention in certain circumstances.

Sozialhilfe Social welfare benefit. Provides the final safety net within the Federal Republic's social security system.

Sozialistische Einheitspartei Deutschlands (SED) Socialist Unity Party of Germany. The dominant political force in the Soviet Zone/GDR. It was founded in 1946 through the enforced merger of the KPD and SPD (see p. 218).

Sozialistische Reichspartei (SRP) Socialist Reich Party. Small neo-Nazi party banned by the *Bundesverfassungsgericht* (see p. 216) in 1952.

Sozialwohnung Social dwelling. The term denotes a house or flat whose subsidised costs should make it affordable for people on lower incomes.

Staatssicherheitsdienst (Stasi) State Security Service. The all-pervasive security service of the GDR responsible for surveillance at home and espionage abroad.

Stammwähler Loyal voter (of one party). A key term in the analysis of electoral behaviour in the Federal Republic.

Standort Deutschland Germany as an (attractive) industrial location. This term is used in debates about the future of the German economy.

Tarifvertrag Wages and conditions agreement. This term relates to the system of national collective wages and conditions bargaining that covers major industries and public services.

Treuhand Privatisation body (for GDR industry). This body was set up in early 1990 to supervise the disposal of GDR state-owned industry.

Überhangmandat Supplementary parliamentary seat. These seats increase the size of the *Bundestag* and are a result of the two-vote system that operates at federal elections. This system is explained more fully in note 1 of Chapter 2.

Verband deutscher Schriftsteller (VS) Writers' Union (in the Federal Republic). This body was established in 1969 to represent the interests of writers. It is now subsumed within the IG Medien (see p. 218).

GLOSSARY

Volkskammer People's Chamber. The largely (at least until 1989–90) powerless parliament of the GDR.

Volkspolizei People's Police. The police force of the GDR. Prior to the official establishment of the NVA (see p. 219) army units were described as the *kasernierte Volkspolizei* (the People's Police in barracks).

Zentrum Centre Party. Largely Catholic party created at the time of the *Kulturkampf* (see p. 218). Was refounded after the Second World War but found itself superseded by the CDU/CSU (see p. 216).

NOTES

INTRODUCTION

1 That German unity was not achieved until 1871 underlines the historical and cultural divisions that have always existed within Germany. In particular, the history of the country was influenced by religious division. Following the Reformation, the principle of *cuius regio, eius religio*, which meant that the inhabitants of an area had to accept the religion of their ruler, led to major strife, culminating in the Thirty Years' War of 1618–48. The end of that war led to greater religious tolerance and allowed Protestants and Catholics to live together more harmoniously so that today there are no sectarian conflicts in Germany of the kind that exist in Ireland. Nevertheless, many areas retain their own cultural identity based on religion. Two notable examples are the traditionally Catholic areas of Bavaria and the Rhineland. That such traditions continued to have a political dimension could be seen in the nineteenth century when after unity Bismarck unsuccessfully tried to reduce the influence of the Catholic Church (an episode known as the *Kulturkampf*) and after 1945 when the Bavarian parliament voted against acceptance of the constitutional arrangements of the new Federal Republic, as laid down in the *Grundgesetz*, because they were deemed too centralistic. Since the Bavarians agreed to tolerate the new order, their refusal never had practical consequences; at the same time, it reflects the different historical traditions within the Federal Republic.

1 THE GERMAN DEMOCRATIC REPUBLIC: THE STATE THAT FAILED

1 The GDR National Anthem was written by the poet Johannes R. Becher, who was GDR Minister of Culture from 1954 to 1958. It refers to 'Deutschland, einig Vaterland' (Germany, single fatherland). This refrain was taken up by demonstrators in 1989.
2 The expression *Nischengesellschaft* was popularised by Günter Gaus, a former journalist, who became the Federal Republic's first permanent

representative (*ständiger Vertreter*) – a term preferred to ambassador as the Federal Republic never regarded the GDR as a foreign country – in East Berlin. His appointment followed the *Grundlagenvertrag* of 1972 between the two German states which established a form of diplomatic relations between them. His account of his experiences is to be found in his book *Wo Deutschland liegt. Eine Ortsbestimmung* (Gaus 1983).

3 The 'leading role of the working class and its Marxist-Leninist party' (i.e., the SED) was enshrined in Article 1 of the 1968 constitution.

4 Lord Acton's famous dictum is: 'Power tends to corrupt and absolute power corrupts absolutely.'

5 Billion is used throughout this book as meaning a thousand million, i.e., the German word *Milliarde*.

6 Following the publication of this work in the Federal Republic, the Stasi intensified its surveillance of Kunze, which included a spyhole bored from a neighbour's flat into his marital bedroom.

7 One critical moment was the avoidance of violence in Leipzig in October 1989 (see Chronology, p. xvi). It is also conceivable that there could have been some kind of coup by the Stasi which would have led to violence.

8 It should not be thought that former members of the National Socialist Party played no role in the GDR. Several achieved the rank of minister, while the satellite party, the NDPD (Nationaldemokratische Partei Deutschlands), was set up specifically to integrate former Nazis and other nationalists into the new society.

2 THE FEDERAL REPUBLIC OF GERMANY (1949–90): THE STATE THAT SUCCEEDED

1 The electoral system of the Federal Republic at federal level combines a mixture of proportional representation and a 'first-past-the-post' system. Voters have two votes, one for an individual standing as a party representative in a constituency and the second for a party, which has drawn up a list of candidates in each *Land*. Half the members of parliament are elected by constituency majority and half through the list. However, the actual numbers of members elected depends on the second vote. If a party gains 50 per cent of the vote in a particular *Land*, it normally gains 50 per cent of the available seats. First of all, the number of members directly elected through first votes is deducted from the number due to a party; the remainder are made up from the list. Within this system it is possible for a party to win more seats on the basis of first votes than is due to it through the proportional second votes. In that case the size of the *Bundestag* is increased through supplementary seats (*Überhangmandate*). The other major features, the 5 per cent clause and the constituency rule, are explained in the main text.

2 A poll commissioned in 1952 found 27 per cent of the population expressing an interest in politics; by 1977 this figure had risen to 49 per cent and to over 50 per cent by the late 1980s.

3 This point was noted by Gabriel A. Almond and Sidney Verba in their seminal study *The Civic Culture. Political Attitudes and Democracy in Five Nations*. They maintained that political satisfaction in Germany is related to 'the specific performance of the system' (Almond and Verba 1963: 251).

4 This is reflected in the titles of major unions which contain the term IG. Examples are IG Metall (for engineering workers) and IG Chemie (for workers in the chemical industry).

5 This system means that there is no distinction between clearing and merchant banks as in Great Britain. *Universalbanken* can indulge in any banking activity and own shares in companies. Their nominal holding is frequently increased because individual shareholders hand over their voting rights to the bank, a practice that has contributed to debates about banks wielding excessive power.

6 The various factors that play a role in this area can be illustrated by one specific example. In 1992, in a dispute over the distribution of the receipts from Value Added Tax (*Mehrwertsteuer*), the *Bundesrat* representatives of the state of Brandenburg, at that time the only *Land* in the former GDR with an SPD government, sided with the CDU-led states as the eastern states were due to receive a generous settlement. This provided the Federal government with a majority for its plans.

7 The issue of abortion dogged (west) German politics for over twenty years. The plans of the SPD/FDP government in the 1970s for freely available abortion within a fixed time scale (*Fristenlösung*) were blocked by the Constitutional Court. There resulted a system whereby abortion was made possible on medical or social grounds (*Indikationslösung*). Since abortion had been made freely available in the GDR, unification called for a new solution. After various attempts, which fell foul of the Constitutional Court, a compromise was reached in 1995 whereby abortion remains technically illegal but is not punished within the first three months of pregnancy provided that, before any abortion is carried out, the woman undergoes counselling.

If the issue of abortion provides an example of the Court taking a conservative line, other judgements in the 1990s have angered conservatives. Not only has it been ruled that soldiers could legally be described as potential murderers, but also in 1995 that the Bavarian practice of placing a cross in every school classroom was unconstitutional, as it offended against the principle of religious freedom. This latter judgement provoked massive protests, not least among those Bavarian politicians who make a public show of their Christian beliefs.

8 The original phrase attributed to Kaiser Wilhelm II was: 'Ich kenne keine Parteien mehr, ich kenne nur noch Deutsche.'

9 The term *nivellierte Mittelstandsgesellschaft* was coined by the sociologist Helmut Schelsky. Ludwig Erhard also made the claim that the Federal Republic was a new kind of classless society.

10 The view, which was undoubtedly shared by most intellectuals at that time, that German authoritarian traditions still persisted in the Federal Republic, was expressed by Wolfgang Koeppen in the volume *Ich lebe*

in der Bundesrepublik. He perceived in the voice of every *Beamter* the tone of traditional Prusso-German authoritarian arrogance (Koeppen 1961: 34). The two statements by Enzensberger and Koeppen reflect genuine changes over the intervening three decades.

11 When the author Günter Walraff published his book *Ganz unten* (*The Lowest of the Low*) (Wallraff 1985), which described his experiences while living disguised as a Turk, his accounts of exploitation and discrimination provoked a massive discussion about the treatment of foreigners in the Federal Republic.

12 A comprehensively modified version of *Ein schwieriges Vaterland* was published following German unity (Greiffenhagen and Greiffenhagen 1993). Both versions quote the part of Heinemann's speech that inspired the title.

3 THE POLITICAL SYSTEM: STABILITY IN DANGER?

1 At present the Federal President is elected by the Federal Assembly (*Bundesversammlung*), which convenes expressly for this purpose. Its membership is made up half from members of the *Bundestag* and half of representatives of the *Länder.*

2 The CDU/CSU split 154 to 146 in favour of Bonn; in the case of the SPD 126 voted for Bonn, 110 for Berlin. Chancellor Kohl was a strong supporter of Berlin, something that might have encouraged some other members of the CDU to vote for a change of capital.

3 Since unification, nominal Protestants are in a majority, whereas in the pre-unification Federal Republic the split between the denominations was much more even. At the time of unification the GDR Prime Minister Lothar de Maizière noted that Germany had become 'more eastern and more protestant' (*'östlicher und protestantischer'*).

4 The development of Berlin as a capital city is sure to be followed with interest. The architecture of the great number of new buildings planned will, for instance, undoubtedly be scrutinised for any echoes of the over-grandiose, heroic style favoured by the Nazis. This was the case in the summer of 1995 when the plans for the new *Bundeskanzleramt* (Office of the Federal Chancellery) were published. As the building is based on a 'modernist' design, it was reasonably well received by liberal sections of the press.

5 Larger local authorities in the Federal Republic are generally responsible for local public transport and the supply of energy.

6 The best current example of such a CDU politician is Norbert Blüm, the Federal Minister of Labour from 1982 to the present. He originally worked for the Opel car company.

7 The musical metaphor reflects the name that was given post-unification to members of the GDR satellite parties: *Blockflöten.* This word literally means recorder (the musical instrument) but primarily reflects that these parties were part of a bloc that was always subservient to the SED.

8 The legality of the *Überhangmandate* is, at the time of writing, under scrutiny from the Constitutional Court. The Court has a record of insisting that each vote should count equally. This means that each party requires the same number of votes to gain one seat. With the *Überhangmandate* in 1994, the CDU/CSU had one member elected per 66,383 voters, whereas the Greens needed 69,859.

9 In accordance with the principle referred to in note 8 above, the Constitutional Court insisted on separate elections in east and west in 1990. Bündnis 90 gained enough votes in the east to have eight parliamentary seats.

10 In the state of Saxony-Anhalt (Sachsen-Anhalt) the *Land* election of 1994 led to the formation of a minority SPD–Green coalition. This has to rely on support from the PDS. To this extent the PDS has been allowed an influence at *Land* government level. The decision to accept such a coalition laid Rudolf Scharping open to the charge that he was collaborating with communists and may well have contributed to the SPD's defeat at federal level later in the same year.

11 The issue of *Politikverdrossenheit* did surface again to a certain extent in 1995 with low turnouts being recorded at *Land* elections, for instance in North Rhine-Westphalia where only 64 per cent voted in comparison with 71.8 per cent in 1990.

12 The 1995 *Land* elections showed a mixed, although generally negative, picture for the FDP. After crossing the 5 per cent hurdle in Hessen in March, it failed to do so in Bremen and North Rhine-Westphalia in May. These results led to the resignation of Kinkel and his replacement by Wolfgang Gerhardt, who, despite an apparent lack of charisma, could claim success in his home state of Hessen. This change of leadership did not, however, help the party in the Berlin *Land* elections of October 1995 when it once more fell far short of the 5 per cent hurdle.

4 THE GERMAN ECONOMY: THE END OF THE 'MIRACLE'?

1 An example of this policy can be seen in the costs involved in the privatisation of the railway carriage and waggon firm Deutscher Waggonbau (DAG), one of whose works in Halle was the setting for large parts of Christa Wolf's 1963 novel *Der geteilte Himmel*. Before the sale to an American company went ahead in 1995 a subsidy of DM500 million was under discussion.

2 For a wide-ranging review of the whole area of regulation in Germany see Dyson (1992).

3 The *Beschleunigungsgesetz für Infrastrukturvorhaben* (Acceleration law for infrastructure projects) was introduced following German unity with seventeen specific projects relating to unity in mind. Its use has subsequently been extended into the area of the pre-1990 Federal Republic.

4 It should be remembered that *Beamte* consist of more than those

NOTES

working directly for the state in ministries and the like at federal and *Land* level. The privileges of being a *Beamter* include non-contributory pensions and normally a job for life. Another peculiarity is that people in this group are paid according to the size of their family. This is because in law they are not paid but 'sustained' (*alimentiert*) by the state. Traditionally, many workers in the post office and on the railways in the Federal Republic enjoyed this status. The complications involved with commercialisation/privatisation mean that at present the state leases *Beamte* to the Deutsche Bahn AG.

5 The extent to which the *Bundesverfassungsgericht* keeps a keen eye on matters relating to taxation could be seen in 1995 when it also ruled that aspects of wealth tax were unconstitutional.

6 Although it would be wrong to deny the existence of this factor, it can be much exaggerated. What is referred to as 'globalisation' is in fact almost exclusively transfers between industrialised countries. Nevertheless, the German economy is affected internationally by the high costs that arise from a strong currency. It was estimated in 1995, for example, that for every pfennig the dollar slipped below $1 = DM1.60 Daimler-Benz was likely to lose DM30 million profit.

5 GERMAN SOCIETY: THE END OF CONSENSUS?

1 An example of such a joke can only be given in German:

Ostdeutscher: Wie komme ich nach Aldi?
Türke: Zu Aldi!
Ostdeutscher: Was, Aldi ist zu?

2 For a fuller discussion of this issue see Southern (1993).

3 The objections of former GDR citizens are reminiscent of those of many Germans to the postwar Nuremberg trials, which were condemned in some quarters as the victors' justice (*Siegerjustiz*).

4 The Huguenot origins of, for example, the first (and only) freely-elected GDR Prime Minister Lothar de Maizière, who later fell from grace because of his links with the Stasi, are clearly visible in his surname.

5 Previously, emigration from Romania had been made possible through financial transfers from the Federal Republic. The odious Nicolae Ceaușescu is reported to have said that Germans were among the country's most important exports.

6 Such workers lived extremely isolated lives in the GDR, being housed in hostel accommodation and therefore largely separately from the GDR's own population. Official protestations of international solidarity did not count when a practical example was required.

7 This figure relates to cases where there was no automatic right to German citizenship, what are officially termed in a good example of bureaucratic German *Ermessenseinbürgerungen* (discretionary naturalisations). The exact figure for 1992 was 37,042 out of a total of 179,904 cases of naturalisation.

227

8 A major survey carried out by *Der Spiegel* in 1994 suggested that young Germans were not entirely free of nationalistic hubris. Forty-five per cent felt themselves, as Germans, to be superior to some other peoples (*Der Spiegel* 38, 1994: 68).

9 How far people of foreign origins should amend their own patterns of behaviour to ease their integration into German society is a difficult question that goes beyond the scope of this discussion.

10 On becoming unemployed an individual obtains 58 per cent (63 per cent if married, plus 5 per cent per child) of his/her former earnings. This entitlement to *Arbeitslosengeld* (unemployment benefit) can last up to three years depending on the previous period of employment. Thereafter there is entitlement to *Arbeitslosenhilfe* (unemployment aid).

11 Each type of secondary school within the tripartite system that generally operates in the Federal Republic (comprehensive schools are comparatively rare) has its own school leaving certificate. In the case of the *Gymnasium* (grammar school) it is the *Abitur*, for the *Realschule* (technical school) the *mittlere Reife* and in the case of the *Hauptschule* (secondary school), the *Hauptschulabschluß*.

12 The number of women in the *Bundestag* following the 1994 election was 177 out of 672, more than in some comparable countries.

13 A complicated diagram to denote the social structure of the Federal Republic in terms of milieu immediately prior to unification can be found in the volume *Sozialkunde der Bundesrepublik Deutschland* which has appeared in numerous editions from 1965 onwards (Claessens *et al.* 1992: 286).

14 An expert discussion of this topic took place in *Die Zeit* in early 1995 under the title: 'Versagt der Sozialstaat' (*Die Zeit* 2, 1995: 17–18).

In this discussion the rates of *Sozialhilfe*, at the time ranging from DM500 monthly for individuals to DM2,000 for a five-person family, are given. The major question is of course whether this is sufficient.

6 THE NEW GERMANY, EUROPE AND THE WORLD

1 The significance of the notes sent by Stalin in 1952, in which he appeared to offer German unification and free elections, has for a long time been a matter of dispute among historians. The issue is whether they were a genuine offer of negotiations or a ploy to delay the integration of the Federal Republic into the western system of alliances.

2 Massive demonstrations mainly by students against these laws were inspired by the way that Hitler and the Nazis had used the emergency powers that existed under the constitution of the Weimar Republic to assume absolute power in 1933.

3 In 1990, the then Minister for Trade and Industry, Nicholas Ridley, had to resign from the Thatcher government following an article in the magazine *Spectator* which revealed the depths of his anti-German sentiments and contained an unsavoury comparison between Chancellor

Kohl and Hitler. The same year Mrs Thatcher initiated a seminar at Chequers during which experts were to brief her and colleagues about the German 'national character'. What emerged into the public domain suggested that many unfavourable views were expressed.

4 The power attributed to the Bundesbank can be seen from the title David Marsh gave to his book on the institution: *The Bundesbank: The Bank that Rules Europe* (Marsh 1992).

5 For a detailed explanation of these conditions see David Marsh, *Germany and Europe. The Crisis of Unity* (1994: 223f.).

6 It can be argued that high interest rates in the Federal Republic depressed demand at home and obliged companies to seek markets abroad, while the same high interest rates also served to deter imports. However, interest rates would have been irrelevant if German industry had not produced goods for which there was a demand throughout Europe and the wider world.

7 The exact words used by de Gaulle in the French National Assembly on 13 June 1963 were 'Les traités sont comme les roses et les jeunes filles – ils ont leurs temps.'

8 A strain was also put on relations in 1985 when Chancellor Kohl invited Ronald Reagan to visit a military cemetery in Bitburg in which a number of SS men were buried. Although this was not a matter of political substance in that no policy issue was involved, the symbolic significance the affair acquired showed the importance of such a dimension in an era of blanket television coverage.

9 Walter Hallstein (1901–82) was a minister in the Ministry of Foreign Affairs prior to becoming President of the European Commission from 1958 to 1967. He was a member of the CDU.

10 The major bone of contention was the renewal of the arms race between the two superpowers in the area of short- and medium-range nuclear missiles. The issue dated back to the days of the SPD-led government, Chancellor Schmidt claiming Soviet superiority in this range of weapons in a speech to the Institute for Strategic Studies in 1977. NATO responded with the 'dual-track' decision. The first track was negotiation; if this failed the second track, the deployment of missiles on the western side, was to be followed. The failure of negotiation and the eventual deployment of missiles led to mass demonstrations in the Federal Republic, particularly in 1983 and 1984.

11 Following his resignation as Federal Chancellor, Brandt chaired a commission on Third World Development whose findings became known as the Brandt Report.

12 Aid from the GDR also had a dubious dimension. The Stasi was involved, for example, in training the secret police of the leftist Mengistu regime in Ethiopia.

13 The phrase that provoked most discussion was 'die Gnade der späten Geburt' (the grace of late birth) by which Kohl referred to his being too young to have been actively involved in the deeds of the Nazis. (He was born in 1930.) Although some found this a felicitous phrase, others inferred that what was meant was that his generation did not have to bear the legacy of what had been done to the Jews.

14 When German involvement in a Libyan project that, it was claimed, was designed to make possible the production of poison gas for eventual use against Israel came to light early in 1991 an American commentator, William Safire, spoke of 'Auschwitz in the desert'.

15 The specially trained unit GSG-9 that ended the hijacking of a Lufthansa flight in Mogadishu in 1977 when the hijackers sought the release of imprisoned Baader–Meinhof/Red Army Faction terrorists was part of the frontier police (*Bundesgrenzgeschutz*) and under the control of the Ministry of the Interior. Accordingly, it is, strictly speaking, inaccurate to see this as a military operation.

7 COMING TO TERMS WITH THE PAST

1 The title King of Prussia was bestowed on Frederick I at the beginning of the eighteenth century. Unlike Brandenburg, East Prussia, which was under the rule of Brandenburg, lay outside the domain of the Holy Roman Empire, no part of which could be ruled by a king. Accordingly, the title King of Prussia was possible, but King of Brandenburg was not.

2 The *Frankfurter Allgemeine Zeitung* (13 April 1995: 33) reported, for example, on the fiftieth anniversary of the liberation of Vienna on how on the 8 April 1945 three officers who had tried to arrange a cease-fire with the advancing Soviet troops were hanged with a placard, 'I negotiated with the Bolsheviks', around their necks.

3 This was reflected in a series of articles in the weekly newspaper *Die Zeit* in early 1985 which dealt with such topics under headings that included 'resistance', 'camps', 'dictatorship', 'expulsion'.

4 The exhibition 'Vernichtungskrieg. Verbrechen der Wehrmacht 1941–1944' ('War of Destruction. Crimes of the Wehrmacht') opened in Hamburg in March 1995 before moving to Berlin, Potsdam and Vienna. A discussion of the issues and a bibliography appeared in the 3 March 1995 edition of *Die Zeit* (10, 1995: 16–20).

5 That this episode remains relatively unknown is suggested by the explanation of the background Rolf Hochhuth gave when referring to it in a 1990 speech about Germany (Keller 1990–1: vol. 1, 57).

6 Denazification tribunals divided those involved into various categories: *Hauptschuldige, Belastete, Minderbelastete, Mitläufer, Entlastete* (major offenders, offenders, lesser offenders, followers, non-offenders).

7 A brief summary of the debate can be found in *Die zweite Schuld* (Giordano 1990: 342ff.). A book devoted to the topic is entitled simply *Historikerstreit* (1995). The large number of editions shows the attention the dispute received.

8 Although Strauß denied ever having said this, it is a frequently quoted statement, which in any case sums up the sentiments of certain rightist groups in the Federal Republic. The reluctance of Strauß to test his claim in the courts also speaks volumes.

8 CONCEPTIONS OF GERMANY AND THE GERMANS

1 The references to lemons and to 'Goldorangen' invoke Goethe's poem 'Mignon I' that celebrates Italy.

2 In this story Wolf is a GDR spy not out of ideological conviction but because of his belief in German unity and his sense that the GDR is disadvantaged by division. His efforts to help the GDR are, however, totally useless, because his existence is known to the intelligence services of the Federal Republic, who make sure he only provides disinformation.

3 These lectures were published in five volumes under the title *Nachdenken über Deutschland* (Keller 1990–1).

4 On 26 April 1995 the *Guardian* (G2: 3) republished the following comment with the date-line 26 April 1945 under the headline 'Germans docile in defeat': 'The Nazi hold on the people is revealed to be of the lightest.' This report from 1945 also contains the comment, interesting in the light of the debate in 1995 discussed on pp. 152–4, 'For many, no doubt, occupation amounts to liberation.'

9 THE INTELLECTUAL CLIMATE SINCE UNIFICATION

1 The *Literaturstreit* can be followed in detail in two volumes which cover more or less the same ground (Anz 1991; Deiritz and Krauss 1991).

2 Both authors have published documentation that shows the surveillance to which they were subjected (Kunze 1990; Loest 1991).

3 The volume edited by Hermann Vinke, *Akteneinsicht Christa Wolf* (*A view of the Christa Wolf Files*), documents Christa Wolf's involvement with the Stasi, both the period of co-operation and the much longer period when she was herself under surveillance (Vinke 1993).

4 Heym's parliamentary career ended in September 1995 in protest against the plans to ensure automatic increases in parliamentary salaries through a change in the *Grundgesetz*. Despite his own party's opposition, he claimed he could not continue because of the poverty being experienced by other fellow citizens.

5 The workings of GDR censorship of literature were the subject of a post-unification exhibition, which also gave rise to a most interesting book (Wichner and Wiesner 1991).

6 Glotz's comments form part of a documentation of reactions to Strauß's essay which, along with the original text, were published in the review of developments in German literary life, *Deutsche Literatur 1993*, part of a series that appears annually (Görtz et al. 1994: 273–314).

7 In the light of the parallel Walser draws between the two groups of 'rebels', it becomes easier to understand why, despite his apparent

NOTES

move to the right, he was prominent in the campaign of the early 1990s for an amnesty for Red Army Faction members held in prison. In fact, it is very difficult to pin any label on Walser, as he also condemned the Gulf War.

BIBLIOGRAPHY

Allemann, Fritz René (1956) *Bonn ist nicht Weimar*, Cologne: Kiepenheuer and Witsch.

Almond, Gabriel A. and Verba, Sidney (1963) *The Civic Culture. Political Attitudes and Democracy in Five Nations*, Princeton: Princeton University Press.

Andersch, Alfred (1977) *Winterspelt*, Zurich: Diogenes.

Anz, Thomas (ed.) (1991) *'Es geht nicht um Christa Wolf'. Der Literaturstreit im vereinten Deutschland*, Munich: edition spangenberg.

Arnim, Hans Herbert von (1991) *Die Partei, der Abgeordnete und das Geld*, Mainz: Hase und Koehler.

—— (1993) *Der Staat als Beute. Wie Politiker in eigener Sache Gesetze machen*, Munich: Knaur.

Arnold, Heinz Ludwig (ed.) (1972) *Deutsche über Deutschland*, Munich: C.H. Beck.

Barthélemy, Françoise, Winckler, Lutz (eds) (1990) *Mein Deutschland findet sich in keinem Atlas*, Frankfurt: Luchterhand.

Becker, Thorsten (1985) *Die Bürgschaft*, Zurich: Ammann.

Bergmann, Peter (1987) *Nietzsche – the Last Antipolitical German*, Bloomington and Indianapolis: Indiana University Press.

Bittermann, Klaus (ed.) (1991) *Liebesgrüße aus Bagdad*, Berlin: Edition TIAMAT.

Böhme, Irene (1982) *Die da drüben*, Berlin: Rotbuch.

Bohrer, Karl Heinz (1990) 'Provinzialismus', *Merkur* 44, 12: 1096–1102.

Böll, Heinrich (1959) *Billard um halbzehn*, Cologne: Kiepenheuer and Witsch.

—— (1963) *Ansichten eines Clowns*, Cologne: Kiepenheuer and Witsch.

—— (1978) *Werke Interviews I (1961–1978)*, ed. Bernd Balzer, Cologne: Kiepenheuer and Witsch.

Borchert, Wolfgang (1990) *Draußen vor der Tür*, Reinbek: Rowohlt (originally published 1956).

Bossmann, Dieter (ed.) (1977) *Was ich über Adolf Hitler gehört habe*, Frankfurt: Fischer.

Brandt, Peter and Ammon, Herbert (eds) (1981) *Die Linke und die nationale Frage*, Reinbek: Rowohlt.

Braun, Volker (1989) *Unvollendete Geschichte*, Frankfurt: Suhrkamp.

233

Broder, Henryk M. (1995) 'In Chor der Gutmenschen', *Der Spiegel*, 39, 29 September 34–9.
Buch, Hans Christoph (ed.) (1978) *Tintenfisch 15 Thema: Deutschland*, Berlin: Wagenbach.
Claessens, Dieter, Klönne, Arno and Tschoepe, Armin (1992) *Sozialkunde der Bundesrepublik Deutschland*, Reinbek: Rowohlt.
Dahrendorf, Ralf (1965) *Gesellschaft und Demokratie in Deutschland*, Munich: Piper (English edition (1968) *Society and Democracy in Germany*, London: Weidenfeld and Nicolson).
Deiritz, Karl and Krauss, Hannes (eds) (1991) *Der deutsch-deutsche Literaturstreit oder 'Freunde, es spricht sich schlecht mit gebundener Zunge'*, Frankfurt: Luchterhand.
Der Spiegel: various.
Deutschland, Deutschland. 47 Schriftsteller aus der BRD und der DDR schreiben über ihr Land (1979) Salzburg and Vienna: Residenz Verlag.
Die Zeit: various.
Döblin, Alfred (1975) *Berlin Alexanderplatz*, Frankfurt: Suhrkamp.
Duve, Freimut, Böll, Heinrich and Staeck, Klaus (eds) (1977) *Briefe zur Verteidigung der Republik*, Reinbek: Rowohlt.
Dyson, Kenneth (ed.) (1992) *The Politics of German Regulation*, Aldershot: Dartmouth.
Enzensberger, Hans Magnus (1961) 'Schimpfend unter Palmen', in Wolfgang Weyrauch (ed.) *Ich lebe in der Bundesrepublik*, Munich: List, pp. 24–31.
—— (1964) 'Am I a German?', *Encounter* 22, 4: 16–9.
—— (1967) *Deutschland, Deutschland unter anderem*, Frankfurt: Suhrkamp.
—— (1969) 'Notstand', *Tintenfisch 2*, Berlin: Wagenbach, 19–20.
—— (1993) *Aussichten auf den Bürgerkrieg*, Frankfurt: Suhrkamp.
—— (1995a) 'Auswärts im Rückwärtsgang', *Der Spiegel* 37: 215–21.
—— (1995b) 'Ich will nicht der Lappen sein, mit dem man die Welt putzt', *Die Zeit*, 5: 47–8.
Fels, Ludwig (1979) '"Und hier ist das Märchen zu ende"', in *Deutschland, Deutschland*, Salzburg and Vienna: Residenz Verlag, pp. 51–9.
Fischer, Fritz (1961) *Griff nach der Weltmacht. Die Kriegszielpolitik des kaiserlichen Deutschland*, Düsseldorf: Droste.
Frankfurter Allgemeine Zeitung: various.
Frisch, Max (1961) *Andorra*, Frankfurt: Suhrkamp.
Gaus, Günter (1983) *Wo Deutschland liegt. Eine Ortsbestimmung*, Hamburg: Hoffmann und Campe.
German Politics: various.
Giordano, Ralph (1990) *Die zweite Schuld oder Von der Last Deutscher zu sein*, Munich: Knaur.
Görtz, Franz Josef *et al.* (eds) (1994) *Deutsche Literatur 1993*, Stuttgart: Reclam.
Grass, Günter (1959) *Die Blechtrommel*, Neuwied: Luchterhand.
—— (1972) *Aus dem Tagebuch einer Schnecke*, Neuwied: Luchterhand.
—— (1979) *Das Treffen in Telgte*, Neuwied: Luchterhand.
—— (1980) *Kopfgeburten oder Die Deutschen sterben aus*, Neuwied: Luchterhand.

—— (1990a) *Deutscher Lastenausgleich*, Frankfurt: Luchterhand.
—— (1990b) *Ein Schnäppchen namens DDR*, Frankfurt: Luchterhand.
—— (1992) *Rede vom Verlust*, Göttingen: Steidl.
—— (1995) *Ein weites Feld*, Göttigen: Steidl.
Greiffenhagen, Martin and Sylvia (1981) *Ein schwieriges Vaterland*, Frankfurt: Fischer (originally published 1979).
—— (1993) *Ein schwieriges Vaterland*, Munich: List.
Greiner, Ulrich (1995) 'Streit muß sein', *Die Zeit*, 42, 13 October: 1.
Grün, Max von der (1967) *Irrlicht and Feuer*, Reinbek: Rowohlt (originally published 1963).
Guardian, various.
Habermas, Jürgen (ed.) (1979) *Stichworte zur 'Geistigen Situation der Zeit'*, 2 vols, Frankfurt: Suhrkamp.
Hahn. H. J. (ed.) (1995) *Germany in the 1990s*, Amsterdam: Rodopi.
Hanesch, Walter, Adany, Wilhelm, Martens, Rudolf, Rentzsch, Doris, Schneider, Ulrich, Schubert, Ursula and Wißkirchen, Martin (eds) (1994) *Armut in Deutschland*, Reinbek: Rowohlt.
Head, David (1995) '"Made in Germany" in the 1990s', in H. J. Hahn (ed.), *Germany in the 1990s*, Amsterdam: Rodopi.
Heine, Heinrich (1978) *Heines Werke in Fünf Bänden*, 5 vols, Berlin and Weimar: Aufbau.
Henschel, Gerhard (1994) *Das Blöken der Lämmer. Die Linke und der Kitsch*, Berlin: Edition TIAMAT.
Herder, Johann Gottfried (1978) *Werke*, 5 vols, Berlin and Weimar: Aufbau.
Heym, Stefan (1991) '"Ich kann doch nicht mein Leben wegerfen". Ein *Zeit*-Gesprach mit Stefan Heym', *Die Zeit*, 50, 6 (December): 64–5.
Historikerstreit (1995), 9th edn, Munich: Piper.
Hochhuth, Rolf (1963) *Der Stellvertreter*, Reinbek: Rowohlt.
—— (1993) *Wessis in Weimar*, Berlin: Volk and Welt.
Hoffmann-Lange, Ursula (ed.) (1995) *Jugend und Demokratie in Deutschland*, Opladen: Leske and Buderich.
Hölderlin, Friedrich (1970) *Werke*, 2 vols, Munich: Hanser.
Ich will reden von der Angst meines Herzens (1991), Frankfurt: Luchterhand.
Jeismann, Michael and Ritter, Henning (eds) (1993) *Grenzfälle. Über neuen und alten Nationalismus*, Leipzig: Reclam.
Keller, Dietmar (ed.) (1990–1) *Nachdenken über Deutschland*, 5 vols, Berlin: Verlag der Nation.
Kielinger, Thomas (1995) 'Defeat or Liberation: How the Germans found their way out of their darkest hour', in *8 May 1945. 50 Years On. Remembering for the Future*, Bonn: Inter Nationes.
Kleist, Heinrich von (1971) *Sämtliche Werke*, Munich: Winkler.
Koeppen, Wolfgang (1961) 'Wahn', in Wolfgang Weyrauch (ed.), *Ich lebe in der Bundesrepublik*, Munich: List, pp. 32–6.
—— (1982) *Das Treibhaus*, 5th edn, Frankfurt: Suhrkamp (originally published 1953).
Kogon, Eugen (1946) 'Gericht und Gewissen', *Frankfurter Hefte* 1, 1: 25–37.

Kolbe, Uwe (1990) 'Ich war nicht darauf vorbereitet ein Deutscher zu sein', in Françoise Barthélemy and Lutz Winckler (eds), *Mein Deutschland findet sich in keinem Atlas*, Frankfurt: Luchterhand, pp. 67–72.

Korte, Karl-Rudolf (1985) 'Der Traum vom "anderen" Deutschland. Schriftsteller leiden am deutschen Weg', in Werner Weidenfeld (ed.), *Nachdenken über Deutschland*, Cologne: Verlag Wissenschaft und Politik, pp. 122–9.

Kunze, Reiner (1976) *Die wunderbaren Jahre*, Frankfurt: Fischer.

—— (1990) *Deckname 'Lyrik'*, Frankfurt: Fischer.

Lamprecht, Helmut (ed.) (1969) *Politische Gedichte vom Vormärz bis zur Gegenwart*, Bremen: Carl Schönemann Verlag.

Lettau, Reinhard (1978) 'Deutschland als Ausland', in Hans Christoph Buch (ed.), *Tintenfisch 15 Thema: Deutschland*, Berlin: Wagenbach.

Loest, Erich (1991) *Die Stasi war mein Eckermann*, Göttingen: Steidl.

Mann, Heinrich (1960) *Essays*, Hamburg: Claasen.

Mann, Thomas (1945) *Germany and the Germans*, Washington: Library of Congress.

—— (1946) *Leiden an Deutschland*, Los Angeles: Pazifische Presse.

—— (1993) *Betrachtungen eines Unpolitischen*, 2nd edn, Frankfurt: Fischer.

Maron, Monika (1992) *Nach Maßgabe meiner Begrifflichkeit*, Frankfurt: Fischer.

Marsh, David (1992) *The Bundesbank: The Bank that Rules Europe*, London: Heinemann.

—— (1994) *Germany and Europe. The Crisis of Unity*, London: Heinemann.

Mechtel, Angelika (1979) 'Deutschland drinnen und draußen', in *Deutschland, Deutschland*, Salzburg and Vienna: Residenz Verlag, pp. 20–8.

Mitscherlich, Alexander and Margarete (1988) *Die Unfähigkeit zu trauern*, 20th edn, Munich: Piper.

Morshäuser, Bodo (1992) *Hauptsache Deutsch*, Frankfurt: Suhrkamp.

Nadolny, Sten (1990) *Selim oder Die Gabe der Rede*, Munich: Piper.

Nietzsche, Friedrich (1980) *Sämtliche Werke*, 15 vols, Munich: DTV/de Gruyter.

OECD (1995) *OECD Economic Surveys 1994/5. Germany*, Paris: OECD.

Owen-Smith, Eric (1994) *The German Economy*, London: Routledge.

Piwitt, Hermann Peter (1978) 'Einen Kranz niederlegen am Herrmannsdenkmal', in Hans Christoph Buch (ed.) *Tintenfish 15 Thema: Deutschland*, Berlin: Wagenbach, pp. 17–24.

Plessner, Helmuth (1974) *Die verspätete Nation*, Frankfurt: Suhrkamp.

Pulzer, Peter (1994) 'United Germany: a normal state', *German Politics*, 3, 1: 1–17.

Richter, Hans Werner (1962) 'Beim Wiedersehen des "Ruf"', in Hans Schwab-Felisch (ed.) *Der Ruf. Eine deutsche Nachkriegszeitschrift*, Munich: DTV.

—— (ed.) (1965) *Plädoyer für eine neue Regierung oder Keine Alternative*, Reinbek: Rowohlt.

Ripper, Werner (ed.) (1974) *Weltgeschichte im Aufriß*, 2 vols, Frankfurt, Berlin and Munich: Moritz Diesterweg.

Sack, John (1993) *An Eye for an Eye*, New York: Basic Books.
Schallück, Paul (1961) 'Zwölf Fragen', in Wolfgang Weyrauch (ed.), *Ich lebe in der Bundesrepublik*, Munich: List.
Scheuch, Erwin K. and Ute (1992) *Cliquen, Klüngel, Karrieren*, Reinbek: Rowohlt.
Schiller, Friedrich (1966) *Werke in drei Bänden*, 3 vols, Munich: Hanser.
Schneider, Peter (1982) *Der Mauerspringer*, Neuwied: Luchterhand.
Schwab-Felisch, Hans (ed.) (1962) *Der Ruf. Eine deutsche Nachkriegszeitschrift*, Munich: DTV.
Schwarz, Georg and Weber, Carl August (eds) (1951) *Wir heißen Euch hoffen. Schriftsteller zur deutschen Verständigung*, Munich: Willi Weismann.
Schwilk, Heimo and Schacht, Ulrich (eds) (1994) *Die selbstbewußte Nation. 'Anschwellender Bocksgesang' und weitere Beiträge zu einer deutschen Debatte*, Frankfurt and Berlin: Ullstein.
Southern, David (1993) 'Restitution or compensation: the property question', *German Politics*, 2, 3: 436–49.
Spengler, Oswald (1993) *Der Untergang des Abendlandes*, Munich: DTV.
Stephan, Cora (ed.) (1992) *Wir Kollaborateure*, Reinbek: Rowohlt.
—— (1993) *Der Betroffenheitskult*, Berlin: Rowohlt.
Stiller, Klaus (1979) 'Deutschland', in *Deutschland, Deutschland*, Salzburg and Vienna: Residenz Verlag, pp. 267–71.
Strauß, Botho (1981) *Paare Passanten*, Munich: Hanser.
—— (1994) 'Anschwellender Bocksgesang' in Franz Joseph Görtz, Volker Hage and Uwe Wittsock (eds), *Deutsche Literatur 1993*, Stuttgart: Reclam, pp. 255–69 (first published 1993)
Süskind, Patrick (1990) 'Deutschland, eine Midlife-crisis', *Der Spiegel* 38: 116–25.
Unseld, Siegfried (ed.) (1993) *Politik ohne Projekt?*, Frankfurt: Suhrkamp.
Vaterland, Muttersprache (1979), Berlin: Wagenbach.
Vinke, Hermann (ed.) (1993) *Akteneinsicht Christa Wolf*, Hamburg: Luchterhand.
Völlger, Winfried (1990) 'Von der Schwierigkeit, ein Deutscher zu sein', in Françoise Barthélemy and Lutz Winckler (eds), *Mein Deutschland findet sich in keinem Atlas*, Frankfurt: Luchterhand, pp. 73–87.
Wallich, H.C. (1955) *Mainsprings of the German Revival*, New Haven: Yale University Press.
Wallraff, Günter (1985) *Ganz unten*, Cologne: Kiepenheuer und Witsch.
Walser, Martin (1960) *Halbzeit*, Frankfurt: Suhrkamp.
—— (1965) *Erfahrungen und Leseerfahrungen*, Frankfurt: Suhrkamp.
—— (1979) 'Händedruck mit Gespenstern', in Jürgen Habermas (ed.), *Stichworte zur 'Geistigen Situation der Zeit'*, 2 vols, Frankfurt: Suhrkamp, vol. 1, pp. 39–50.
—— (1982) *Versuch, ein Gefühl zu verstehen und andere Versuche*, Stuttgart: Reclam.
—— (1987) *Dorle und Wolf*, Frankfurt: Suhrkamp
—— (1994a) *Vormittag eines Schriftstellers*, Frankfurt: Suhrkamp.
—— (1994b) 'Über freie und unfreie Rede', *Der Spiegel*, 45, 130–8.
Weidenfeld, Werner (ed.) (1985) *Nachdenken über Deutschland*, Cologne: Verlag Wissenschaft und Politik.

Weidenfeld, Werner and Korte, Karl-Rudolf (eds) (1993) *Handbuch zur deutschen Einheit*, Bonn: Bundeszentrale für politische Bildung.
Weiss, Peter (1965) *Die Ermittlung*, Frankfurt: Suhrkamp.
Weizsäcker, Richard von (1986) *Reden und Interviews (1)*, Bonn: Presse- und Informationsamt der Bundesregierung.
Wellershoff, Dieter (1979) 'Deutschland – ein Schwebezustand', in Jürgen Habermas (ed.), *Stichworte zur 'Geistigen Situation der Zeit'*, 2 vols, Frankfurt: Suhrkamp, vol. 1, pp. 77–114.
Weyrauch, Wolfgang (ed.) (1961) *Ich lebe in der Bundesrepublik*, Munich: List.
Wichner, Ernst and Wiesner, Herbert (eds) (1991) *Zensur in der DDR*, Berlin: Literaturhaus Berlin.
Wirtschaftswoche (1995), 4.
Wolf, Christa (1963) *Der geteilte Himmel*, Halle: Mitteldeutscher Verlag.
—— (1968) *Nachdenken über Christa T.*, Halle: Mitteldeutscher Verlag.
—— (1983) *Kindheitsmuster*, 8th edn, Berlin and Weimar: Aufbau.
—— (1990) *Was bleibt*, Frankfurt: Luchterhand.
Zahl, Peter-Paul (1978) 'Die andauernde Ausbürgerung', in Hans Christoph Buch (ed.), *Tintenfisch 15 Thema: Deutschland*, Berlin: Wagenbach.

FURTHER READING

Part I Divided Germany

(The further reading for Part I deliberately contains texts that were written prior to 1990. Readers of these texts will obtain a sense of how the two pre-unification German states were viewed during the time of their existence.)

Baker, Kendall, Dalton, Russell J. and Hildebrandt, Kai (1981) *Germany Transformed. Political Culture and the New Politics*, Cambridge, Mass.: Harvard University Press.
Benz, Wolfgang (ed.) (1983) *Die Bundesrepublik Deutschland. Geschichte in drei Bänden*, Frankfurt: Fischer.
Childs, David (1983) *The GDR: Moscow's German Ally*, London: George Allen and Unwin.
Fulbrook, Mary (1992) *The Two Germanies 1945–1990*, Basingstoke: Macmillan.
Glaessner, Gert-Joachim (1992) *The Unification Process in Germany*, London: Pinter.
Hancock, M. Donald and Welsh, Helga A. (eds) (1994) *German Unification: Process and Outcomes*, Boulder, Westview Press.
Inglehardt, Ronald (1977) *The Silent Revolution*, Princeton: Princeton University Press.
Jesse, Eckhard (1986) *Die Demokratie der Bundesrepublik Deutschland*, 7th edn, Berlin: Colloquium Verlag.
Jesse, Eckhard and Mitter, Armin (eds) (1992) *Die Gestaltung der deutschen Einheit*, Bonn and Berlin: Bouvier.

238

Kloss, Günther (1990) *West Germany. An Introduction*, 2nd edn, Basingstoke: Macmillan.
Lehmann, Hans Georg (1988) *Chronik der DDR. 1945/49 bis heute*, 2nd edn, Munich: C.H. Beck.
—— (1989) *Chronik der Bundesrepublik Deutschland. 1945/49 bis heute*, 3rd edn, Munich: C.H. Beck.
Liebert, Ulrike and Merkel, Wolfgang (eds) (1991) *Die Politik zur deutschen Einheit. Probleme, Strategien, Kontroversen*, Opladen: Leske and Buderich.
Ludz, Peter C. (1980) *Die DDR zwischen Ost und West*, 4th edn, Munich: C.H. Beck.
McAdams, A. James (1993) *Germany Divided: From the Wall to Reunification*, Princeton: Princeton University Press.
Osmond, Jonathan (ed.) (1992) *German Reunification. A Reference Guide and Commentary*, Harlow: Longman.
Smith, Gordon (1987) *Democracy in Western Germany*, 3rd edn, London: Heinemann.
Sontheimer, Kurt (1971) *Grundzüge des politischen Systems der BRD*, Munich: Piper.
Turner, Henry Ashby Jr (1992) *Germany from Partition to Reunification*, New Haven and London: Yale University Press.
Weber, Hermann (1991) *DDR: Grundriß der Geschichte*, Hanover, Fackelträger.

Part II Facing the future

Adam, Hermann (1992) *Wirtschaftspolitik und Regierungssystem der Bundesrepublik Deutschland*, Bonn: Bundeszentrale für politische Bildung.
Andersen, Uwe and Woycke, Wichard (eds) (1995) *Handwörterbuch des politischen Systems der Bundesrepublik Deutschland*, 2nd edn, Bonn: Bundeszentrale für politische Bildung.
Backes, Uwe and Jesse, Eckhard (1993) *Politischer Extremismus in der Bundesrepublik Deutschland. Das Standardwerk in Aktualisierter Fassung*, Berlin: Propyläen Verlag.
Bade, Klaus J. (1994) *Ausländer, Aussiedler, Asyl. Eine Bestandsaufnahme*, Munich: Beck.
Baring, Arnulf (ed.) (1994) *Germany's New Position in Europe. Problems and Perspectives*, Berg: Oxford.
Beyme, Klaus von (1993) *Das politische System der Bundesrepublik Deutschland nach der Vereinigung*, 7th edn, Munich: Piper.
Craig, Gordon (1991) *The Germans*, Harmondsworth: Penguin.
Fritsch-Bournazel, Renata (1992) *Europe and German Unification*, Oxford: Berg.
Geißler, Rainer (1992) *Die Sozialstruktur Deutschlands*, Opladen: Westdeutscher Verlag.
Gutjahr, Lothar (1993) *German Foreign and Defence Policy after Unification*, London: Pinter.

Hesse, Joachim Jens and Ellwein, Thomas (1992) *Das Regierungssystem der Bundesrepublik Deutschland*, 7th edn, Opladen: Westdeutscher Verlag.
Kennedy, Ellen (1995) *The Bundesbank*, 2nd edn, London: Pinter.
Lippert, Barbara and Stevens-Ströhmann, Rosalind (1993) *German Unification and EC Integration*, London: Pinter.
Markovits, Andrei S. and Gorski, Philip S. (1993) *The German Left: Red, Green and Beyond*, Cambridge: Polity Press.
Mintzel, Alf and Oberreuther, Heinrich (eds) (1992) *Parteien in der Bundesrepublik Deutschland*, Opladen: Leske and Budrich.
Nave-Herz, Rosemarie (1993) *Die Geschichte der Frauenbewegung in Deutschland*, Bonn: Bundeszentrale für politische Bildung.
Padgett, Steven (ed.) (1993) *Parties and Party Systems in the New Germany*, Aldershot: Dartmouth.
Paterson, William E. and Southern, David (1991) *Governing Germany*, Oxford: Blackwell.
Schäfers, Bernhard (1995), *Gesellschaftlicher Wandel in Deutschland*, 6th edn, Stuttgart: Enke.
Scharf, Thomas (1994) *The German Greens. Challenging the Consensus*, Oxford: Berg.
Smith, Gordon and Paterson, William E. (1992) *Developments in German Politics*, Macmillan: Basingstoke.
Tatsachen über Deutschland (1995) Frankfurt: Societäs Verlag.

Part III The search for identity

Balfour, Michael (1992) *Germany: The Tides of Power*, London: Routledge.
Bullivant, Keith (1994) *The Future of German Literature*, Oxford and Providence, RI: Berg.
Carr, William A. (1991) *A History of Germany 1815–1990*, 4th edn, London: Arnold.
Craig, Gordon A. (1981) *Germany 1866–1945*, Oxford: Oxford University Press.
Fulbrook, Mary (1990) *A Concise History of Germany*, Cambridge: Cambridge University Press.
Glaser, Hermann (1991) *Kleine Kulturgeschichte der Bundesrepublik Deutschland*, 2nd edn, Bonn: Bundeszentrale für politische Bildung.
Hahn, H.J. (1995) *German Thought and Culture*, Manchester: Manchester University Press.
James, Harold A. (1990) *A German Identity 1770–1990*, London: Weidenfeld and Nicolson.
Kohn, Hans (1965) *The Mind of Germany*, London: Macmillan.
Krockow, Christian Graf von (1990) *Die Deutschen in ihrem Jahrhundert 1890–1990*, Reinbek: Rowohlt.
—— (1993) *Scheiterhaufen. Größe und Elend des deutschen Geistes*, Reinbek: Rowohlt.
Parkes, K. Stuart (1986) *Writers and Politics in West Germany*, Beckenham: Croom Helm.

Taylor, A.J.P. (1961) *The Course of German History*, London: Methuen.
Williams, Arthur and Parkes, Stuart (eds) (1994) *The Individual, Identity and Innovation. Signals from Contemporary Literature and the New Germany*, Bern: Peter Lang.
Williams, Arthur, Parkes, Stuart and Smith, Roland (eds) (1991) *German Literature at a Time of Change 1989-1990*, Bern: Peter Lang.

INDEX

242